# From Mountain Man
## to Millionaire

Missouri Biography Series

William E. Foley, Editor

# From Mountain Man
## to Millionaire

### The "Bold and Dashing Life" of Robert Campbell

William R. Nester

**University of Missouri Press** Columbia and London

**Library of Congress Cataloging-in-Publication Data**

Nester, William R., 1956–
   From mountain man to millionaire : the "bold and dashing life" of
Robert Campbell / William R. Nester.
       p.   cm. — (Missouri biography series)
   Includes bibliographical references (p.   ) and index.
   ISBN 0-8262-1218-2 (alk. paper)
   1. Campbell, Robert, 1804–1879.   2. Pioneers—West (U.S.)—
Biography.   3. Fur traders—West (U.S.)—Biography.
4. Businessmen—Missouri—Saint Louis—Biography.   5. Saint Louis
(Mo.)—Biography.   6. Fur trade—Rocky Mountains—History—19th
century.   7. Missouri—History—Civil War, 1861–1865.   I. Title.
II. Series.
F592.C263N47   1999
978'.02'092—dc21                                          98-54962
[B]                                                           CIP

⊗™ This paper meets the requirements of the
American National Standard for Permanence of Paper
for Printed Library Materials, Z39.48, 1984.

Text design: Elizabeth K. Young
Jacket design: Mindy Shouse
Typesetter: Bookcomp, Inc.
Printer and binder: Thomson-Shore, Inc.
Typefaces: Palatino, Impact

To John and Valerie
Two great friends and adventurers of mind and spirit

# Contents

Acknowledgments . . . . . . . . . . . . . . . . . . . . . . . . . . . . . . . . . . . . . . . . xi
Introduction . . . . . . . . . . . . . . . . . . . . . . . . . . . . . . . . . . . . . . . . . . . . 1
1  Old and New Worlds (1804–1825) . . . . . . . . . . . . . . . . . . . . 4
2  The Shining Mountains (1825–1829) . . . . . . . . . . . . . . . . . . 13
3  Worldly Triumphs (1829–1833) . . . . . . . . . . . . . . . . . . . . . . 50
4  Fort William (1833–1834) . . . . . . . . . . . . . . . . . . . . . . . . . . . 82
5  A Home and Family of His Own (1835–1845) . . . . . . 110
6  Wealth, Power, and Tragedy (1846–1859) . . . . . . . . . . 161
7  Civil War (1860–1865) . . . . . . . . . . . . . . . . . . . . . . . . . . . . . . 198
8  New Directions (1865–1879) . . . . . . . . . . . . . . . . . . . . . . . . 224
Robert Campbell Family Lifespans . . . . . . . . . . . . . . . . . . . . . 249
Bibliography . . . . . . . . . . . . . . . . . . . . . . . . . . . . . . . . . . . . . . . 251
Index . . . . . . . . . . . . . . . . . . . . . . . . . . . . . . . . . . . . . . . . . . . . . . . 267

# Acknowledgments

I especially wish to acknowledge the wonderful research help given by Jeff Huntington, the Campbell House Museum Executive Director, and Charles Brown, the Mercantile Library's Research Librarian, as well as the various research assistants at the Missouri Historical Society and the very sweet, knowledgeable, and devoted docents at the Campbell House.

I offer my deepest appreciation to renowned historians William Foley and Robert Utley, Campbell House board member Don Bergman, and University of Missouri Press editor John Brenner for their meticulous proofreading of my manuscript and the many suggestions they made for its improvement.

From Mountain Man
to **Millionaire**

# Introduction

To those familiar with the history of the trans-Mississippi fur trade, such names as Jedediah Smith, William Sublette, Jim Bridger, Tom Fitzpatrick, William Ashley, and Jim Beckwourth are well known. Biographies have been written about all of these men, as well as about a host of lesser luminaries. And what of Robert Campbell? While armchair and professional historians alike have undoubtedly heard of him, few know much about him.[1]

Campbell's relative obscurity is a pity, but it is understandable. He did not embark on any odysseys that mapped new territory. No scandals swirled about him. He was not a crack shot or hunter, unusually brave in battle, of Herculean strength or girth, nor a teller of tall tales.

Yet Robert Campbell was immensely successful in fulfilling nearly every ambition that seized him and in overcoming nearly every challenge he met, and his actions were heroic by any measure. Born in 1804 in Ireland, he emigrated to the United States in 1822; a year later he entered the fur trade, in which he rose steadily from trapper to brigade leader to partner, all within a half dozen years. During that time he raised his rifle against many a charging Blackfoot; trekked through the snowbound Rockies in midwinter to carry word from one stranded brigade to another; frequently risked his life for his comrades, including a wounded Bill Sublette at the Battle of Pierre's Hole; and outwitted such worthy rivals as the Hudson's Bay Company's Peter Skene Ogden,

1. The only significant published work on Campbell is a brief article: Harvey L. Carter, "Robert Campbell," in Leroy R. Hafen, ed., *Trappers of the Far West: Sixteen Biographical Sketches*. There are also two unpublished works: Marlene Hawver, "Robert Campbell: Expectant Capitalist," and Stephen F. Huss, "Take No Advantage: The Biography of Robert Campbell." Fortunately, there is a rich hoard of primary sources penned by Campbell himself and his associates. Research for this book was done at three primary places in St. Louis: the Campbell House Museum, the Missouri Historical Society, and the St. Louis Mercantile Library.

American Fur Company partisans Kenneth McKenzie, Henry Vander-burgh, and Andrew Drips, or independent traders such as Nathaniel Wyeth. Few mountain leaders were as successful, daring, and skilled as Robert Campbell.

By the mid-1830s, Campbell had accumulated enough wealth to embark on new careers. Retiring from the mountains, he devoted the rest of his life to investments in banking, merchandise, and railroads that simultaneously deepened his own riches and helped develop the region's economy. It was said that his name was as financially good on a banknote as that of the U.S. Treasury secretary. Though he never ran for public office, he served as a powerful voice of reason and modera-tion, helping to bridge impassioned, bitterly splintered political factions, especially during the Civil War.

During his nearly six decades in America, from 1822 until his death in 1879, Campbell helped shape a succession of fascinating historical epochs—the fur trade era in the Rockies, the transformation of St. Louis from frontier town to booming industrial metropolis, and Missouri's bloody Civil War and Reconstruction. Along the way, he formed deep and enduring friendships with most of the prominent frontier leaders of that time. Hold up a mirror to Campbell's long, eventful life and you see reflected the nation's essential events, issues, and individuals during those decades.

He accomplished all this through hard work, intelligence, luck, and, above all, sterling character. Throughout his life, Campbell's friends and associates persistently noted his character. The accumulation of vast wealth did not corrupt Campbell as it has so many others. His life was free of scandal in an age of unbridled capitalism when virtually any means could be tried to acquire wealth and use its power. Campbell was a philanthropist, diverting huge sums to, among many others, victims of the Irish potato famine during the 1840s and Native Americans during the 1870s. Yet his brilliantly successful life as a businessman and philanthropist was marred by personal tragedy. As a devoted husband and father, he had to endure the deaths of ten of his thirteen children.

Though Robert Campbell's papers remain largely intact, few of them offer penetrating glimpses into his mind. He was not an unusually reflective or philosophical man. He did, however, leave us with one especially insightful observation on New Year's Day, 1833, when he was high up the Missouri River in a trading post opposite the Yellowstone River. As if the drudgery and danger of a wilderness post and his responsibility for the lives and fortunes of a score of engagés were not burdensome enough, Campbell's enterprise was locked in a struggle for the Indian trade with the American Fur Company's Fort Union, a half dozen miles away. He concluded the three-month journal that detailed his travails with the words, "all worldly gain is but dross."[2]

That epigram summed up Robert Campbell's outlook on life. Although he struggled his way up from rags to riches, he never lost faith in the Calvinist belief that God was the author of every individual's fate, and that thus all worldly successes should honor God. That belief had been driven into him from his earliest days. Inscribed above the front doorway of his childhood home, Aghalane, in County Tyrone, Northern Ireland, was the motto, "vix la nostra voce": "I scarcely call these things our own." The phrase captured the humble piety, hard work, and deep appreciation with which he and his family viewed their worldly success. God was the ultimate source of their accomplishments; in striving constantly to better themselves, they honored God and his gifts to them. Campbell personified the ideal of Calvinist capitalism.

Late in his life, Robert Campbell characterized his decade in the Rocky Mountain fur trade as "a bold and dashing life."[3] The intervening decades had dimmed his memories of the near constant drudgery and hardship broken by moments of sheer terror as Indians or grizzly bears threatened. Nor did his introspective character at first seem "bold and dashing" in comparison to such colorful contemporaries as Joe Meek, Bill Williams, or Sir William Drummond Stewart, to name a few.

Yet, in a profound sense, the saying captures Robert Campbell's character. It took boldness to plunge repeatedly into the wilderness, and later into real estate, merchandise, steamships, railroads, and other enterprises in hopes of greater financial returns. And Campbell was quietly dashing—an intelligent, handsome, magnetic individual who shunned swagger and conceit. As much as anything, he accumulated wealth and fame because he was a natural leader whose decisions inspired his partners and employees alike to contribute all they could for their mutual success. By that measure, Robert Campbell did indeed enjoy a bold and dashing life.

2. George R. Brooks, ed., "The Private Journal of Robert Campbell," 115.

3. Drew Alan Holloway, ed., *A Narrative of Colonel Robert Campbell's Experiences in the Rocky Mountain Fur Trade from 1825 to 1835 (as dictated to William Fayel)*, 24.

# Old and New Worlds (1804–1825)

**W**hen Robert Campbell was born on February 12, 1804, he entered a harsh feudal and colonial world that dragged nearly every one of the four and a half million Irish into squalor, despair, and repression. Virtually all Irish were peasants who eked out an existence on estates owned by English or Anglican Irish landlords; about 0.2 percent of the population owned estates of two thousand or more acres, which together accounted for two-thirds of all Irish land. The Ireland of that era has often been described as a Catholic country ruled by Anglicans. Laws restricted the ability of Catholics, who numbered three of every four people, to own land, participate in politics, gain an education, or even practice their religion.[1]

Campbell was among the few Irish fortunate enough to escape such extremes of poverty and repression. As "dissident" Presbyterians, the Campbells were forced to tithe the Anglican Church and were effectively barred from Parliament, but they were allowed to own land. Nothing, of course, kept the Campbells from nurturing the flame of an ancient but long noble heritage; though the family tree is obscure, the Campbells are possibly related to the Argyle clan that fled Scotland to northern Ireland with other Presbyterians to escape forced conversion to Anglicanism in the mid–seventeenth century. Even more misty are the origins of the maternal side of Campbell's family; the boast that they

---

1. D. George Boyce, *Nineteenth-Century Ireland: The Search for Stability*, 6; L. M. Cullen, *Life in Ireland;* Andrew Hadfield and John McVeagh, eds., *Strangers to that Land: British Perceptions of Ireland from the Reformation to the Famine;* E. Estyn Evans, *Irish Folkways;* Thomas W. Freeman, *Ireland: Its Physical, Historical, Social, and Economic Geography;* Conrad Gill, *The Rise of the Irish Linen Industry.*

were descendants of the Scottish king, Robert II, may be no more than a family legend.[2]

No ancestry, however noble, can alone sustain a family. No one visiting the Campbells would have mistaken them for nobility. Robert Campbell grew up in a yeoman farm family whose lifestyle was at best spartanly comfortable. His father, Hugh, received the deed to the 180-acre farm named Aghalane, which means "wide meadow" in Gaelic, from his father on February 16, 1780. It then took Hugh a half dozen years before he could save enough hard-earned money to build Aghalane House on his land. When his house was completed, Hugh must have thought it well worth the wait. The stone two-story house had six double-hung windows across the upper front, three chimneys across the roof ridge, a single front door and five slightly larger windows across the lower front, and a similar set of windows across the house's rear. All of that glass displayed a financial means that was prosperous if not ostentatious—each window was taxed. The roof was thatched with flax; the walls were lime-washed. Hugh proudly recorded his feat in a plaque above and to the left of the front door that read, "Hugh Campbell built this House in the year of our Lord 1786." Above and to the right, another plaque prominently displayed the Argyle family coat of arms and the inscriptions "Most Noble Duke Argyle" and "Vix la Nostra Voce" ("I scarcely call these things our own"). The Campbell motto conveyed its central values—duty, hard work, and gratitude to God.[3]

Hugh needed a large house in which to shelter all of his children (eleven are recorded), though they did not all live together at once. His first wife, Catherine Denny, gave birth to five children before she died. Hugh's second wife and Robert's mother was Sarah Elizabeth Buchannan, who had six children: Ann (1795–1876), Hugh (1796–1879), Andrew (1797–1868), Elizabeth (1801–1824), James Alexander (1802–1823), and finally Robert (1804–1879). Though he was the youngest, Campbell would grow up to become the family's emotional and financial backbone.

2. Most of the information on Robert's early life was taken from the various documents in the Campbell Family Papers, Missouri Historical Society (MoHiS) and the Campbell House Foundation collection, as well as Huss, "Take No Advantage," 1–15.

3. "Aghalene House, Home of the Campbells of Aghalene" (museum brochure). Genealogical Chart of the Campbell Family, Campbell Family Papers, MoHiS. The Campbell Houses in Ireland and America are perhaps the only example of museums devoted to one family's history on two continents. Aghalane was saved from the brink of demolition in 1985 and moved to the Ulster-American Folk Park in Camphill, Omagh County, Tyrone, Northern Ireland.

Although Elizabeth and James died young, Campbell's other siblings were remarkably long-lived for a time when doctors at best were lucky to achieve Hippocrates' first commandment—to cause no harm. Campbell himself would live for seventy-five years, dying on October 16, 1879. Of those who survived to become adults, only Ann never married. Incurable diseases killed Elizabeth and James; strong genes apparently explain the others' longevity. Both parents enjoyed long, vigorous lives. Hugh was born around 1748 and died sixty-two years later on November 2, 1810. Sarah was born in 1766 and died eighty-five years later on October 9, 1851. Despite their longevity, those Campbells who endured were not immune from health problems. Andrew battled against and frequently succumbed to alcoholism throughout his life. As a boy, Campbell had lung problems, exacerbated by the peat fires that smoldered in the family hearth. It was a common Irish affliction. Surviving letters reveal that the Campbells were a very close, loving family. As the family's "baby," Robert Campbell undoubtedly received no end of affection and indulgences.[4]

The Campbell farm probably grew flax, potatoes, and oats in the surrounding fields and various vegetables in their garden, and raised a menagerie of milk cows, horse, oxen, chickens, sheep, pigs, rabbits, and geese. About one-fourth of the Campbell land was peat bogs, which supplied fuel for heat, light, and cooking. Food, equipment, and livestock were stored in various outbuildings behind the house, forming a courtyard. Those crops or livestock not consumed at home were sold or traded in the nearby market towns. Most income came from sales of spun flax or woven linen to the mills in nearby Ulster, while lesser amounts probably came from wool or linen actually spun or woven on the farm. The Campbells also received rents from tenants on their land.[5]

In all, the farm was prosperous enough to pay the way of the eldest son, Hugh, to medical school in Edinburgh in 1812. Unlike Hugh, Robert never went to college. His education was confined to that meted out by the minister at the nearby Eden Mill meetinghouse. He probably learned much more from his literate mother and siblings at home.

Like any farm child, from an early age Campbell spent much of his time helping other family members with various chores. At that time,

4. Little is known about Robert Campbell's half-siblings. They seem to have scattered to their own homes by the time he reached adulthood since there is no mention of them in his letters.
5. Deane C. Douglas, *The Ulster County;* Liam Kennedy and Philip Ollerenshaw, *An Economic History of Ulster;* P. McAleer, *Townland Names of County Tyrone.*

much of the flax production could be done on the farm. The stalks were first retted or allowed to rot in shallow flooded fields along the Glenelly River that flowed through the Campbell land. After days submerged in water, the flax was dragged out, combed, dried on rafters, and then boiled, steps which provoked a nasty stench that filled the air and clung to clothing. The flax was then spun, reeled, and woven by separate hand-operated machines probably located in the kitchen, which provided warmth and light in the winter. Campbell also undoubtedly helped cut the peat into twenty-pound rectangles and hauled it to a drying area.

Nature, the industrial revolution, the end of the Napoleonic Wars, and medical advances combined to batter the Campbells and most other Irish families. Crop failures devastated Ireland in 1816 and 1817, briefly raising food prices and bringing malnutrition to many and starvation to some. Overall, prices dropped with demand after Napoleon's final defeat in 1815. Technological advances allowed textile factories to destroy cottage weaving across the British Isles. Even smallpox inoculations were a mixed blessing: over the coming decades, the population growth from tens of thousands of people spared by inoculations created an ever greater demand for food from a land whose production was limited and often blighted. Ireland's population density was already Europe's greatest, and it would worsen.

These economic calamities robbed the Campbells of their hope that Hugh could become a doctor, let alone that the other sons could go to college. Hugh had to drop out of medical school after his first year. The Campbells thus fell into a vicious cycle—they were too poor to invest in education or business that could improve their living standards. For Hugh and eventually Robert, America became the salvation for those whose ambitions and very lives were stymied in Ireland.

Although Campbell undoubtedly carried vivid memories of his father all his life, he never got to know him; not long after Campbell entered his sixth year, his father died. Ten years separated Robert from his oldest brother, Hugh, who became like a father to him. Over the decades, Hugh would attempt to guide Robert with advice of varying degrees of help or hindrance, and more positively with job offers. Robert picked up many of Hugh's characteristics. The two brothers were thought "of the same stripe: sober, honest, conscientious, and hard-working."[6]

Hugh has been described as "one of those countless figures who inhabit the shadowy wings of the stage of history. That he is visible at

6. George R. Brooks, "The Journal of Hugh Campbell," 241, 241–68.

all today is due to the light of recognition reflected from his younger brother Robert."[7] Hugh's contribution to history is greater than that. In fact, the Campbell brothers illuminated each other. We are indebted to Hugh for the fascinating glimpses he provides into the Campbell family dynamics and into Robert's character, activities, and aspirations through his lifelong correspondence and business association with his brother and others. Even more important, Robert Campbell might never have sought his fortune and fame in America had not Hugh led the way.[8]

On June 19, 1818, Hugh sailed from Londonderry aboard an American-bound ship appropriately named the *Perseverance*. He settled first in Milton, North Carolina, where he became a merchant, and later in Raleigh. In the three years after Hugh left for America, the letters and journal that he sent home inspired Robert to follow. More than adventure pulled Campbell from the nest; he was also gently pushed as his older brothers, Andrew and James Alexander, could barely support themselves on the family's limited land.

In spring 1822, shortly after he turned eighteen years old, Campbell sailed on the *Climax* from Londonderry to Philadelphia, via Saint John, New Brunswick. The roundabout route actually cost less than a direct voyage. London imposed tariffs on shipping between Britain and America to discourage immigration to its recent enemy and former colony. The *Climax* carried not only forty men and twenty women immigrants but also "small . . . stores belonging to 25 heads of families," "sundry packages," and seventy tons of plaster.[9] Ships like the *Climax* specialized in transporting immigrants, offering standard fares and providing berths and meals of salt beef or pork, potatoes, and hardtack. Immigrants brought their own bedding and extra foods. In what for many was their first exercise in democracy, the passengers elected a captain to represent them to the ship captain and a cook to prepare their meals.

On June 27, 1822, Campbell disembarked at Philadelphia. The thrill that surged through him during his voyage probably took a long time to subside after he set foot in the New World. He soon learned that the differences between Ireland and America were vast. America was an excellent place for an enterprising young man to find almost any kind of livelihood, even for a weaver, which he had called himself in the *Climax*'s

7. Ibid., 241.
8. Kirby Miller, *Emigrants and Exiles;* William Forbes Adams, *Ireland and Irish Emigration to the New World from 1815 to the Famine.*
9. Manifest of the Ship Climax, Campbell House Foundation Collection.

manifest. Philadelphia would prove to be very good for Campbell. He would eventually spend a good portion of his life there cutting business deals, visiting Hugh and his future sister-in-law Mary after they moved to the city, and courting the girl who would become his wife.

Philadelphia was the nation's leading wholesale center throughout the 1820s. Its population was larger than New York's and just as enterprising, while its location on the central seaboard with a good road heading west to the Ohio Valley accounted for its sales volume. Within a year of arriving in America, Campbell would travel the westward road already followed by tens of thousands of others. In 1817 alone, thirteen thousand wagons with $16 million worth of goods set off down the rutted 240 miles of road from Philadelphia to Pittsburgh. The overland trip usually took sixteen days. In Pittsburgh, goods were piled on flatboats, keelboats, or steamboats and conveyed downriver to hamlets and towns along the Ohio and Mississippi Rivers. Merchants then sent furs and other commodities back to Philadelphia to pay off their debts and renew the buying-and-selling cycle. With the opening of the National Road from Cumberland, Maryland, to Wheeling, Virginia, in 1818, Baltimore became a serious rival to Philadelphia, but never its commercial equal. New Orleans tended to be the destination for bulky loads of grain or lumber that could be conveyed by flatboat. Steamboats eventually could make the New Orleans to St. Louis run in seven or eight days. Yet even that swift passage could not make up for the extra month or more it took ships sailing from Europe to reach New Orleans rather than the East Coast, and the subsequent higher freight and insurance rates. Although St. Louis merchants could find goods in New Orleans, they generally preferred to journey to Philadelphia with its greater selection, cheaper prices, better credit, and more reliable sellers. Being closer to Europe, the merchants of New York and Boston could shave off some transportation costs on goods coming from the East. But they were that much farther from western markets. During the 1810s and 1820s, New York and Boston supplied slivers of the western trade. The opening of the Erie Canal in 1825, however, would help New York catch up to Philadelphia.[10] It would not take Campbell long to understand these economic dynamics and the opportunities they provided to entrepreneurs.

How Robert Campbell spent his first year in America is unknown, though he seems to have found employment as a clerk in Philadelphia. Whatever he did could not have exceeded the importance of meeting

10. Lewis E. Atherton, *The Pioneer Merchant in Mid-America*, 52, 67–68.

John O'Fallon in 1823. O'Fallon was well connected to St. Louis society; by the marriage of an aunt he counted among his uncles William and George Rogers Clark. It was Indian Superintendent William Clark who had appointed O'Fallon the sutler at Council Bluffs in 1821. O'Fallon had come east to Philadelphia to market his furs and buy goods for the next year's trading. Impressed with Campbell's accounting and personal skills, O'Fallon offered him a job as an assistant clerk for the Council Bluffs post. Campbell eagerly accepted. He wrote Hugh of his good fortune and asked to borrow two hundred dollars to tide him over until he received his salary. Hugh sent him the money. Campbell then helped O'Fallon to purchase supplies and convey them all the way west to Council Bluffs.

To get to Council Bluffs, Campbell would have to pass through St. Louis, which had been the gateway to the West ever since Pierre Laclède and Auguste Chouteau founded it in 1764. St. Louis was a colorful, bustling frontier town when Campbell disembarked at the muddy levee in the fall of 1823 and eagerly strode its streets. The city's 1821 directory noted that 5,500 people lived in the town and an additional 4,232 in the county.[11] Most were Americans, but the 155 original French families played an important role in the economy and society, while a variety of other nationalities crowded the town.

One image from his arrival lodged deeply in Campbell's mind, and he was able to recall it decades later. Appropriately, it concerned Indians. Despite St. Louis's growing cosmopolitanism, it was still a frontier town at heart. Delegations from various tribes constantly arrived to smoke and negotiate with William Clark and then departed laden with gifts. To an Irish lad not long off the boat, the sight of Indians was richly exotic. Campbell described one such Indian delegation that especially tickled him: they "all bought umbrellas and walked in Indian file, bare headed with the umbrellas spread over them, making a ludicrous appearance. The first thing they had done on reaching town was to buy up all the red umbrellas."[12]

As a new state with a growing population, Missouri was a promising place for an enterprising man like Campbell to make his fortune. Furs, lead, and trade goods were the state's economic pillars; furs accounted

11. John A. Paxton, *The St. Louis Directory and Register Containing the Names, Professions, and Residence Heads of Families and Persons in Business . . .* , quoted in John Francis McDermott, ed., *The Early Histories of St. Louis*, 66–70.

12. Quoted in Holloway, ed., *A Narrative*, 4.

for about one-fourth of St. Louis's wealth throughout the 1820s. Campbell's timing could hardly have been better. After a decade of economic depression during and following the War of 1812, the fur trade was experiencing unprecedented expansion as the demand for pelts raised their price to prewar levels. Eager for profits, the Missouri, Columbia, and French fur companies pushed into the upper Missouri River watershed in 1821. Their rivalry would rage all the fiercer the following year when the Ashley-Henry Fur Company crowded into the field. The newcomers would surpass the others in the wealth they exploited from the mountains. And Robert Campbell would join in creating and sharing that wealth.

His introduction to the trade came during the winter of 1823–1824 at Bellevue near the Platte River mouth. As he huddled in blankets near a smoky fire, his lung problems returned, probably with a share of homesickness. In the spring, he embarked downriver to work in O'Fallon's St. Louis store. O'Fallon introduced Campbell to the city's leading doctor, Benjamin Farrar, who advised him that "your symptoms are consumptive and I advise you to go to the Rocky Mountains. I have before sent two or three young men there in your condition, and they came back restored to health and healthy as bucks."[13] Although Campbell continued to work for O'Fallon, he began looking for a clerk position in one of the other fur companies.

Having established himself in America, Campbell received news from home that threatened to destroy all his hard-won gains. His brother, James Alexander, had died. In a January 1825 letter, Hugh urged Robert to "make preparations for revisiting Ireland. [You] will there be a help and solace to our weak and afflicted family and must never more think of leaving them . . . Are you well? Is it merely due to your unsettled situation that you don't write oftener? . . . I trust you will be in a situation to return to Ireland, without assistance from me . . . Now, Robert, may God be with you and . . . be an honor to your friends and the pride of a brother who . . . esteems you above all friends (except a beloved mother) on earth."[14] The letter was deeply revealing of the relationship between the two brothers. Hugh expressed his deep love and respect for his brother, yet as family patriarch following their father's death, he did not hesitate to order his brother to return home.

13. Hugh Campbell to Robert Campbell, January 31, 1825, Campbell Papers, Mercantile Library Association (MLA).
14. John Wiley to Robert Campbell, May 8, 1825, Campbell Collection, MoHiS.

As if his brother's letter were not pressure enough, Campbell received a similar message from family friend Robert Wiley: "Your mother will no doubt be again disconsoled at [Hugh's] departure . . . It is to be expected that you can quit this country with less regret than Hugh—he has been here longer and has become perfectly acquainted with the habits of the people . . . Shortly after his return it will be in his power to embark in business on his own . . . you would have to spend some years yet in an apprenticeship . . . for those reasons it appears much more proper that you should repair to your mother."[15]

The arguments made both practical and emotional sense. As the older, more established brother, Hugh should stay in America while Robert should rejoin his aggrieved family. How long Campbell struggled with the choice of staying or returning is unknown. In the end, he chose his health and career over the demands of his family and wrote Hugh of his decision. Hugh accepted that choice but admonished Robert, "For God's sake take care of yourself let nothing induce you to risk your health."[16] Yet, in that same letter Hugh broke the news to Robert that their sister Elizabeth had died.

With these tragedies and the subsequent guilt over not being with his loved ones hanging over him, Campbell worked even harder to fulfill his ambitions and his family's hopes. Soon he had written a triumphant letter to Hugh, repaying the two-hundred-dollar loan and recounting his boss's satisfaction in his work. Hugh replied: "Do you know how proud I feel to hear that you please your employers? . . . This is the only true test of merit. While in a respectable situation we ought not to be contented with doing our duty . . . we ought to identify our interest with that of our employer and act accordingly."

That unabashed praise must have dissolved any lingering remorse plaguing Campbell. Hugh had certainly hit the nail on the head. Campbell's various employers over the next decade would find few workers who could match and none that could exceed his devotion. Now debt-free and an experienced trader, he redoubled his efforts to sign up with a trapping brigade headed west. In the fall of 1825 he would finally seize the opportunity that he had been impatiently awaiting.

15. Hugh Campbell to Robert Campbell, September 26, 1824, Campbell Collection, MoHiS.
16. Hugh Campbell to Robert Campbell, June 12, 1825, Campbell Papers, MLA.

Chapter 2

# The Shining Mountains (1825–1829)

**W**hen Campbell headed west in November 1825, the Rocky Mountain fur trade was expanding after years of stagnation.[1] During the decade he spent in the mountains, he would rise steadily in prominence and prosperity, first as a clerk, then as a brigade leader in fur companies owned by others, and finally as a partner in his own firm. He was also fortunate to enjoy as mentors and role models two brilliant fur trade leaders: William Henry Ashley, who demonstrated relentless efforts to fulfill a strategic business vision, and Jedediah Smith, who taught Campbell wilderness survival skills and exhibited the ability to inspire hardened, fiercely independent men to follow him to the ends of the earth and death's door if need be. Robert Campbell's life cannot be understood apart from those two men and the development of the fur trade before he first entered it.

Ashley surpassed all his rivals as a brilliant frontier capitalist. Through ceaseless, fearless, and often ruthless enterprise, Ashley rose from obscure, humble origins into enormous wealth and status. He was the quintessential "expectant capitalist" who successfully invested in a range of promising fields.[2] No matter what the enterprise, he knew how

1. For studies of the fur trade era, see Hiram Martin Chittenden, *The American Fur Trade of the Far West*; Paul Crisler Phillips, *The Fur Trade*; Fred Gowans, *Rocky Mountain Rendezvous: A History of the Fur Trade Rendezvous, 1825–1840*; John E. Sunder, *The Fur Trade of the Upper Missouri, 1840–1865*; Hafen, ed., *Trappers of the Far West*; LeRoy R. Hafen, ed., *Mountain Men and Fur Trappers of the Far West: Eighteen Biographical Sketches*; Leroy R. Hafen, ed., *Fur Traders and Mountain Men of the Upper Missouri*; David J. Wishart, *The Fur Trade of the American West, 1807–1840: A Geographical Synthesis*; Dale Morgan, *Jedediah Smith and the Opening of the West*.
2. Richard M. Clokey, *William H. Ashley: Enterprise and Politics in the Trans-Mississippi West*. William H. Goetzman, "The Mountain Man as Jacksonian Man."

to command the loyalty, if not the affection, of others. After fighting his way into the tight ranks of the elite, Ashley was rewarded by those other rich, powerful men with a succession of public offices and duties. Campbell would follow much the same path.

Most important, Ashley revolutionized the fur trade. It was Ashley who, in 1825, inaugurated the annual Rocky Mountain rendezvous of free trappers whose needs and furs were conveyed by pack train. In doing so, Ashley shed the enormous fixed costs of trading posts and employees. Trading posts may have been safer places to store men, goods, and furs, and were easy to find for trappers and Indians alike, but they were enormously expensive to maintain. Trading posts were anchored to the Missouri River and its few navigable tributaries such as the Yellowstone. If a region's beaver or buffalo were hunted out, it was costly in time and money to abandon a post, carry the tons of supplies to a more promising location, and build a fort there. In contrast, rendezvous sites could be determined year to year, depending on the most convenient place for the trapping brigades and Indian bands to converge with the caravans. If one region's beaver played out, trapping brigades simply packed their animals and rode elsewhere. Keelboats were the trading post's lifeline, bringing up supplies and carrying down furs and robes. Yet keelboats were actually a far riskier means of transportation than pack animals. While snags sank numerous keelboats with their expensive cargos, no supply caravan was ever lost to nature or to Indian attack. Likewise, the annual cost to maintain small armies of engagés in the field was enormous; free trappers cost a fur company nothing. While engagés received a salary no matter how much they produced, a free trapper's livelihood depended on garnering as many furs as possible. When competition pushed up the price of beaver pelts in the early 1830s, the fur companies simply inflated the cost of the goods sold to the free trappers.

That is not to say that the succession of fur companies anchored along the Missouri River lost money. Overall, however, their profit margin was thinner than those of Ashley and his successors in the decade between 1823 and 1833. After that, high profits tilted back toward the Missouri River trade. By then, the American Fur Company had swamped its rivals and reaped huge monopoly profits. Buffalo robes had soared past beaver pelts in demand and price. The whims of fashion had withered the demand for beaver while overtrapping had exhausted its supply. While the handful of surviving beaver dammed distant mountain streams, seemingly endless numbers of buffalo roamed the nearby plains. Indians could easily bring the robes into one of the dozen trading posts along the Missouri River. Although the river still claimed many a cargo, the bulky robes were much easier to convey by keelboat and, beginning in 1832, by steamboat. Campbell would succeed first in the rendezvous fur trade and later in the Missouri River robe trade.

It was Jedediah Smith who not only recruited Campbell but also, recognizing his intelligence and accounting skills, made him his clerk. Smith was a model of exemplary character, prowess, and will. He had survived an Arikara attack and a grizzly that had nearly mauled him to death. He had repeatedly threaded the wilderness alone or with a comrade to take messages between Ashley's far-flung trapping and supply brigades. Five years older than Campbell and with two more years of wilderness experience, Smith became Campbell's mentor, teaching him about Indians, animals, trapping, and survival. With their common interests and values, the two became close friends.

On October 30, 1825, Campbell left St. Louis with Smith, 70 men, and 160 pack animals carrying twenty thousand dollars' worth of goods. Campbell's virtue must have been sorely tempted as the party passed west through the hamlets and farms en route to the frontier. Jim Beckwourth admitted that "before we left the settlements, our party made free use of the bee-hives, pigs, and poultry belonging to the settlers; a marauding practice commonly indulged in by the mountaineers, who well knew that the strength of their party secured them against any retaliation on the part of the sufferers."[3]

The trapping party headed west along the Kansas River and northeast up the Republican Fork. January snowstorms buried them. With their pack animals dying, they reached and sheltered in an abandoned Pawnee village. Smith sent back "Black" Moses Harris and Jim Beckwourth with a message to Ashley to send a relief expedition with more pack animals.

3. Jim Beckwourth as told to T. D. Bonner, *The Life and Adventures of James P. Beckwourth*, 36. See also the *Missouri Advocate* and *St. Louis Enquirer*, October 29, 1825, *Missouri Republican*, St. Louis, October 31, 1825, in Dale L. Morgan, *The West of William H. Ashley*, 38–39; for conflicting numbers and explanations of Smith's brigade, see Morgan, *Jedediah Smith*, 175, 408n.

How accurate were the accounts of a man known to be a "gaudy liar"? Actually, his biography was largely truthful and his "stretchers" were relatively rare. See Oswald's introduction along with Elinor Wilson, *Jim Beckwourth: Black Mountain Man, War Chief of the Crows, Trader, Trapper, Explorer, Frontiersman, Guide, Scout, Interpreter, Adventurer, and Gaudy Liar*.

They spent a miserable two months in the Pawnee village. Half the men deserted, and nearly all the rest considered following. Campbell recalled that they

> suffered very much for want of provisions. One-third of our mules died that winter, and we sent back for more mules to St. Louis. Some of our men knew where the Indians had formerly cached their corn, and they dug it up. When the Pawnees returned to their village, they having gone out on the Buffalo hunt, we paid them for so much of the corn as we had taken . . . The chief of the Republican Pawnees was Ish-Ka-ta-pa. Mr. Smith and myself staid in his lodge. We had no interpreters. We lived on the corn taken from the caches, and killed some buffalo bulls on the Smoky Hill Fork while going out. That was the only meat we had except that we got occasionally a turkey.[4]

In March, Smith led his party from the Republican to Grand Island on the Platte River and waited there for Ashley. Like many a plains river, the Platte has been described as being "a mile wide and an inch deep." Yet, with the spring snowmelt, the Platte could be a "fussy, foaming, seething thing . . . like some big bragging men I have seen, all blubber and belly."[5] Campbell, Smith, and the others must have spent many an hour gazing down that river, wondering if the message had ever reached Ashley, and if so whether he would rescue them, and gazing up those swirling waters, pondering their fate if they ever did trek the hundreds of miles that separated them from the Rocky Mountains.

Harris and Beckwourth in fact did carry their message to Ashley. The word that Smith's expedition had bogged down and required rescuing chagrined Ashley for more than business reasons. Beckwourth recounts the recently married Ashley's "reluctance to tear himself away from the delights of Hymen." Nonetheless, Ashley immediately began to organize a supply caravan. Before leaving St. Louis, he wrapped his commercial venture in messianic gloss to an admiring *St. Louis Enquirer* reporter. After laying claim for discovering the South Pass, which allowed an easy traverse of the Rocky Mountains, Ashley declared that he was now after something other than wealth—he hoped to find the legendary Buenaventura River, which was said to flow to the Pacific Ocean.[6]

4. Holloway, ed., *A Narrative*, 19.
5. Dale Morgan and Eleanor Towles Harris, eds., *The Rocky Mountain Journals of William Marshall Anderson*, 87.
6. Bonner, *Beckwourth*, 33. "New Route to the Pacific Ocean, discovered by Gen. William H. Ashley, during his late Expedition to the Rocky Mountains," *Missouri Advocate, St. Louis Enquirer*, March 11, 1826, Morgan, *Ashley*, 140–41.

Ashley's twenty-five-man party set off on March 8, 1826, and reached Smith's men on April 1. Beckwourth reported that he

> found the men, twenty-six in number, reduced to short rations, in weakly condition, and in a discouraged state of mind. They had been expecting the arrival of a large company with abundant supplies, and when we rejoined them without any provisions, they were greatly discouraged. General Ashley exerted himself to infuse fresh courage into their disconsolate breasts, well knowing, however, that, unless we could find game, the chances were hard against us . . . Our allowance was half a pint of flour a day per man . . . We numbered thirty-four men, all told, and a duller encampment, I suppose, never was witnessed. No jokes, no fire-side stories, no fun; each man rose in the morning with the gloom of the preceding night filling his mind; we built our fires and partook of our scanty repast without saying a word.[7]

It was a miserable beginning to Campbell's mountain career, and he must have often bitterly regretted ever leaving St. Louis.

Ashley imposed military-style order on his men as they headed up the Platte River. The men were divided into messes of eight to ten, with a man in charge of each. Supplies were distributed to that leader, who then split them among his mess mates. Camps were drawn in a square with the pack animals staked inside at night and guards patrolling outside. The men piled their packs, saddles, and the supplies in a surrounding wall behind which they slept, ate, or lounged until it was time to move on. In the morning scouts rode a wide circle around camp, and if no Indians were spotted the pack animals were then taken out for fresh water and grass. On the march, scouts were sent out on all sides to scour the countryside for Indians or game.[8]

Where the Platte River curled south from its headwaters, Ashley's party headed up the Sweetwater River, traversed South Pass, followed the Sandy and Green down to Ham's Fork, and up it to Cache Valley on the Bear River. Along the way, the men engaged in some late spring trapping. Exploration for fresh beaver grounds and new routes was as important as trapping. One party was dispatched to see if a rumored river—the "Buenaventura"—linked the Great Salt Lake with the Pacific Ocean. Campbell "went to Willow or Cache valley in the spring of 1826, and found the party just returned from their exploration of the

7. Bonner, *Beckwourth*, 37–38.
8. Ashley to Gen. A. Macomb, March 1829, 21st Cong., 2d sess., *Senate Document* 39 (Serial 203), 107.

lake, and [concluded] that it was without any outlet."⁹ The revelation
that the Buenaventura was no more than a mountain myth must have
disappointed everyone, especially Ashley and his lieutenants, whose
enterprise could have been enriched by an easy trade route to California.

Around the first of July, Ashley's trapping brigades that had wintered
in the Rockies and the newer arrivals converged into Cache or Willow
Valley. For two weeks, the ragged trappers would enjoy a range of
bacchanalian delights. Jim Beckwourth leaves us this vivid account:

> The absent parties began to arrive, one after the other. Shortly after, General
> Ashley and Mr. Sublet[te] came in, accompanied with . . . pack mules, well
> laden with goods and all things necessary for the mountaineers and the
> Indian trade. It may well be supposed that the arrival of such a vast amount
> of luxuries from the East did not pass off without a general celebration.
> Mirth, songs, dancing, shouting, trading, running, jumping, singing, racing,
> target-shooting, yarns, frolic, with all sorts of extravagances that white men
> or Indians could invent, were freely indulged in. The Unpacking of the
> medicine water contributed not a little to the heightening of our festivities.¹⁰

The arrival of friendly Indians such as the Flatheads, Shoshones,
Bannocks, and Nez Perces to the rendezvous was essential for its success.
The Indians brought in their own packs of furs for which they received
goods at grossly inflated prices. The fur company leaders not only
unashamedly gouged the Indians as badly as the white trappers but
also skillfully played off the tribes against each other. By supplying
the friendly tribes west of the Rockies with guns, they helped check
the Blackfeet on the eastern side. The more economically dependent a
tribe became on the whites, the less likely its warriors would be to raid the
trapping brigades. For the Indians it was a Faustian bargain. While the
trade enhanced each tribe's living standards, it eroded their traditional
cultures, and, periodically, devastated their populations through the
transmission of plagues.¹¹

Most trappers welcomed the Indians, especially their women, who
were sought both for immediate sexual release and, for many, marriage.

9. Robert Campbell to G. K. Warren, April 4, 1857, *Reports of Explorations and Surveys to Ascertain the Most Practical and Economic Route for a Railroad from the Mississippi River to the Pacific Ocean* (Washington: Government Printing Office, 1861), 11:35.

10. Bonner, *Beckwourth*, 107.

11. W. R. Jacobs, "The Indians and the Frontier in American History—A Need for Revision," 43–56; Jeanne Kay, "The Fur Trade and Native Population Growth," 2265–87; Nick P. Kardulias, "Fur Production as a Specialized Activity in a World System: Indians in the North American Fur Trade," 25–60; Lewis Saum, *The Fur Trader and the Indian.*

Nearly all the tribes enjoyed very uninhibited attitudes about sex—the Cheyenne excepted. While there are tantalizing hints in his letters that Campbell dallied with Indian women, none suggest that he ever "packed a squaw." Well over half of his comrades, however, did marry into a tribe. By one account, the first wives of 40 percent of mountain men were Indian women, and a further 15 percent were women of mixed heritage.[12]

The vivid memories that Campbell recorded about rendezvous characteristically had more to do with sustenance than sex:

> When the supplies were brought up in the Summer, about two pounds of bread each . . . only then did they have bread. Flour cost one dollar for a pint cupfull. The trappers would make a feast of batter fried in melted buffalo tallow—a sort of fritter and call their friends around to partake. Each man brought his pan and his knife, and very little liquor would be sold out— except to the old trappers. The single men among the trappers would mess half a dozen together. The air was pure and perfectly healthy . . . It was a bold and dashing life.[13]

Certainly Robert enjoyed all the antics of the men, although he gives us no details of his own indulgences. Among those who impressed Robert the most was Bill Fallon, "a strong, athletic man, as spry as a cat, and a great horseman. His weight was 200 pounds. He could mount a horse on the run and pick up a sixpence from the ground while on the gallop."[14]

At the 1826 rendezvous, Campbell met William Lewis Sublette, the man who would become his closest friend and business partner.[15] Born in Kentucky in 1799, Sublette was five years older than Campbell and brought to their relationship not only two tough years of wilderness experience but also a hearty, daredevil exuberance. The two hit it off, with each absorbing the other's strengths: Campbell's prudence and Sublette's daring, combined with their shared vision of wringing adventure and riches from the wilderness. Within five years they would broaden their friendship into a legal partnership that brought them wealth and entry into St. Louis's elite circles. For now, however, they

12. William R. Swagerty, "Marriage and Settlement Patterns of Rocky Mountain Trappers and Traders," 159–80; Jennifer S. H. Brown, *Strangers in Blood: Fur Trade Company Families in Indian Country*; Sylvia Van Kirk, *"Many Tender Ties": Women in Fur Trade Society in Western Canada, 1670–1870*; John C. Jackson, *Children of the Fur Trade: Forgotten Metis of the Pacific Northwest*.
13. Holloway, ed., *A Narrative*, 23–24.
14. Ibid., 20.
15. John E. Sunder, *Bill Sublette: Mountain Man*.

were just two young men revelling in the rough companionship, danger, and exhilaration of the mountains.

Along with the others, Campbell and Sublette must have gazed enviously at the wealth Ashley was packing on his mules. Ashley's haul was even greater in 1826 than it had been the previous year; he traded for 125 packs of beaver worth sixty thousand dollars in St. Louis. As historian Richard Clokey explained it, Ashley

> paid his trappers $3 a pound for their pelts at the rendezvous, or $2 a pound to those who accepted a basic salary as well, and he hoped for a price of $5 a pound in St. Louis. His transportation expenses now amounted to $1.12 1/2 a pound, leaving him with an ordinary margin of profit of 80 or 90 cents. When combined with the resale profit on supplies, that figure was reasonable for a stable business operation. But his risks were . . . great at every step of the way.[16]

A staggering number of Ashley's men died—anywhere from twenty-seven to sixty men from 1822 to 1826—in helping to reap that fortune.[17]

Ashley chose to get out while he was ahead. On July 18, 1826, with Robert Campbell serving as legal witness, William Ashley sold his share to the new partnership of Jedediah Smith, William Sublette, and David Jackson. Beneath the three partners were the lieutenants: Campbell, Tom Fitzpatrick, Jim Bridger, Moses Harris, and Jim Beckwourth, although none were then investors in the new company. Under the agreement, Ashley handed over the $16,000 worth of goods he had brought to rendezvous, along with the command of forty-two trappers. After the accounts were figured, the partners owed Ashley $7,821. In addition, Ashley promised to supply them with $7,000 to $15,000 worth of goods at the July 1, 1827, rendezvous as long as he received their order on or before March 1. To prevent being gouged, the partners shrewdly got Ashley to fix a price for each item. Both sides agreed to sell only to each other.[18]

Ashley would serve as the chief backer for Smith, Jackson, and Sublette until they dissolved their partnership in 1830. In eastern markets, Ashley purchased their goods and sold their furs. The partners would either "pay me in Beaver fur delivered in that country at three dollars pr. pound or I am to receive the fur, transport the same to St. Louis and have it disposed of on their account, deducting from the amount of sale one

16. Clokey, *Ashley*, 171.
17. Sunder, *Sublette*, 64.
18. William H. Ashley, to Jedediah S. Smith, David E. Jackson, and William L. Sublette, Articles of Agreement, July 18, 1826, Morgan, *Ashley*, 150–52.

dollar twelve & half cents per pound for transportation, and place the net proceeds to their credit."[19] Ashley also served as the partners' primary financial backer, charging them 6 percent annual interest on banknotes they wrote on his name. It would prove to be a lucrative arrangement for all parties.

The partners decided to split their enterprise into two large brigades. One led by Smith would head southwest, largely for exploration. The other by Jackson and Sublette would head north, largely for trapping, although, of course, both would combine the two objectives.[20]

Campbell accompanied the northbound party to known trapping grounds. They first trapped the upper Snake River watershed, then traversed the divide into Jackson Hole and up into the Yellowstone plateau region. Trapper Daniel Potts leaves an amusing account of a companion's misadventure with Yellowstone's geysers: "One of our men visited one of these while taking his recreation—there at an instant the earth began a tremendous trembling, and he with difficulty made his escape when an explosion took place resembling that of thunder. During our stay in that quarter I heard it every day."[21]

Campbell recalled his own amusing incident that autumn of 1826: "We came across the tracks of a bear, and while following it, Jim Bridger, who was in advance, saw a smoke on the head waters of the Missouri. We, Sublette, Bridger, and myself, determined to see what it was. As we habitually had to be on the alert when hostile Indians were suspected in our vicinity, we dashed along, until we came to a place where the Indians had camped a month before, leaving some burned logs, from which the smoke still issued. The exploit became known for a long time in camp as " 'the battle of the burned logs.' "[22]

Such amusements only briefly diverted the men from the misery of wading the icy mountain streams and ponds in which they set their traps. Campbell offers this succinct description of the process

> for trapping the beaver . . . The beaver has a little bag under the tail, or more properly an oil sac near the anus. The trapper takes this castoreum from the

19. Ashley to [B. Pratte and Co.], October 14, 1826, Ashley Papers, MoHiS.

20. For details on Smith's adventures, see Harrison Clifford Dale, *The Explorations of William H. Ashley and Jedediah Smith, 1822–1829;* George R. Brooks, ed., *The Southwest Expedition of Jedediah Smith: His Personal Account of the Journey to California, 1826–1827;* and Morgan, *Jedediah Smith.*

21. Daniel Potts to brother, July 8, 1827, reprinted in Donald McKay Frost, ed., "Notes on General Ashley, the Overland Trail, and South Pass," 63.

22. Holloway, ed., *A Narrative,* 26.

sac, and uses it as bait . . . They take a piece of willow, strip off the bark and wash it, so as to leave no scent, as the beaver's sense of smell is exquisite, and then put castoreum on it. The willow is attached to the trap and floats over it, when the beaver is attracted to the smell approaches and is caught. The animal flounders about until drowned, but if he gets on the bank, with the trap, he has been known to bite off his feet to regain his liberty. The trappers generally set out from camp with eight traps each. When they moved camp they cached what provisions were not necessary for the hunt, as dependence was made on game. Arriving at good hunting ground a stop was made of some two or three days in a place, or even for one day. They then set their traps for three or four miles up and down the stream . . . It was the habit, to have out two-thirds trapping, and the other taking care of camp, no matter how large the party would be.[23]

Though steel traps were the most common means of taking beaver, the mountain men also shot them as they swam or clubbed them on land or in their lodges. While the trappers were scattered for miles along nearby streams and ponds, those left in camp would keep busy stretching and scrapping hides, grazing the horses, repairing equipment, and keeping a sharp eye out for Indian raiders, while the rest scattered, usually in pairs, for miles to search out beaver. Most trappers took about 120 skins a year.[24]

Trappers skinned a wide range of animals, including muskrats, otters, foxes, martens, sables, wolves, bears, deer, elk, and raccoons. Beaver pelts, however, were the most highly valued by American and European furriers and thus the primary target. Beavers have two layers of fur: the long, brown outer fur and an underlayer of short, fibrous hairs. The underlayer was used for felt, which was molded into the tall, short-brimmed hats so fashionable among the well-to-do in Europe and America. Trapping occurred in late fall or early spring when beaver pelts were at their thickest and the waters ice-free. Pelts and other skins were then pressed into packs that weighed roughly a hundred pounds each. The typical beaver pack included sixty to seventy pelts and the buffalo pack about ten robes.[25]

Beaver flourish best in sluggish streams and ponds surrounded by willow and aspen, a primary source of food and building materials for dams and lodges. After mating in February, the female beaver gives

23. Ibid., 23, 25.
24. F. J. Young, ed., "The Correspondence and Journals of Captain Nathaniel Wyeth, 1831–36," *Sources of the History of Oregon*, 1:60–61.
25. C. E. Hanson, Jr., "Castoreum," *The Museum of the Fur Trade Quarterly* 1 (1965): 3–7.

birth to two to four cubs by May or June. Two and a half years later, the surviving beaver will reach maturity, weighing thirty to sixty pounds. Trapping aside, beaver populations naturally fluctuate. During prolonged droughts, parasites such as tularemia and pseudotuberculosis concentrate in the water and kill off beaver. Mild winters also can exact a toll; more babies survive and diseases are bred in the crowded lodges and ponds. If left alone, beaver populations will rebound from these natural catastrophes.[26]

Unregulated trapping, however, upset this balance. By scouring the same valleys year after year, trappers destroyed their own livelihood over the long term. Ashley clearly recognized how short-sighted all this was, and advocated "leaving the streams undisturbed for five or six years" after trapping a valley, which would allow the beaver to "be found as numerous as when first trapped." As sensible as such a scheme was, it would have been impossible to implement in the free-for-all marketplace. Only where the Hudson's Bay Company enjoyed a monopoly, as in the Canadian Rockies and the Northwest, was regulation possible. In fact, Sir George Simpson, the Hudson's Bay Company's manager in that region, instituted just such a conservation policy for the Hudson's Bay Company as early as 1821.[27]

To trap and survive in the mountains, a man needed some essential clothing and equipment consisting of

> one Animal upon which is placed one or two [blankets] a riding Saddle and bridle a sack containing six Beaver traps a blanket with extra pair of Mocasins his powder horn and bullet pouch with a belt to which is attached a butcher Knife a small wooden box containing bait for Beaver a Tobacco sack with a pipe and implements for making fire with sometimes a hatchet fastened to the Pommel of his saddle his personal dress is a flannel or cotton shirt (if he is fortunate enough to obtain one, if not Antelope skin answers the purpose of over and under shirt) a pair of leather breeches with Blanket or smoked Buffaloe skin, leggings, a coat made of Blanket or Buffaloe robe a hat or Cap of wool, Buffaloe or Otter skin his hose are pieces of Moccasins made of Dressed Deer Elk or Buffaloe skins with his long hair falling loosely over his shoulders complete his uniform.[28]

26. Wishart, *Fur Trade*, 27–29; J. M. Cowan, "The Fur Trade and the Fur Cycle: 1825–1857," 19–30; Alfred Morrell, *Beaver Behavior*.

27. W. H. Ashley to Dale L. Morgan, ed., *Ashley*, 177–78. Arthur J. Ray, "Some Conservation Schemes of the Hudson's Bay Company, 1821–50: An Examination of Resource Management in the Fur Trade," 49–65.

28. Aubrey L. Haines, ed., *Journal of a Trapper: Osborne Russell*, 82.

After trapping through the Yellowstone plateau, Sublette and Jackson decided to venture over the divide into what was considered the West's richest fur grounds—the Three Forks region, where the Jefferson, Madison, and Gallatin Rivers join to form the Missouri River. That region was also the most dangerous—it was the southern end of Blackfeet country, which stretched all the way north along the Rocky Mountain's front range to the Saskatchewan River. No tribe warred more fiercely or incessantly against the Americans than the Blackfeet, in part because of a cultural proclivity for aggression and in part because the whites had befriended their enemies. Campbell explained that the "Blackfeet were always at war with us because they were at war with the Snakes, the Crows, the Flatheads, and the neighboring tribes. They had fierce contests, and great care was taken to avoid them when on their marauding expeditions. They would cut up bear's feet, and use them as moccasins to steal up and capture horses."[29]

Three bands composed the Blackfeet or Siksikauwa tribe: the Siksika or Blackfoot in the north, the Kainah or Bloods in the center, and the Piegans or Pikuni in the south. A fourth Algonquian-speaking band, the Atsina or Gros Ventres, lived among the Blackfeet but were more closely related linguistically and culturally to the Arapaho, whom they frequently visited. The dialects spoken by the Blackfeet and Gros Ventres were not understood by more recent Algonquian-speaking arrivals to the plains such as the Cheyenne, Crees, and Ojibwas. The Gros Ventres were the most aggressive of the four bands, and many of their raids were attributed to the Blackfeet.

These four bands may have arrived on the northwest plains as early as the seventeenth century. By the mid–eighteenth century, they had begun trading with whites and had acquired horses and guns, which enabled them to hunt buffalo and enemies more efficiently. The Blackfeet drove tribes such as the Shoshone, Flathead, and Kutanai west of the Rockies. With more food and fewer enemies the Blackfoot population expanded steadily, making them virtually invincible not only along the front range but wherever their war parties raided. Physically, the Blackfeet "are more of a Herculean make—about middling stature, with broad shoulders and great expansion of chest. The skins of their dresses are chiefly black or of a dark brown color. They have black leggings or moccasins, from which comes the name Blackfeet."[30]

29. Holloway, ed., *A Narrative*, 25; John C. Ewers, *The Blackfeet: Raiders on the Northwest Plains*.
30. Michael MacDonald Mooney, ed., *George Catlin Letters and Notes on the North American Indians*, 121.

The Blackfeet were fiercely independent and tended to murder any strangers who entered their land. By the late eighteenth century, however, the Hudson's Bay Company had managed to forge an uneasy peace with them. The British had no choice but to do so since the Blackfeet occupied a strategic region on the northwest plains that split the Hudson's Bay Company's Columbia and Saskatchewan River operations. The Blackfeet were willing enough to trade with the Hudson's Bay Company, but they would permit no trapping in their territory. The Blackfeet themselves did not trap beaver, which were sacred to them, although they did not hesitate to trade skins or plews looted from others. Mostly, the Blackfeet hunted other fur animals as well as buffalo.

Shortly after Campbell and his brigade entered the Three Forks region, a Blackfoot war party picked up their trail and stalked the trappers to their winter camp in the Cache Valley. All along, the Blackfeet tried to cut off stray trappers or steal horses. Potts describes one such encounter:

> two others and myself pushed on in the advance for the purpose of accumulating a few more Beaver and in the act of passing through a narrow confine in the Mountain we . . . met plumb in face a large party of Blackfeet Indians, who not knowing our numbers fled into the Mountain in confusion and we to a small grove of willows where we made every preparation for battle after which finding our enemy as much alarmed as ourselves we mounted our Hourses which were heavyly loaded we took the back retreat. The Indians raised a tremendious Yell and showered down from the Mountain top [and] almost cut off our retreat. We here put whip to our Horses and they pursued us in close quarters until we reached the plains where we left them behind on this trip one man was closely fired on by a party of Black feet several others were closely pursued.[31]

It seemed impossible to shake the Blackfeet. One day while the brigade wintered in Cache Valley at the Snake River forks, "the Blackfeet came in the day time and took the two fastest horse, belonging to our Iroquois . . . They got the start and we could not follow." After the theft the trappers redoubled their watch. The care paid off. The Blackfeet tried again and "came up one night, but our Iroquois understood the signs. We had our animals picketed and guarded at night and always had three reliefs in nights. Every man had to mount guard except the leader of the expedition."[32]

31. Daniel Potts to Brother, July 8, 1827, Morgan, *Ashley*, 162.
32. Holloway, ed., *A Narrative*, 24.

With Blackfeet and other hostile Indians lurking near, the trappers suffered constant tension broken by sheer terror when war cries and arrows tore the air. Winter brought its own miseries. Holing up for month after month in cramped, frozen, smoky, makeshift huts was hellish. The winter trapped them like animals, sapped them to the dregs of their stamina and sanity. Cabin fever must at times have reached near murderous proportions. Even the best story lost its vigor after the dozenth retelling. Pranks that would have amused in easier circumstances might provoke fistfights instead. Resentments boiled over real and imagined slights. Even the most hardened trapper must have mourned ever leaving his family and friends now half a continent away. How did they keep from going mad in that icy straitjacket?

Forced enrollment in the "Rocky Mountain College" certainly eased the boredom, if anyone in their party had anything to teach. Those who could read taught those who could not. Charred sticks stratched letters on bark sheets. A well-worn edition of Shakespeare's plays, the Bible, or some other literary work was a godsend, stimulating endless debates over the meaning of passages or dilemmas of the characters.

Gambling was the only real excitement for those snowbound men. Betting their meager fortunes or falling deeper into debt through endless rounds of the game hand helped pass the time. Such activities relieved but a fraction of the monotony. Enormous relief and high jinks exploded when the snows of the last winter storm began to melt and brigade leaders called on the men to pack up.

While Campbell and his comrades dragged beaver from their traps, dodged Blackfeet, and huddled around smoky fires in the Rockies, Ashley returned to St. Louis with fifty men and a hundred pack animals loaded with furs. He then took a hard survey of the competition. Only the Hudson's Bay Company competed directly with Ashley and his successors in the Rockies, but the British company proved a dangerous rival. Sir George Simpson, the Hudson's Bay Company commander between the Pacific Ocean and Rockies, ordered his annual brigades launched from Flathead Post or Nez Perce Post into the Rockies to trap out the region and create a "fur desert" between the British and American realms and "poison the minds of the Indians . . . against us."[33]

33. William H. Ashley to Joseph Charless, St. Louis, June 5, 1827, Morgan, *Ashley*, 166. See also William H. Ashley to Benton, January 11, 20, 1829, William H. Ashley to General Alexander Macomb, Commander in Chief, U.S. Army, March 1829, S. W. Foreman to John H. Eaton, Secretary of War, St. Louis, May 1829, ibid., 183–88, 189–94, 195–96.

In 1824, violence had almost begun between American and British parties camped in the same valley when the Hudson's Bay Company leader, Peter Skene Ogden, displayed the Union Jack. Each side claimed the other was trespassing on their national territory. Actually, both were violating Mexican sovereignty. A score of enraged Americans led by Johnson Gardner stormed into Ogden's camp and not only forced him to haul down his flag but also induced twenty-nine of his trappers to defect with promises of higher prices for their furs. Tensions had continued to simmer whenever the rivals found themselves trapping the same streams.

Of the three American firms Ashley had faced since 1822, none had tried to trap the Rockies after the massacre of a Missouri Fur Company party led by Michael Immell and Robert Jones in 1823; the company folded in 1825. The two surviving rivals clung to posts on the Upper Missouri. The French Company of Pierre Chouteau and Bernard Pratte barely retained Fort Lookout in the heart of Teton Sioux territory. Kenneth McKenzie's Columbia Fur Company had been more successful; its Fort Kiowa and Fort Tilton reaped a modest annual collection of furs and robes. Both companies maintained posts in the Council Bluffs area near the Platte River mouth. All three firms would eventually be devoured by a fourth.

It was John Jacob Astor's American Fur Company that posed the greatest threat to Smith, Jackson, and Sublette, and to their backer, Ashley.[34] Astor's firm dominated the trade on the American side of the Great Lakes and controlled the marketing for most fur sales funneled through New York City. As early as 1808, when he incorporated the American Fur Company, Astor had envisioned monopolizing the trade across the continent. He had first tried to enter the western fur trade in 1810 when his newly formed Pacific Fur Company dispatched overland and sea expeditions to the Columbia River valley. After a series of setbacks, he was forced to sell out to the Hudson's Bay Company in 1813 in the midst of the War of 1812. Undaunted by the failure, he never lost his dream of expanding his fur empire east of the Mississippi River to engulf the entire West. Meanwhile, he directed his American Fur Company's Northern Department to crush all rivals in the Great Lakes and upper Mississippi Valley regions.

On May 6, 1822, Astor celebrated the destruction of a major fur trade rival—the U.S. government. The factory or government trading

---

34. Kenneth Wiggins Porter, *John Jacob Astor: Business Man.*

post system had been created in 1796 to discourage private traders from impoverishing and debauching the Indians through price gouging and liquor sales. The twenty-eight factories that were eventually established tried to undersell private traders and uphold laws that forbade trading liquor to the Indians. Underfunded by Congress, the factory system was more an irritant than a threat to the American Fur Company and other traders. Nonetheless it was a "monster" worth slaying. Without it, profits would soar. Astor enlisted the support of Missouri Senator Thomas Hart Benton and succeeded in twisting enough arms and greasing enough palms in Congress to get a bill passed that abolished the government factory system.

That same year Astor sent his junior partner, Ramsey Crooks, to St. Louis to establish a branch of the American Fur Company known as the Western Department. Crooks began negotiations with local fur companies to acquire a stake on the Missouri River. While the fur companies themselves spurned his advances, their key supplier and marketer, Stone, Bostwick, and Company, which had been pushed to bankruptcy's brink by years of fierce pounding by the American Fur Company, surrendered. When Astor bought out Stone, Bostwick, and Company on April 1, 1823, he acquired a potential stranglehold on Ashley's and Henry's partnership, as well as on other St. Louis ventures. Crooks renewed his negotiations with Chouteau and Pratte to acquire B. Pratte and Company, better known as the French Fur Company; they sold out in January 1827. That same year, in July, Crooks bought out the Columbia Fur Company. Astor consolidated the two firms and named his newest conquest the Upper Missouri Outfit of the Western Department of the American Fur Company. Robert Campbell could not possibly know it at the time, but the American Fur Company's Upper Missouri Outfit and its successors would be his nemesis for nearly three decades.[35]

Astor already had a financial hook into Ashley when he took over Stone, Bostwick and Company, and he sunk another after acquiring B. Pratte and Company. Unfortunately, Ashley had begun negotiating for a joint venture with B. Pratte and Company only three months before it sold out to Astor. On October 14, 1826, Ashley suggested to Pierre Chouteau, Jr., and Bernard Pratte that they invest in an 1827 trapping expedition. Following up a talk he had had with Pratte several days earlier, Ashley proposed "an equal participation in the adventure . . . The expedition I propose sending in the spring will consist of about

35. Porter, *Astor*, 734–67; David Lavender, *Fist in the Wilderness*, 341–43, 471.

forty Men one hundred twenty mules & horses, the merchandise &c necessary to supply them for twelve months, and that to be furnished Messrs Smith Jackson & Sublett, all of which must be purchased for cash on the best terms."[36] Pratte and his partners spurned Ashley's offer.

In January, Ashley went east on a buying trip. From Lancaster, Pennsylvania, he wrote to Chouteau, offering more details for his proposal:

> I will accompany the expedition as far as I may deem absolutely necessary, and receive for my personal services . . . two hundred & fifty dollars pr. month which sum is to be paid by due me by the hunters west of the mountains . . . they accounting to me . . . at whatever price I receive [the pelts] in that country which is in no case to exceed three dollar pr. pound . . . the said B. Pratt will account to me for and pay the same at St. Louis . . . Pratte & Co will not suffer any person trading for them at [Taos] or other . . . places, directly or indirectly to interfere with the business in the same section of the country.[37]

In other words, Ashley offered Pratte and Company a partnership in return for agreeing to withdraw from all its other operations. The man drove a tough bargain.

A letter from Chouteau apparently crossed Ashley's in the mail, for in it he did not mention the latter's demand that Pratte and Company withdraw from all other operations. Instead, Chouteau spoke of their earlier talks and concluded that a deal "would be to our mutual advantage," but asked for time to consider it. The sticking point, as revealed in "all our conversations on the subject . . . has always been to decide who should conduct the Expedition. If this question were once decided, I have no doubt that we could come to an agreement."[38] Chouteau's words are ambiguous, but he seems to at once laud Ashley's leadership for such an expedition while hinting that someone from Pratte and Company should actually command it.

By February 28, Ashley was back in St. Louis wrangling with Pratte and Chouteau over his proposals.[39] Two deals hung in the balance by March 1, 1827: Ashley was on the verge of cutting a deal with Pratte and Chouteau, which in turn depended on whether he received a merchandise order and 1827 rendezvous location from Smith, Sublette,

36. Ashley to B. Pratte and Co., October 14, 1826, Morgan, *Ashley,* 158–59.
37. Ashley to B. Pratte and Co., February 2, 1827, ibid., 160.
38. Pierre Chouteau, Jr., to William H. Ashley, Philadelphia, February 10, 1827, ibid., 160–61.
39. William H. Ashley to Bernard Pratte, St. Louis, February 28, 1827, ibid., 161.

and Jackson by that date. The March 1 deadline passed with no word from the partners.

Ashley could not know that word from the partners was merely a few days away. On New Year's Day, William Sublette and Moses Harris set off from the camp with hopes of reaching St. Louis before the March 1 deadline.[40] It was an extraordinarily reckless gamble. The two men had to trudge their way on foot through a thousand miles of wilderness during the middle of winter and reach St. Louis in two months. They tramped off through the drifts in snowshoes, accompanied by a pack dog. Along the way, they found no buffalo and little water or firewood until they reached the Sweetwater River. They rested briefly at a Pawnee village on the Platte River, then continued downriver. Buffalo and other game were elusive. A little farther, Sublette traded a knife for a dried buffalo tongue from a party of Pawnee. They were so hungry at Grand River that they greedily devoured a raven one of them had shot. At starvation's brink, they debated eating their faithful dog. Sublette finally agreed. Harris managed to throttle the dog, and its meat sustained them for two days. Starvation soon hovered again; they staved it off by killing a rabbit. They reached the Kaw village, where they traded a pistol for a horse. The race ended on March 4 when they stumbled into Ashley's home in St. Louis.

The disclosure that Ashley was trying to mount a joint expedition with the opposition must have badly jolted Sublette. How much could Ashley be trusted after all? Four months before the March 1 deadline, Ashley had begun negotiations that would have dissolved their July 1826 agreement! But within two days of Sublette's arrival everything fell into place. Ashley dropped the plan for his own expedition, which made less financial sense after he had heard Sublette's tales of his men having garnered a mountain of furs that now merely awaited shipment back to civilization. Although Sublette technically had voided the 1826 agreement by missing the deadline by three days, Ashley agreed to honor it. Doing so was hardly a sacrifice for Ashley; he stood to make a nice pile of money from the deal. Yet he still wanted to split the costs, risks, and profits with Pratte and Company. Chouteau and Pratte agreed.

Once hands were shaken, the plans moved quickly. Ashley had already lined up most of the supplies, pack animals, and men. On March 8, 1827, Ashley advertised for fifty engagés to be employed in the mountains for a year at wages of $110. A mere week later, on March 15,

40. Sublette Recollection Recorded by Matthew Field, 1843, ibid., 163.

the supply caravan left St. Louis with fifty men, a hundred packhorses carrying $6,500 of goods, and a four-pounder cannon slung between two mules. Ill health and business duties forced Ashley to turn back at Lexington. Sublette had tarried in St. Louis to recuperate from his arduous journey and apply for a trading license. On March 26, he met with Indian Superintendent William Clark to receive a two-year trading license for his firm, capitalized at $4,335 and bonded with $3,000. He caught up to the plodding caravan west of Lexington.[41]

Meanwhile, across the Rockies, the scattered winter camps broke up and the men began trapping. Campbell's party "started on a hunt to the waters of the seeds-ke-dee-agie (Prairie Hen River) now called Green River. The name is very euphonious, as pronounced by the Indians. It was called Verde (green) by the Mexicans."[42] The season proved another lucrative one for most as they gradually trapped their way toward that year's rendezvous at Bear Lake, to be held during the first two weeks of July 1827.

The whites present were a mix of free trappers, who received the mountain price of $3 a pound for their furs, and engagés, most of whom made $200 and some $110 a year. As a clerk and lieutenant, Robert received both a fixed salary of $500 and the mountain price for any furs he dragged in. Even the most successful trapper saw his profit disappear with the inflated prices for essential and luxury goods alike. Ashley had marked up the goods that he sold the partners by roughly 50 to 75 percent, and in some cases by even more. For example, gunpowder cost $1.50 a pound in St. Louis and $2.50 when delivered to rendezvous; lead was raised from $1 to $1.50, coffee and tobacco from $1.25 to $2, vermillion from $3 to $6, beads from $2.50 to $5, three point blankets from $9 to $15, cotton stripes per yard from $1.25 to $2.50, calico from $1 to $2.50, scarlet cloth from $6 to $10, and blue cloth from $5 to $8. The partners in turn "sold their goods one third dearer than Ashley did."[43]

The partners made little money on their fur sales. They paid the free trappers $3 a pound, the same price they received for those furs from Ashley. Depending on how many or few furs the engagés took, the partners either made or lost money on them. Then the partners had to deduct the salaries of a half dozen lieutenants such as Campbell, whose

41. Sunder, *Sublette*, 73; William H. Ashley to B. Pratte and Co., April 4, 11, 14, 1827, Morgan, *Ashley*, 164–66.

42. Holloway, ed., *A Narrative*, 25–26.

43. Morgan, *Jedediah Smith*, 232. Potts to brother, July 8, 1827, Frost, ed., "Notes on Ashley," 67.

leadership more than made up for their cost. Any profits for the partners and Ashley alike came from marking up merchandise prices.

In all, the white and Indian trappers brought in 7,400 pounds of beaver pelts and 95 pounds of castoreum for $3 a pound, and 102 otter skins for $2 a pound. In return, the partners sold the men $22,690 worth of goods. In St. Louis, Pratte and Company bought from Ashley those same furs for $33,150 or $4.75 a pound. In all, the partners cleared their debt with Ashley and made a slender profit. Ashley, in contrast, rode off with at least $10,580.72. These lessons were not lost on Campbell.[44]

The Americans scored an important diplomatic coup at the rendezvous when they forged a peace agreement among themselves and the Shoshone and Utes. Before then war parties from both tribes, but especially the Shoshone, had stolen horses and even killed trappers. For the remainder of the fur trade era, those two nations lived in peace with the trappers–with some notable transgressions.

And then there were the Blackfeet. One day nearly 120 Blackfeet charged the camp's outskirts and killed a Shoshone warrior and his wife. The camp was in an uproar as men snatched up rifles or saddled horses to drive off the attackers. The Utes, Shoshones, and six whites rode out against the Blackfeet, who retreated to a patch of woods on the plain. The Blackfeet finally fled, leaving six dead and perhaps carrying off others. The Shoshone lost three killed and three wounded. Campbell recalled that of the six trappers who gamely waded into the battle, "Tullock was wounded on the wrist, and his hand withered from the effects of the wound . . . Sublette behaved bravely. I staid in camp in charge of everything. the families of those killed disposed of all the bodies. One of them placed a buffalo robe on Sublette's tent and said to him, 'You are a great warrior . . .' "[45]

As the trappers recovered their wits from that scare, another surprise, this one pleasant, greeted them. Smith and two other men staggered into the rendezvous on July 3. After trekking parts of the Sevier, Virgin, and Colorado River canyons they had struck across the Mohave Desert to the Mexican settlements, and then north up California's Central Valley, where Smith had left the expedition to return to rendezvous for more men and supplies.

44. *Missouri Observer,* October 17, 1827; Morgan, *Jedediah Smith,* 233; Gowans, *Rendezvous,* 26.

45. Robert Campbell, Morgan, *Ashley,* 168; see Beckwourth's exaggerated account in Bonner, *Beckwourth,* 71–73.

The rendezvous broke up on July 13. Smith had tarried but ten days when he set off again for California accompanied by eighteen men. Rather than retrace his tortured trek across the Great Basin, he would reach his men by the previous year's roundabout route. This time the partners would not see each other until the 1829 rendezvous, when Smith would stagger back with word of even greater disaster. Sublette led a party north into the Blackfeet country. Jackson headed back to Missouri with the caravan. In St. Louis he and Ashley would quickly buy up twenty thousand dollars' worth of goods, gather a pack train and wranglers, and lead it back to the mountains that autumn. Those supplies would be a godsend to the parties that received them.

Campbell now commanded his own trapping brigade. Leading the Iroquois and a mélange of white trappers, he led his party through the heart of Blackfeet country via the headwaters of the Missouri and Columbia Rivers, especially the beaver-rich Deer Lodge and Bitter Root Rivers. In the Big Hole Valley they encountered an immense buffalo herd. While the Indians accompanying his party rode off to "surround" the buffalo, a trapper managed to catch a beaver, which the party's French cook roasted. Campbell "ate a small piece to quiet my appetite, as I had had nothing to eat for a day or two. Just after I ate, I felt pains, as did all the others who ate. The beavers were poisoned from eating the wild parsnip. Hence the name of the river, Malade . . . The result of the 'Surround' was that the Indians came in with any quantity of buffalo meat but none of us would enjoy it. We had pains in the neck, head, and other disagreeable sensations in the stomach and bowels."[46]

Entering Cache Valley, they discovered a Blackfoot village. With their horses exhausted, they had no choice but to camp nearby. Campbell recalled that

> some of our men went to the village and found they had fortifications built up to protect them. The Blackfeet came into our camp and we were suspicious of trouble. We started off early in the morning to go on the Snake river, and the Indians followed us. At a little creek I brought our men under shelter of a bank. The Indians attacked us, and our men fired upon them. Old Pierre [an Iroquois trapper] was killed. He had advanced too far. One of the most notable incidents was that we had a Flathead Indian and a squaw accompanying us. He started to fight the Indians. His squaw followed and cheered him on. The poor fellow was shot through the head, but we brought him into camp. He lived four or five days after he was shot. The eventful

46. Holloway, ed., *A Narrative*, 29.

valley in which Pierre met his fate, has perpetuated his name, "Pierre's Hole." We remained there several days. We found a portion of Old Pierre's remains—a portion of his feet—in the Blackfeet village after they left. Whilst we remained there, two Indians, who had been out stealing, were coming down in an opposite direction. The Iroquois shot them, and they were the first Indians that I saw scalped. The Iroquois put their feet on the dead body, fastened their fingers in the hair, and running the knife around the skull, yanked the scalp off in an instant. It was a horrid sight.[47]

Following the fight, the Iroquois decided to return to the Flathead camp, leaving Campbell with a Flathead and a French Canadian. The three men camped in Willow Valley. A few days after arriving, Campbell

went out on my mule to hunt. Whilst I was gone a party of Crows that had been visiting the Snakes at Salt Lake took four of our horses; the Indian and Frenchmen whom I had left in charge concealing themselves. (Two years later I saw the horses in the Crow village). When I returned to camp it was deserted. After a while my Flathead Indian discovered me . . . and said he thought I and the Frenchman were killed . . . The next morning I went off to reconnoiter these same Indians between Willow valley and Salt Lake, and saw the Indians camped there. My Flathead said if I would give him a knife, he would go down in the night and steal a horse to replace the one he had lost. He offered to steal one for me also. I objected, and dissuaded him from making the attempt. We remained in the Mountains for three days, to keep out of their way. We then came back into the valley and found our trapper party. They found the Frenchmen that they supposed had been killed. His name was James Fourness and he lived . . . until he was over one hundred years old.[48]

That winter of 1827–1828 was one of the worst on record. Those who survived it would shiver at the mere thought of the utter misery of those frigid, snowbound short days and long nights. Brigade leaders ceaselessly fought through the snowdrifts and subzero temperatures to keep their enterprise alive. Campbell

took a party and went over to Sweet Water Lake where we had made a cache the previous summer. A terrible snow storm came on which lasted several days. We had to go to Soda Springs on Bear river, a long distance out of the way. The result was, all our animals died from starvation. The snow was four feet deep . . . It was one of the most severe winters ever known. I cached my goods there and went back to camp in Willow or Cache valley. I then

47. Ibid., 30.
48. Ibid., 30–31.

disposed of my goods there to the trappers and started back on snow shoes, with four dogs and a train which I got from the hunters. On the second day, all gave out except the half-breeds. We travelled on to the mouth of the Pontneuf where Fort Hall was subsequently built. There I found Mr. Samuel Tullock with a party of trappers and a brother [Pinckney] of Sublette was with him—also Mr. Peter [Skene] Ogden, with a portion of Hudson's Bay trappers, all encamped together snow bound. They could go no further.[49]

Although he does not mention Robert Campbell's name, Ogden records that on February 17, 1828, there arrived "two Americans . . . accompanied by one of their Traders and two men, they met on the Pontneuf River, near its sources . . . he also informed me, they had a skirmish with the Black Feet, and old Pierre the Iroquois Chief who deserted from me four years ago was killed and cut into pieces."[50]

Campbell's arrival was an enormous relief to those Americans stranded with Ogden. In the weeks before he had appeared, the Americans had failed to muster a war party against the Shoshone and were unsuccessful in three attempts to struggle through the snowbound mountains and join Campbell. Now Campbell tried to enlist Ogden and his Hudson's Bay men in a joint attack against the Shoshone. Ogden demurred, though he agreed wholeheartedly that retribution was necessary.[51]

The winter storms could no more stifle the rivalry between the Americans and British than it could the Indian danger. Ogden worried that the Americans would try to lure away his trappers by offering higher prices for their pelts. In fact, the opposite had happened. Two of Campbell's men deserted to Ogden, who undoubtedly felt a barely suppressed glee when he rejected Robert's pleas that they be returned. After all, a mere four years earlier, another American party had humiliated him when they enticed more than a score of his men to desert to their side. Then he had been helpless. Now the tables were turned, although the stakes were far lower. Campbell settled the affair in his favor the following day when he "had a long conference with the two trappers who joined me last fall, and both have consented to return."[52]

Their plight worsened when yet another winter storm reburied them, hemming in Campbell and his men. To further complicate the difficulties,

49. Ibid., 31.
50. T. C. Elliot, ed., "Peter Skene Ogden—Journal of Snake Expedition, 1827–28, 1828–29," February 17, 1828.
51. Ibid., January 22, 1828.
52. Ibid., February 20, 1828.

a party of Shoshones arrived to pitch their lodges half a mile from camp; they proved to be "Starving and very troublesome." Campbell was determined to rejoin his men before the snow melted: "I then prepared to leave to join my party, who were with the Flatheads, on Flathead river. We packed our bedding on the dog train. I had two half-breeds . . . with me. We carried no tent for ourselves." He and his men finally struggled away on February 23. The most information that Ogden could pry from Campbell was that they were heading for Flathead country. He remarked that "they have certainly a long Journey before them, but are well provided for it, while here they were very silent regarding the object of their journey."[53]

It would be another month before Tullock embarked with his brigade. Shortly after Tullock and his men left on March 26, they were "attacked by Blackfeet on the Portneuf river. The attack occurred in the morning, and they were robbed of all their horses, and had four men killed, Sublette's brother [Pinckney] among them."[54]

Campbell recalled his party's rugged journey north:

> At night we shovelled off the snow with our snowshoes, for the dogs tent. We killed buffalo to live on. We fed our dogs at night so that their food could digest, while they were at rest. We passed through Shoshone Cove, and crossed the Bitterroot river. All the country to the West was free from snow . . . We went down the Mountain to the plain. We hung up our snow-shoes on a tree, and made little sacks for saddlebags, where there was no snow. We crossed the Hellsgate to Wild-Horse Mountain, and found the party who had left us the season before, feeding off the flesh of wild horses. It was very good food. There were no buffalo in that part of the country. The flesh of the young colt is delicious. They had wild onions for a condiment. I had been forty-four days on snow-shoes and my ankles became lame when I took them off. We hunted and trapped along and came to Sweet Water lake again.[55]

The spring trapping through Flathead country was successful, but plagued with difficulties. As if all the challenges of wilderness survival were not harsh enough, the gunpowder brought to the 1827 rendezvous was of very poor quality, "so bad, that it became a saying, that the men would snap the gun and lay it down on the ground, before it went off."[56]

53. Holloway, ed., *A Narrative*, 32. Elliot, "Odgen," February 23, 1828.
54. Holloway, ed., *A Narrative*, 32.
55. Ibid., 32–33.
56. Ibid., 33.

Misfires were common, and could be disastrous if game was scarce or if trappers were under attack from bears or Blackfeet. The word of the trappers' weakness spread among all the mountain tribes, friendly and hostile. Yet they managed to dodge Blackfeet throughout their spring hunt.

Ironically, to their horror, they ran into several hundred Blackfeet warriors only a half dozen miles from the July 1828 rendezvous. Campbell recalled,

> we were at the foot of the Lake and going up towards the head. In the morning we were attacked by the Blackfeet just as we were starting from camp. Four of the trappers who had been up at the head of the Lake came down and had joined me the night before. They managed to get some good powder. My cook, who had the tents packed on the horses was found killed early in the morning. I led the party and got to a Willow Spring and prepared for defense. We fought for four hours. We knew of four Blackfeet being killed by our fire. Presuming on our poor powder they charged on us and were shot down. We didn't get their scalps. We then found that our ammunition was getting short. We were cut off. The Indians flanked us and got in ahead of us.[57]

Campbell and his men reached some rocks where they sheltered and opened fire. They were safe for now. But they were already nearly out of ammunition.

Campbell gathered his men and offered a solution to their dilemma:

> We knew that the encampment at the head of the Lake—18 miles distant—had ammunition, that we sorely needed. The question was, how to get out, and get a communication with the camp. I proposed that I would go through to the encampment with two horses. A little Spaniard volunteered to go with me and we started. We dashed right in the face of the enemy! As it is not their mode to stand a charge, they separated. We dashed on, and as they saw this they gave way and fled before our onset. They knew that we would soon reach reinforcements, and in turn surround them. We went on at a gallop; I and the little Spaniard. We were going at such speed, that my horse fell with me. The whole of my face was skinned. Reaching the encampment, I started back immediately with reinforcements and a supply of ammunition, and rejoined the balance of our party. The Indians had disappeared as soon as they saw we went out for help. We lost half a dozen horses in the fight, but got off safely, except with the loss of one man killed and two or three wounded.[58]

57. Ibid., 33.
58. Ibid., 33–34.

The Blackfeet escaped with five thousand dollars' worth of pelts, forty horses, and other goods. Six or eight Blackfeet were killed or wounded; among Campbell's men, one man (the cook) was killed and two others were wounded. Campbell's loss of a small fortune just miles before it could have been safely sheltered in camp would have caused him bitter disappointment, although it probably did not linger. The disaster was all too typical for the mountains.

Did the battle and Campbell's role in it occur as he told it? If Campbell's account were the only one available, there would be no sources to refute it. But there are actually four surviving accounts of the battle. Daniel Potts's version was the most immediate, having been written in a letter to his brother in October 1828. William Ashley's account was given two years later in testimony before Congress. Jim Beckwourth's was dictated to his biographer, Thomas D. Bonner, in 1856. Campbell's was the most removed from the experience, having been dictated to Fayel in 1870.[59]

Although all four accounts agree on most points, in two crucial details, Campbell's version departs from the others. One is the distance from the battle back to camp. Potts estimated the distance to be about sixteen miles, just two miles shy of Campbell's account. Beckwourth does not give the total distance but mentions reaching a relief party about five miles from rendezvous. Ashley's account differed the most, stating the battle was only a few miles from rendezvous. If the ambush was indeed sixteen or eighteen miles away, the messengers would have probably run their horses into the ground before they reached the relief party. Indeed, in Campbell's version his horse stumbled and he suffered a bruised face.

The biggest discrepancy, however, is over just who made that ride. Campbell and Beckwourth stake rival claims to be among those two riders who took word to the rendezvous and brought back the reinforcements that drove off the Blackfeet. Beckwourth claims he stepped forward when Campbell called for volunteers:

> Campbell then said that two had better go, for there might be a chance of one living to reach the camp. Calhoun volunteered to accompany me, if he had his choice of horses, to which no one raised any objection. Disrobing ourselves, then, to the Indian costume, and tying a hankerchief around our heads, we mounted our horses as fleet as the wind, and bade the little band

59. Daniel T. Potts to Robert Montgomery Potts, October 13, 1828, Morgan, *Ashley,* 181; William Ashley to Thomas H. Benton, January 20, 1829, 20th Cong., 2d sess., *Senate Document 67* (Serial 181), 13; Bonner, *Beckwourth,* 101–7; Holloway, ed., *A Narrative,* 33–35.

adieu . . . we dashed through the ranks of the foe before they had time to comprehend our movement. The balls and arrows flew around us like hail, but we escaped uninjured. Some of the Indians darted in pursuit of us, but, seeing they could not overtake us, returned to their ranks . . . When about five miles from the camp we saw a party of our men approaching us at a slow gallop. We halted instantly, and, taking our saddle-blankets, signaled to them first for haste, and then that there was a fight. Perceiving this, one man wheeled and returned to the camp, while the others quickened their pace, and were with us in a moment, although they were a mile distant when we made the signal. There were only sixteen, but they rushed on, eager for the fray, and still more eager to save our friends from a horrible massacre. They all turned out from the camp, and soon the road was lined with men, all hurrying along at the utmost speed of the animals they bestrode . . . The Indians were surprised at seeing a reinforcement, and their astonishment was increased when they saw a whole line of men coming to our assistance. They instantly gave up the battle and commenced a retreat. We followed them about two miles, until we came to the body of Bolliere—the old man that had been slain; we then returned, bringing his mangled remains with us . . . On our side we lost four men killed and seven wounded . . . From the enemy we took seventeen scalps . . . We also lost two packs of beaver, a few packs of meat, together with some valuable horses . . . The battle lasted five hours, and never in my life had I run such danger of losing my life and scalp.[60]

If we had only the accounts of Campbell and Beckwourth, the matter would be easily resolved. Campbell was a model of modesty and veracity; Beckwourth had a reputation for at times stretching truths into exaggerations and even outright myths. Yet those views themselves may have been exaggerated. The "gaudy liar" Beckwourth actually told the truth much more often than not. Campbell's account might be explained by a memory dimming with age or even as a tall tale to impress the admiring young greenhorn who transcribed his autobiography.

Potts's version is too vague to support either side:

A party of about one hundred Blackfeet mounted attacked thirty odd of our hunters with their familys this engagement lasted for upwards of three hours when a couple of our men mounted two of their swiftest horses dashed through their ranks of the horrid tribe where the balls flew like hail and arrived with express at our camp in less than one hour a distance of more than sixteen miles in this we had one man killed & two wounded one child lost. that of the enemy six or eight killed and wounded.[61]

60. Bonner, *Beckwourth*, 104–6.
61. Potts to Potts, October 13, 1823, Morgan, *Ashley*, 181.

It is Ashley's version that seems to weigh heavily on Beckwourth's side of the ledger:

> Mr. Campbell had a valuable collection of furs, and intended . . . setting to join the rest of the Americans. This circumstance induced Mr. C. to use all possible expedition on his march. Notwithstanding, when within a few miles of the rendezvous, he discovered two or three hundred Indians in pursuit of him; he and party succeeded in reaching some rocks near at hand, which seemed to offer a place of safety. The Indians, who proved to be Blackfeet warriors, advanced, but were repulsed with the loss of several of their men killed; they would, no doubt, have ultimately succeeded in cutting off the whites, had they not been so near the place of rendezvous, where, in addition to 60 or 70 white men, there were several hundred Indians friendly to them, and enemies of the Blackfoots. This fact was communicated to the assailants by a Flathead Indian, who happened to be with Mr. Campbell and spoke the Blackfoot language. At the same time, the Indians saw two men, mounted on fleet horses, pass through their lines, unhurt, to carry the information of Mr. C's situation to his friends. This alarmed the Indians, and produced an immediate retreat.[62]

Although Ashley mentions Campbell three times elsewhere in the narrative, the two riders who "carry the information of Mr. C.'s situation to his friends" are nameless. That would seem to preclude Campbell as one of the riders. If Campbell did ride to the rescue, it is possible but improbable that Ashley was ignorant of it. A feat like that by a brigade leader would have been forever enshrined in mountain lore. Trappers would have demanded that he retell his story at campfires for years thereafter. Ashley himself did not attend rendezvous yet would have later heard of Campbell's feat from those who excitedly recounted the entire battle.

If Campbell was among the riders, why would he, a brigade leader, leave his men, especially with ammunition nearly spent and the poor gunpowder causing as many misfires as sure shots? Perhaps he would ride off if no one else was willing to volunteer. Yet he does not mention leaving anyone else in charge. The identity of the other rider is just as conflicting—he mentions "a little Spaniard," while Beckwourth attributes a "Calhoun."

Could Campbell's memory have faded forty-two years after the event? His mind was still vigorous in 1870. Even with more than four decades between the battle and his retelling, he could hardly have mistaken such an important adventure as riding through several

---

62. Ashley to Benton, January 20, 1829, *Senate Document 67*, 13.

hundred Blackfeet eager for his scalp. If Beckwourth was telling the truth, did Campbell deliberately tell a tall tale to the admiring William Fayel? The rest of his narrative to Fayel is either verifiable or certainly rings true. Should we doubt his version of the Blackfeet battle? The truth, of course, will never be known.

After its exciting beginning, the 1828 rendezvous did not match the excesses of the previous encounters. Jackson had shepherded a caravan to the mountains during the autumn of 1827 and had distributed those supplies to the scattered trappers and Indians. Without fresh supplies, especially liquor, the 1828 rendezvous must have been a disappointment for most of those whites and Indians who gathered at Bear's Lake. Worse, there was no sign of Jedediah Smith. It was as if the Southwest had swallowed him up and refused to spit him out as it had the previous year. Only the Blackfeet attack on Campbell's brigade had allowed the boys to cut loose a year's worth of pent-up stresses.

As if the lack of fresh goods were not bad enough, a rival appeared at camp. The previous summer, Joshua Pilcher, Lucien Fontenelle, William Henry Vanderburgh, Charles Bent, and Andrew Drips had pooled seven thousand dollars, enough to equip a small party for the mountains. With Pilcher in command, they had led 45 men and 104 horses out of St. Louis in August. While crossing South Pass, a Crow party ran off their horses, forcing them to cache the supplies. That winter, the brigade trapped and camped the Green River valley. The following spring, they managed to trade enough horses from a Shoshone band to ride back to South Pass and raise their cache. Snowmelt had seeped into the cache and rotted most of the goods. With sour hearts, Pilcher and Company trudged into that year's rendezvous.[63]

Despite the previous year's losses, the 1828 summer rendezvous proved lucrative indeed for the partners. Bound for St. Louis, Sublette led a caravan packed with "7,107 1/2 pounds of beaver valued at $5.00 per pound; 49 otter skins at $3.00 apiece, 27 pounds of castorem at $4.00 per pound, and 73 muskrats at 25 cents each, the total value being $35,810.75. This sufficed to pay various debts, including $9,010.40 owing Ashley for the second outfit of 1827, and leave a 'Ballance due S.J.&S. this 26th day Octr 1828' of $16,000."[64]

63. Pilcher to Secretary of War, 1830, 21st Cong., 2d sess., *Senate Document* 39 (Serial 203), 7–8.
64. Morgan, *Jedediah Smith,* 302. Ashley Account with Smith, Jackson, and Sublette, October 1, 1827 to October 25, 1832, Sublette Papers, State Historical Society of Missouri, Columbia (MoSHi).

While Sublette headed east, the plan was for Jackson to lead a brigade into Flathead country and Campbell to take a trapping party into Crow country. Campbell hesitated to accept the command. After all, he had spent nearly four continuous years in the mountains, exposed to nearly constant dangers from man, beast, and weather. By that summer of 1828, he had understandably "intended returning to St. Louis that year and quit the country." When they got wind of his intention, the partners and lieutenants begged him to stay. So Campbell "was prevailed on to go over into the country of the Crows, as a partner with Bridger and others."[65]

He was lucky to have Jim Bridger in his brigade. Bridger had first ventured into the mountains in 1823, a year and a half before Campbell. By all accounts, he was among the most skilled of the mountain men in hunting, trapping, tracking, and diplomacy with the Indians. A want of formal education had prevented Bridger from becoming a lieutenant for the partners, for it was said that "he was perfectly ignorant of all knowledge contained in books, not even knowing the letters of the alphabet; put perfect faith in dreams and omens, and was unutterably scandalized if even the most childish of the superstitions of the Indians were treated with anything like contempt or disrespect; for in all these he was a firm and devout believer."[66]

An air of more than usual anxiety must have hung over the partners as they shook hands and rode off in different directions. For the three previous years, first Ashley and then the partners had enjoyed a monopoly at the annual rendezvous, while their only mountain rival, the Hudson's Bay Company, largely confined its trading posts and brigades to the northern Rockies. Now Pilcher and company had appeared like a bear in their honey tree. The partners could take some solace that so far their rivals' venture was a disaster. Following rendezvous, Fontenelle, Vanderburgh, and Bent returned to St. Louis with only sixteen beaver packs. Ignorant of where the best beaver streams lay, Pilcher and Drips could only trail the more experienced partners. Pilcher and his men tagged along behind Jackson's brigade while Drips's party followed Campbell's. Pilcher's strategy largely spoiled Jackson's without enriching himself. Hudson's Bay Company Governor Simpson reported that during the winter, Jackson and Pilcher were encamped near Flathead Lake, close to the Hudson's Bay Company's Fort Colville, but "had very few Skins,

65. Holloway, ed., *A Narrative*, 35.
66. David L. Brown, *Three Years in the Rocky Mountains*, 12; J. Cecil Alter, *Jim Bridger*.

and of those few, about half fell into our hands in exchange for necessary supplies."[67]

It would be the Crow rather than Drip and his men who troubled Campbell's twelve-man brigade. They evaded Drips's pursuit and "commenced trapping on Powder river, and our operations extended on the Tongue, Big Horn, and tributaries." It was a bold strategy. Although the Crows rarely killed the whites, they strove constantly to steal their horses and anything else they could lay their hands on. No whites had trapped their country for two years after two Crow were killed by Sublette's party when they tried to run off some horses. Campbell's party managed to avoid any Crows until they reached "the Cache River at Po-po-agie where it joins the Wind river, and I made a cache there to put in my beaver. A war party of Crows that had been down to the Cheyennes and Arapahoes, were returning and found my cache. They took 150 skins."[68]

Three bands composed the Crow or Absaroka: the River Crow or Minespere (Dung on the River Banks) on the lower Bighorn River, and the Arcaraho (Where Many Lodges Are) and Erarapi'o (Kicked in their Bellies), both in the Wind River valley and known as Mountain Crow. The Siouan-speaking Crow were closely related to the Hidatsa and often visited and traded with them at their earthen lodge village on the Missouri River. Mountain Crow warriors had stolen Campbell's fur cache.

Campbell suspected but would not know exactly who stole his furs until he arrived at the Crow village where he hoped to trade goods and spend the winter. In late autumn, as he and his men rode into the village where the Wind River bends into the Bighorn River, the entire population pressed closely around them, shouting and gesturing. It must have been quite a colorful sight. The trappers reckoned that the Crows were not just the West's best horse thieves but that they also prepared the best pelts, lodges, and clothing. The painter George Catlin described Crow lodges as cured "almost as white as linen and [they] beautifully garnish them with porcupine quills, painting, and ornamenting them in such a variety of ways as renders them exceedingly picturesque. Highly ornamented and fringed with scalp-locks, one of these lodges is sufficiently large for forty men to dine under." In all, the Crows were an artful, dandyish, licentious people.[69]

---

67. *Part of the Dispatch from George Simpson Esq Governor of Rupert's Land to the Governor & Committee of the Hudson's Bay Company, London* (London and Toronto: 1947), 55–56; Cabanne to Chouteau, September 22, 1828, Morgan, *Ashley,* 176.

68. Holloway, ed., *A Narrative,* 35.

69. Mooney, ed., *Catlin,* 119–20. Robert H. Lowie, *The Crow Indians.*

Few among the Crows were more vain than their chief, Long Hair. Campbell was taken to Long Hair's lodge to smoke, eat, and negotiate. The appropriately named chief allowed Campbell to measure

> his hair . . . and found it to be ten feet and seven inches in length, closely inspecting every part of it . . . and satisfying [himself] that it was the natural growth. On ordinary occasions his hair is wound with a broad leather strap . . . then folded up into a . . . block of some ten or twelve inches in length . . . which when he walks is carried under his arm or placed in his bosom within the folds of his robe. But on any grand parade or similar occasion, his pride is to unfold it, oil it with bear's grease, and let it drag behind him, some three or four feet of it spread out upon the grass, and black and shining like a raven's wing.[70]

As Campbell met with Long Hair, a war party came in "with some scalps and were having great rejoicings. They held a great dance, in which the braves boasted of their exploits. Among other things they boasted of having found my cache."[71]

Campbell immediately protested to Long Hair the theft of his party's furs. After some reflection, Long Hair proved to be understanding of his plight:

> The old chief then came into my lodge and said to me, "Have you been catching beaver?"
> "Yes!" I answered.
> "What do you do with it?" asked the chief.
> "Put it in the ground," said I.
> "Where is it?" he inquired.
> I drew a plan of the ground, where my beaver had been cached.
> The old chief then said, "You talk straight about it!"
> He said for four years they had had no whites trading among them and a war party found this place where the beaver was cached. "They opened it," said the chief, "and brought some along. They tell me they brought 150 skins. Now don't let your heart be sad. You are in my lodge and all these skins will be given back you. I'll neither eat, drink, nor sleep till you get all your skins. Now count them as they come in!"
> He then mounted his horse and haranged the village, saying to his people that they had been a long time without traders, and they must not keep one skin back. Then the squaws and old men would come and pitch the beaver skins into my lodge until nearly all were returned.

70. Mooney, ed., *Catlin*, 123–24.
71. Holloway, ed., *A Narrative*, 35.

The son-in-law of the chief said to me, "Tell the old chief the skins were all in and if any are missing, I'll give you the balance." I then told the old chief the skins were all in, and the next day I invited two or three men into my lodge to satisfy him, from their inspection, that the skins were all right. The old chief becoming satisfied, then broke his fast.[72]

Campbell regained his furs but lost one of his men, Jim Beckwourth. According to Beckwourth, the Crow begged him to stay with them when another trapper in the party, Caleb Greenwood, jokingly told them that he was a long-lost tribal member. The Crow enticed Beckwourth with promises of women, horses, and great status. Jim naturally decided to stay. The mistaken identity further eased relations between Campbell's party and the Crow. Campbell thus willingly released Beckwourth from the party with a promise to pay his $271.17 1/2 debt to the partners in beaver at three dollars a pound.[73]

As the spring of 1829 freed the frozen streams, Campbell split his party into two: "One party had all their horses stolen by the Blackfeet. There were five in my party, with Fitzpatrick, who now found us. We stood guard every night." Nonetheless, Blackfeet killed four of his men— Ezekiel Abel, Philip Adam, Kuke Lariour, and Peter Spoon, at Bad Pass of Big Horn. "At the end of the hunt we struck for the Red Buttes, in order to meet Sublette coming up. Not meeting him, I went to Sweet Water and over to Wind River, where we had our rendezvous."[74]

Sublette had left St. Louis on March 7 with ninety-five hundred dollars' worth of goods, fifty-five men, and more than one hundred pack animals. The caravan reached the Popo Agie rendezvous around July 1. It was Joe Meek's first rendezvous, and he recalled that the site was picked because it had

> grass for the animals, and game for the camp. The plains along the Popo Agie, besides furnishing these necessary bounties, were bordered by picturesque mountain ranges, whose naked bluffs of red sandstone glowed in the morning and evening sun with a mellowness of coloring charming to the eye of the Virginia recruit. The waving grass of the plain, variegated with wild flowers; the clear summer heavens flecked with white clouds that threw soft shadows; the lodges of the Booshways, around which clustered the camp in motley garb and brilliant coloring; gay laughter, and the murmur of soft Indian voices, all made up a most spirited and enchanting picture,

72. Ibid., 35–36.
73. Wilson, *Jim Beckwourth*, 48; see Beckwourth's questionable but vivid account in Bonner, *Beckwourth*, 139–376.
74. Holloway, ed., *A Narrative*, 36.

in which the eye of an artist could not fail to delight. But as the goods were opened the scene grew livelier. All were eager to purchase, most of the trapper to the full amount of their year's wages; and some of them, generally free trappers, went in debt to the company to a very considerable amount, after spending the value of a year's labor, privation, and danger, at the rate of several hundred dollars in a single day.[75]

Sorrow haunted that bucolic setting and the trappers' boisterous antics. There was again no sign of Jedediah Smith, who had been absent now for two years. Most assumed that he and his men were dead. And violence exploded as it had at every previous rendezvous. Campbell vividly recalled an "unpleasant incident" involving

> a great bully of a Frenchman, named Bray [who] when Sublette came up, gave out liquor. He had been out with Samuel Tullock, got disatisfied, and became quarrelsome, under the influence of drink. He abused Tullock and said he had but one hand, but could knock him down. He asked Sublette if his pistol was loaded. He kept on with his abuse, when Tullock struck him a blow with his fist. The Frenchman fell over and never breathed. It was justifiable though. Mr. Tullock did not intend killing the man. The Frenchmen in camp took Bray's part, but drinking liquor in camp was all stopped. We buried the man there. The difficulty produced a terrible damper in camp.[76]

Amidst the pall cast over rendezvous by Bray's death, Smith's absence, and the liquor prohibition, Campbell received two letters that added to whatever bitter doubts and guilt he may have felt about his career. The letter from his brother Hugh had been written nearly two years earlier but stung just as deeply:

> Your resolution not to return to Ireland shall be respected. I shall neither urge nor hint my former wishes on that matter in the future. Indeed to my surprise it was not approved of at home, for nearly the same reason you advanced . . . As to your prospects of your settling down in a steady pursuit of a fixed mercantile business I can only say that such is my most ardent wish . . . At present I will just remark that to me and all your friends any change from your present unsettled life would be for the better. . . . allow me to say explicitly that your present pursuits neither meet the apprivation of myself nor any real friends you have. In the name of an affectionate mother and sister I conjure you to abandon it. On receipt of this—no matter where it may find you—no matter how deeply entangled in your dangerous avocation, I entreat you to leave all and return to me . . . Return again Dear

75. Frances Fuller Victor, *The River of the West*, 48–49.
76. Holloway, ed., *A Narrative*, 37.

Robert to a life of security and call on me for anything I can command. Can it be possible Robert, that you who are raised amidst peace and quiet should devote yourself to a course of life nearly allied to one of blood sheds and rapine? And for what? The gratification of the love for adventure or the excitement of staking life and liberty against fortune? For shame my brother. In the honor of your good mother desist and return to me . . . I beseech you to return to civilization and security. Do not refuse me.[77]

In demanding that Campbell abandon his career and "return to civilization and security," Hugh clearly thought he was imparting wisdom to a dear but wayward brother. His concern for Robert's safety was certainly understandable. The danger was great and the financial rewards a roll of the dice under the best of circumstances. Yet, it is difficult to tell what was more important to Hugh, swelling his own ego or ensuring Robert's safety. Then there is another possibility. Was not Hugh shirking his own duty to his family? After all, he was much closer to Ireland than his brother yet demanded that Robert be the one to journey home and take care of family matters. Regardless, in modern parlance, Hugh would be considered domineering and egotistical.

The letter from his sister Anne was just as discouraging:

I wonder what keeps you in such a dangerous place. What can compensate for the deprivations you must endure in that wilderness, the want of society—fatigue of the chase, and worse than every day hazard in your life. Think how happy you might be here . . . You say you will probably reside in St. Louis should you return this summer. I think neither the Rocky Mountains nor St. Louis fits you. In the former you have to encounter every peril particularly the treachery of the Indians (unless indifference to the defense of your life) you should not attempt to kill any of them, for it would be a sin. In the latter place your health suffered and what grander power or wealth all is nothing without health.[78]

Anne's concern was unburdened by any need to control Robert; she was sincerely worried about his safety and ultimate happiness. Still, she was asking him to abandon his career to come home and take care of his family.

From the moment Campbell had headed west from Philadelphia five years earlier, he had wrestled with his decision. He had refused repeated pleas by Hugh and other family members to return to Ireland. Instead, he had disappeared into the Rocky Mountains and trapped on streams

77. Hugh Campbell to Robert Campbell, October 27, 1827, MoSHi.
78. Anne Campbell to Robert Campbell, June 5, 1827, MLA.

whose waters eventually flowed into the Pacific Ocean. Yet four years of continuous strain over trying to survive a barrage of wilderness dangers and reap a harvest of furs had sapped his enthusiasm. He had mulled getting out the previous year but his comrades had prevailed on him to remain. The letters from Hugh and Anne seem to have tipped the balance between their demands that he return to Ireland and his friends' arguments that he stay in the mountains. Campbell split the difference. After a visit to his family in Ireland and Hugh in Philadelphia, he would return to St. Louis with his small fortune and there sink his roots.

The partners incorporated his decision into their strategy. Sublette's younger brother, Milton, took Campbell's place as brigade leader and led forty men into the Big Horn and Yellowstone country. William Sublette led a brigade northwest to link up with Jackson and his men. That left Campbell to convey the caravan back toward St. Louis on July 18.

Meanwhile, the second rendezvous of 1829 opened at Pierre's Hole on August 20 when Sublette's caravan snaked down the pass south of the Tetons and reached David Jackson's brigade. To Sublette's joy, Jedediah Smith was with Jackson. Smith recounted the series of disasters and challenges that had killed off most of his men in the two years since he and Sublette had parted at the 1827 rendezvous. As in 1826, Smith's party lost most of their pack animals through the rugged plateau country leading from the Sevier River over to the Virgin and then down the Colorado to the Mohave village during 1827. The Mohaves turned on them and killed ten of Smith's men while they crossed the Colorado. With the other survivors, Smith finally reached his men in northern California and then headed north toward Oregon. Umpqua wiped out all but Smith and three other men. They managed to reach Fort Vancouver, where Hudson's Bay Governor Simpson sent out delegations to the Indians to force them to return any stolen pelts and equipment. Simpson then bought these from Smith for $2,369.60. That was all Smith brought back to rendezvous after his three-year oddysey.

While the second rendezvous of 1829 played out, Campbell plodded east with the caravan. He reached St. Louis in August and handed over 4,076 pounds of beaver, 7 otter skins, and 14 pounds of castoreum to Ashley. The pelts were later sold on consignment in New York for $5.25 a pound, grossing $22,500. The partners saw none of that. It all went to pay off debts to Ashley and other creditors. When that year's account was settled the partners still owed one thousand dollars to Ashley alone.[79]

79. Ashley Account with Smith, Jackson, and Sublette, April 1829 to October 1830; James Aull to Tracy and Wahrendorff, August 20, 1829, Sublette Papers, MoSHi.

Returning to St. Louis after four years in the wilderness surely jostled Campbell's senses. He must have reveled in simple pleasures long denied such as hot baths, a warm bed, and a cornucopia of well-cooked foods with which to fill his belly. Perhaps most satisfying was that he could relax his constant vigil against hostile men, beasts, and weather. He did not tarry long in St. Louis, however. Soon he was on the trail again, this time bound for the land of his birth.

# Worldly Triumphs (1829–1833)

**M**uch had happened to Campbell's family in the years since he had received those last letters from Hugh and Anne. A letter from Hugh met him in St. Louis. Hugh was now happily married and living in Richmond, Virginia: "Mary is everything I could wish and more than I had hoped to possess. With her the path of life seems strewn with flowers." Not all the news was good. Younger brother Andrew still succumbed to the temptations of excessive drink, procreation, and spending: "It appears that his family increases faster than his means of supporting it. There seems to be amongst them all a want of system and economy and the finish of their affairs which . . . vexes . . . me as it is injurious to their interest."[1] Andrew's excesses aside, everyone else was fine and eager to hear from Robert, or better yet, to receive him back home.

Heading east made business sense as well as family sense. Campbell had determined to work for himself rather than someone else. But he needed connections and capital to establish his own business. Although highly respected in the mountains, he was as yet unknown back east. As for capital, he had some saved but would spend much of it on his extended trip to the East Coast and Ireland, and in contributions to his family. Another year or two in the mountains would be vital for garnering enough capital to strike off on his own. So he went first to Philadelphia to make the rounds of prominent merchants, discussing the demand for pelts, the supply of trade goods, and the odds of successfully breaking into an already crowded, cutthroat field.

He then visited Hugh and his new sister-in-law in Richmond. Mary was all the wonderful things of which Hugh had lyrically written, and

1. Hugh Campbell to Robert Campbell, August 15, 1829, Campbell Papers, MLA.

she and Robert quickly became close, affectionate friends. He spent week after relaxing week enjoying their company, often discussing business and politics with Hugh and playing backgammon with Mary. They spoke of Hugh and Mary moving to America's business capital, Philadelphia. The brothers could establish a powerful enterprise if Robert gathered furs and Hugh sold them in return for trade goods.[2]

But those dreams were mere possibilities. For now, Campbell would return to his boyhood home. On March 9, 1830, he embarked on the *William Thompson* for Ireland. Like so many who revisit their past after traveling the world for years, he probably weathered a barrage of conflicting emotions, especially as he contrasted America's violence, dynamism, and opportunities with Ireland's poverty and stagnation.

It was a joyous homecoming. But after settling in, Campbell found himself immersed in those tics and squabbles that afflict every family. Most disruptive was the wastrel Andrew's threat to dispute Elizabeth's will of her property to Anne. Along with the rest of the family, Robert delicately took Anne's side and eventually helped Andrew accept Elizabeth's wishes. Hugh supported Robert in settling the conflict in Anne's favor. In a July 5 letter, Hugh wrote of his "opinion that there is nothing contained in [their father's will] to debar our sisters from bequeathing their portions as they may think proper."[3]

Another problem arose: the family was united in conniving to keep Robert home, and he had to gently but firmly reject their entreaties. To the family chorus imploring Robert to stay, Hugh as usual added his own voice. Not long after arriving, Robert received a letter in which Hugh urged him "to advise against encouraging any person to visit the United States—and above all, to place yourself under no obligation to such as are resolved to come on."[4] This was quite an about-face from the business possibilities they had mulled in Richmond.

The family's determination to retain him must have terribly discouraged Campbell. After all, he was a grown man who had risked much, suffered, and then thrived in the American wilderness. His family could not fathom how profoundly those experiences had changed his life. His mother, brothers, and sisters naturally saw him as the shy adolescent boy who had left home to seek his fortune in America; no matter how

2. Hugh and Mary Campbell to Robert Campbell, April 19, 1830, ibid.
3. Hugh Campbell to Robert Campbell, July 5, 1830, ibid.
4. Hugh Campbell to Robert Campbell, April 19, 1830, ibid.

much he tried to convey to them his experiences, they could think of him in no other way.

Through his letters, Hugh unwittingly undercut the campaign to keep his brother in Ireland by passing on news of Robert's mountain friends, and general American business and political trends. Of national politics, Hugh wrote that "Congress is still in session. And the Jacksonites continue the majority in both houses. I think the hero's popularity is on the decline and that he will be opposed successfully in offering again for the presidency. Clay, Van Buren and Calhoun are spoken of by their respective adherents. We never heard of so much unprofitable debating as the succession as Congress seems to be 'all talk and no cider.' "[5]

Although most Americans of the era disdained political parties or "factions," it was human nature to ally with those of a like mind or interest. Americans were divided between two orientations that would eventually coalesce into the Democratic and Whig Parties. Andrew Jackson and his supporters championed the decentralized agrarian republic that Thomas Jefferson had advocated a generation earlier, and favored loose credit and the elimination of the United States Bank. Although the Federalist Party of Alexander Hamilton had died following the War of 1812, its idea of an active government that tried to guide the nation's economic development by promoting industry, trade, transportation, communication, and the United States Bank's tight credit and strong currency policies had endured with Henry Clay's "American System" of the 1820s and 1830s.

Campbell himself was divided politically; as a westerner he sentimentally leaned toward Jackson, but as a hard-nosed businessman he preferred Clay. His views mirrored those of William Ashley, who favored rechartering the Bank of the United States, government assistance in improving the nation's highways and canals, and a strong tariff to nurture American industries. Yet that did not stop Ashley from favoring "the reelection of Gen. Jackson, in preference to any other man."[6] Such were the contradictions of many businessmen in the Democratic Party of that era. Campbell would soon be an active Democratic Party member.

Campbell's old mountain friends not only missed his company but also savored his business and leadership skills. A letter arrived from William Sublette in fall 1830 in which he called for a business partnership

5. Ibid.

6. William H. Ashley to Nathan Kouns, Chairman of the Administration Committee of Correspondence, for Callaway County, Missouri, St. Louis, September 20, 1831, Morgan, *Ashley*, 206–7.

between them. Campbell reluctantly had to decline for the present. Another bout with consumption as well as family problems anchored him to Tyrone County. Learning of his affliction, Jedediah Smith wrote Hugh inquiring after Campbell's health.[7]

Cooped up in his childhood home surrounded by his adoring but demanding family, Campbell must have thought often about the hearty companionship and adventures that he had experienced in those magnificent western mountains and endless plains. During his brief absence, dramatic events had changed the fur trade. In 1830, Sublette had led ten oxen-pulled wagons hauling thirty thousand dollars' worth of goods, eighty-one men, and twelve beef cattle and a milk cow to that year's rendezvous on the Wind River. The American Fur Company dispatched their own caravan to rendezvous, led by Lucien Fontenelle, Andrew Drips, and Joseph Robidoux, but it arrived after Sublette had sold off his wares to his own men, the free trappers, and Indians. The mountain men scoffed at the greenhorns. It took years to acquire the trapping expertise needed to make money in the Rockies. Most assumed the American Fur Company would bankrupt itself trying to squeeze into a region dominated by veterans. That view would be proved wrong.

The partners reaped an enormous harvest that year, selling enough goods and garnering enough furs to not only pay off their debts to Ashley and other creditors but also gain a large fortune. They decided to quit trapping while they were ahead. It had been apparent all along that enriching oneself in the mountains rested on selling highly inflated goods at rendezvous rather than working the streams. To do so, however, required financial investments and organizational talents that few possessed. The partners had accumulated those assets.

Besides, the three men had wearied of the constant hardship, danger, responsibility, and fear they lived with in the mountains. The material losses alone the partners had suffered from July 1826 to July 1830 had been enormous—$43,500 that included 480 horses worth $28,000, $10,000 of goods, $1,000 of traps and other equipment, and $4,500 in furs stolen by the Indians. Indians had also killed forty-three of their men.[8]

On August 4, Smith, Jackson, and Sublette sold out to Tom Fitzpatrick, Jim Bridger, Milton Sublette, Henry Fraeb, and Jean Baptiste Gervais, the leaders of what became known as the Rocky Mountain

7. Jedediah Smith to Hugh Campbell, November 24, 1830, Campbell Letters, MoHiS.
8. Smith, Sublette, and Jackson to William Clark, July 1830, Sublette Papers, MoHiS; Smith, Jackson, and Sublette to John Eaton, Secretary of War, October 29, 1930, both in Morgan, *Jedediah Smith*, 337–48.

Fur Company. The price was $15,532.23, which would be paid for with beaver pelts before June 15, 1831. Sublette, Smith, and Jackson returned with their caravan to St. Louis on October 10, 1830, with 170 packs of fur worth $84,499.14. Once again Ashley marketed their furs, earning $2,500 for shipping and handling, $2,114 or 2.5 percent commission on the sale, and 6 percent on money they owed him. Still, after paying off their debts to Ashley and others, the three partners could split the then sizable fortune of $53,920.92![9]

In 1830, the western fur trade was split into four distinct but connected regions, three of which were monopolized by three different companies. The Rocky Mountain Fur Company largely controlled the central Rockies, the American Fur Company the Missouri River, and the Hudson's Bay Company the Northwest. Then there was the Santa Fe trade, in which scores of aspiring companies and individuals competed to sell goods in an ever more saturated Mexican market and to buy furs dragged in by free trappers ranging across the southern Rockies and the Southwest. With their impregnable positions in their respective realms, the American Fur Company and the Hudson's Bay Fur Company posed a threat to the Rocky Mountain Fur Company.

The seemingly secure position of Smith, Sublette, and Jackson had been challenged by Pilcher and Company as early as 1828. Although that threat had dissolved almost as soon as it had arisen, it was a harbinger of things to come. During the early 1830s, a half dozen firms, including the American Fur Company, had invaded the central and northern Rockies. Only one of those companies would survive—by the mid-1830s, the American Fur Company had destroyed all its opposition, including the Rocky Mountain Fur Company.

In 1830, however, those who trapped the central and northern Rockies saw the Hudson's Bay Company as by far the greater threat. As far as American national interests were involved, they were right. Shortly after returning to St. Louis, Smith, Sublette, and Jackson jointly penned a letter to Secretary of War John H. Eaton that revealed the nature of the British threat to the American West. The Hudson's Bay Company enjoyed a monopoly, cheap labor, and duty-free trade goods, and were stripping American territory of its fur wealth. They had to be stopped.[10]

9. John O'Fallon to Robert Campbell, June 30, 1831, Campbell Letters, MoHiS; Ashley Account with Smith, Jackson, and Sublette, 1830, Sublette Papers, MoHiS.
10. Smith, Sublette, and Jackson to Eaton, October 29, 1830, Morgan, *Jedediah Smith,* 347–48.

Washington failed to heed their warning. It would be another fifteen years before the U.S. government, bolstered by the growing number of settlers in Oregon, felt confident enough to challenge the British company's position in the Northwest. Until then the Hudson's Bay Company steadily and insidiously drained the region's wealth and poisoned Indian minds against the Americans.[11]

Having vented their fears and filled their pockets, Sublette, Smith, and Jackson must have felt enormous relief and satisfaction as they settled into a long, comfortable St. Louis winter. On March 10, 1831, Sublette bought 446 acres of land on the River des Peres, a half dozen miles west of St. Louis, for three thousand dollars; on April 26 he paid four thousand dollars for an adjacent 333-acre area known as Sulphur Springs. Smith too tried to settle down, buying a mansion on Federal Avenue and two slaves to serve him. How Jackson spent his money remains unknown, but it is probable that he indulged a good deal in luxurious living.[12]

Yet the dust had no sooner settled around them than they were eager to stir up some more. All three were in their early thirties, still vigorously healthy, stifled by city life, and itching to roll the dice on the quest for adventure and wealth. In early 1831, Sublette and Jackson formed a new partnership, this one geared to exploiting the Santa Fe trade. Smith decided to accompany Jackson and Sublette on their Santa Fe expedition. All three men applied for and received passports.

The first wagons of their expedition left St. Louis on April 1; the rest embarked by April 10. Sublette, Jackson, and Smith organized their caravan at Lexington. Their combined force included eighty-five men and twenty-three mule-drawn wagons, of which ten belonged to Sublette and Jackson, two to Smith, and the rest to other hopeful traders. There they were joined by Fitzpatrick, who had returned from the mountains to organize that year's rendezvous supply caravan. The partners informed Fitzpatrick that the shelves were bare in St. Louis so he need not go there, and that they could only sell him what was left over after they had displayed their goods in Santa Fe's plaza. Fitzpatrick had no choice but to tag along.

Hardship and tragedy plagued the caravan. Shortly after they reached the tallgrass prairies, Pawnees killed a straggler. Near the

11. Frederick Merk, *Albert Gallatin and the Oregon Problem;* Frederick Merk, *The Oregon Question: Essays in Anglo-American Diplomacy and Politics;* Samuel Flagg Bemis, *John Quincy Adams and the Foundations of American Foreign Policy.*

12. Sunder, *Sublette,* 94; Morgan, *Jedediah Smith,* 324.

Arkansas River, the partners ordered the cannon unlimbered, loaded, and fired at a war party of Comanche and Gros Ventres that had massed to attack them; the war party slipped off beyond cannon-shot but continued to shadow them. When they reached the Cimarron Cutoff, drought had dried all the streams and threatened to kill all their animals. On May 27, Smith volunteered to scout for a spring. In his decade in the wilderness he had survived one peril after another, including three massacres. This time the luck or divine guidance that had protected him for so long fled with the approach of a Comanche war party. Smith killed the chief before dying. The caravan pushed on, ignorant of Smith's fate and shadowed by that war party of Comanches and Gros Ventres.

The Santa Fe market proved a bust. A decade after Becknell had opened up the Santa Fe trade, the field had been picked fairly clean. The competition was fierce and well established. Newcomers stood little chance of making money. Those who did marshaled their caravans down to Chihuahua, nearly a thousand miles farther south. This neither Sublette nor Jackson was prepared to do. Instead, while Fitzpatrick took his pick of six thousand dollars' worth of their unsold goods and headed north to rendezvous, Sublette and Jackson dissolved their partnership. Jackson formed a partnership with David Waldo to trade in the Southwest, then headed on to California to procure horses and mules. Sublette tarried for weeks in Santa Fe trying to sell off the rest of his goods before, disillusioned, he returned to St. Louis. There he turned over to Ashley fifty-eight hundred pounds of furs and hides. Impressive as that haul seemed, he did not make a dime from it. After it was sold, Sublette and Jackson still owed Ashley seventy-one hundred dollars, while Sublette alone had racked up a debt to Ashley of twenty thousand dollars.[13]

Meanwhile, Campbell had returned to St. Louis in June 1831 via Richmond, where he had visited with Hugh and Mary. He had arrived too late to participate in any of that year's trading ventures but just in time to learn of Smith's death. The news must have deeply grieved him. The two had been the closest of friends ever since Campbell joined Smith's party as his clerk in November 1825. Their friendship was a refuge not only from the constant danger, but also from the "Society . . . of the Roughest kind, Men of good morals seldom enter into business

13. Ashley Account with Jackson and Sublette, March 29, 1931; April to November 1831, Sublette Account with Ashley, January to August 1831, Sublette Papers, MoHiS; Clokey, *Ashley*, 183–88.

of this kind." Over the years their ties remained powerful despite all the time they remained apart. When they shook hands and bid each other good-bye at the Bear Lake rendezvous in 1827, it would be the last time Campbell ever saw Jedediah Smith. Although he was partners and friends with William Sublette and David Jackson, Jedediah Smith was closest to Robert Campbell. It was to Campbell that Smith had hoped to entrust the disposal of his property.[14]

Jedediah's last words to Campbell came to him indirectly. In a November 24, 1830, letter to Hugh Campbell, Smith wrote of the

> great reason to feel thankful to You My Dear Sir, for the trouble you put your Self on my account—but, with pain did I peruse that part of your Epistle, which Speaks of the ill health of My much valued Friend—Oh is it possible I Shall never again See him in the Land of the living? My Prayer to Almighty God, is, that I may again be allowed the Privilege of passing some time in company with my Friend—I have not written directly to Robert, for this reason, I thought Your Letters would be more certain of their place of destination [Ireland], consequently it would be better for us to correspond, as, in the mean time I shall be in pleasant converse with two friends in stead of one.[15]

Sublette's return in September probably boosted Campbell's spirits and business prospects. Campbell's savings had dwindled since he had left St. Louis for Ireland. His only hope to raise a fortune large enough to invest in a sustainable business lay in beaver streams a thousand miles westward. Sublette, meanwhile, had abandoned hope of making money in the Santa Fe trade and had decided to return to doing what he knew best—supplying rendezvous. To do so meant deepening his debt to Ashley. It also meant finding a new partner. That partner had to be a hardened mountain veteran and sophisticated businessman. The obvious choice was Robert Campbell. When Sublette popped the question, Campbell quickly agreed to throw in, but as his lieutenant and clerk rather than as partner. Before they could enter a formal partnership, Campbell would have to acquire a far larger stake, Sublette would have to pay down his debts, and together they would have to prove to creditors that they could secure the rendezvous trade.

With Campbell in tow, Sublette turned once again to Ashley for financial backing. Ashley was in the midst of a fierce political struggle.

14. Jedediah Smith to his parents, December 24, 1829, Solomon Simons to Peter Smith, November 22, 1829; Jedediah Smith Sr. to Peter Smith, February 16, 1830, Morgan, *Jedediah Smith,* 349–51.

15. Jedediah Smith to Hugh Campbell, November 24, 1830, Morgan, *Jedediah Smith,* 357.

Missouri was split not only between what would become the Democrat and Whig Parties but also between the old-guard "junto" rooted in the French families and the "central clique" or "Boonslick Democrats." During the 1820s, the "central clique" elbowed aside the "junto" as Missouri's ruling political and economic elite. Ashley was among the latecomers who leaned toward the central clique rather than the junto that had once excluded him. In 1831, he ran for a seat in Missouri's General Assembly against junto candidate Robert W. Wells. To overcome Wells, Ashley tried to bridge the philosophical chasm by campaigning for the populist Jackson's reelection but also for federal funding of infrastructure such as roads, the rechartering of the United States Bank, and a protective tariff for industry, all of which Jackson and his followers shrilly opposed. Ashley won by a narrow margin, 212 votes of 10,000 cast, gaining majorities in St. Louis and the other towns while Wells captured the rural counties. Ashley's victory was a boost for Sublette and Campbell. Ensconced in Washington, Ashley could keep a close eye on markets and supply the partners with the goods they needed.[16]

So the friends wintered at Sublette's Sulphur Springs plantation just outside of St. Louis, laughingly or mournfully recalling mountain adventures while organizing a supply caravan for the 1832 rendezvous. Word from the eastern markets, however, was discouraging. European hat styles were rapidly shifting from beaver felt to silk. The price for beaver dropped with the demand: from $5.50 when 1831 opened to $4.50 at its close. Savvy merchants believed the price might well continue to fall. Frederick Tracy wrote Ashley, "There is little demand for the article & I do not see any prospect of improvement."[17] But with mounting debts to various creditors, the partners had no choice but to forge on in hopes that they struck it rich or at least broke even.

Fur prices aside, predictably, the family chorus tried to call Campbell home when he wrote them of his plans. With gentle sarcasm, Mary wondered how Robert could "leave the charming ladies of St. Louis particularly the interesting French dames or rather damsels for the fair or rude sex of the mountains. But who knows, it may give you the greatest pleasure to meet with some of the squaws that you left to mourn your absence." Campbell rejected his family's siren call. However, he did have something worth passing on to them besides memories. His April 10,

---

16. Clokey, *Ashley*, 207–14. For an excellent summary of that era's politics, see Robert Shalhope, "Thomas Hart Benton and Missouri State Politics: A Reexamination."

17. Frederick Tracy to William Ashley, June 8, 1832, Sublette Papers, MoHiS.

1832, will split his Irish land among Hugh, Andrew, and Anne, and made provisions for his St. Louis wealth to repay his debt to Hugh and pay any balance due his men.[18]

There may have been several reasons behind Campbell's willingness to spurn the "charming ladies of St. Louis." First of all, he was still a young buck of twenty-eight, an age when the thrill of mountain adventure, wondrous beauty, and discovery, and of boisterous, rugged comrades and "rude sex" with uninhibited Indian women, could easily outweigh the drudgery, misery, and terror that so often accompanied wilderness survival and enterprise. Then there was a practical reason— he had spent nearly all his savings. A trusted friend had offered him a job that employed his skill as a clerk, trapper, and brigade leader. If all went well, he would make more money than ever before.

And, perhaps most important of all, the era in which Campbell lived demanded that he be among those few exalted "self-made men," an ideal coined by Henry Clay, rather than follow the herd who "live lives of quiet desperation," as Henry David Thoreau later put it. While Campbell could have easily signed on as a clerk in some St. Louis merchant house and led a stable, respectable, but financially modest life, the mountains offered a chance to get rich quick. Ashley, for example, had won fortune, fame, and power after only a few perilous years in the mountains. Smith, Sublette, and Jackson too had reaped affluence from those distant streams. Like most who gamble, Campbell's mind tended to fix on the few who had won, rather than the hundreds who had barely eked out an existence and the scores who had been gruesomely killed by frostbite, grizzlies, or Indians. It was a gamble to be sure, but the potential payoff was great.[19]

On April 25, 1832, William Clark granted William Sublette and Robert Campbell a trading license for the "Blackfeet, Crows, Snake, Flatheads, Kiowas, Cheyenne, Comanches, Arapahos, Utaws and other tribes in the region of the Rocky Mountains." Among the mountain of standard trade goods packed in Sublette's ten wagons were 450 gallons of whiskey. The shipment was formally legal. William Clark had granted Sublette a special license to pack whiskey for his "boatmen" and "not to be used in trade or barter or given to Indians." The liquor license was given

18. Mary Campbell to Robert Campbell, March 3, 1832, and Robert Campbell's Will, April 10, 1832, Campbell Papers, MLA.
19. For the classic study, see Irwin G. Wyllie, *The Self-Made Man in America: The Myth of Rags to Riches.* See also David C. McClelland et al., *The Achievement Motive;* John William Ward, *Andrew Jackson: Symbol for an Age;* Carl N. Degler, *Out of Our Past: The Forces that Shaped Modern America;* David C. McClelland, *The Achieving Society.*

with a wink and a nod. No "boatmen" were necessary for the overland trip. The license was a transparent fiction that allowed Sublette to sell whiskey at rendezvous. Sublette most likely paid Clark under the table for the license; how much remains unknown.[20]

Sublette must have been jubilant as he shook hands with Clark. He had acquired not only a liquor license and a huge array of goods to sell at rendezvous but also a controlling interest in the Rocky Mountain Fur Company. Although the new firm had been operating for less than two years, it was already badly ailing, a condition Sublette did not hesitate to exploit. The mountain men who had gathered at the 1831 rendezvous had waited for Fitzpatrick's supply caravan in vain. Joe Meek recalled that the men "had exhausted the stock of goods on hand. The camp was without blankets and without ammunition; knives were not to be had; traps were scarce; but worse than that all the tobacco had given out, and alcohol was not! In such a case as that what could a mountain man do?"[21]

Fitzpatrick did not reach one of his partners, Henry Fraeb, until long after the brigades and free trappers had forlornly scattered through the Rockies. While Fitzpatrick immediately headed back east to order the next year's goods, Fraeb snaked the supply caravan through the mountains in an often vain attempt to reach his isolated trapping brigades. Fitzpatrick brought few pelts back with him to St. Louis when he arrived in late autumn; with nothing to get for their furs, the trappers had saved them for the 1832 rendezvous. By loaning money and supply goods to Fitzpatrick on credit, Sublette placed himself in the same controlling position over the Rocky Mountain Fur Company that Ashley had won over Smith, Sublette, and Jackson. With two years' worth of pelts waiting at rendezvous, Sublette stood poised to reap possibly the biggest haul of furs and profits yet from the mountains. A creeping resentment must have begun to sour Fitzpatrick's long friendship with Sublette as he and four of his men joined the caravan.

The caravan left St. Louis on April 25. Campbell recalled, "I again started out for the Indian country, taking out with me a small outfit of goods, blankets, clothes, and only five men and fifteen horses. Ten of the horses were loaded with merchandise. I accompanied Mr. William Sublette, who led a party of fifty men. Sublette was taking out goods to furnish the firm of Milton Sublette, Fitzpatrick and Bridger in exchange for beaver." In all, Campbell had invested $363.75 in his packhorses,

20. Sunder, *Sublette*, 102.
21. Victor, *River of the West*, 99.

upon which he heaped a wide array of goods including blue and scarlet cloth, butcher and scalping knives, small bells, rifles, mackinaw blankets of various widths, vermillion, powder horns, awls, beads, handsaws, bridles, combs, buttons, sugar, ink, letter paper, quills, flints, calico, flannel, calico shirts, copper kettles, lead, beaver traps, axes, branding irons, wool socks, curry comb, spoons, rope, flour, coffee, Spanish saddles, belts, and various other items. For himself, he invested $12 in a bay, and armed himself with a rifle for $17 from P. Carmer, $3 for a sight, and $30 for two Hawken pistols. His guns would prove as useful as his trade goods.[22]

The rendezvous to which Sublette and Campbell headed would prove to be the most competitive, profitable, dangerous, and rowdy of them all. Several fur companies and suppliers jousted for profit and power; the Rocky Mountain and American fur companies would be the largest rivals, followed by Sublette and Campbell. At Independence, another rival joined Sublette's caravan, Bostonian Nathaniel Wyeth and his twenty-five followers. Sublette diplomatically called those greenhorns "men of theory, not of practice."[23]

Sublette, Campbell, Fitzpatrick, and Wyeth must have looked on anxiously while another company readied itself and beat them into the field. On May 1, 1832, Captain Benjamin Bonneville, on leave from the army, led 110 men toward the Rockies. In the upper Green Valley he would build a supply post, derisively called Fort Nonsense by his own men and more experienced trappers alike. In all, Bonneville's trappers were not very successful, but they drained furs and scared game away from the Rocky Mountain Fur Company and the others in the field.

Sublette's caravan did not depart from Independence until May 13. It included eighty-six men and three hundred head of livestock. The caravan followed the well-worn route west via the Missouri, Kansas, and Blue Rivers, then over the divide to the Platte. For Campbell the "trip was more prosperous than usual, having taken every precaution which past experience had taught us to provide for every emergency. We had two steers and fifteen sheep, beside the usual supplies of bacon, meal, flour, &c. to meet our wants, until we reached the Buffalo . . . To those, who are not amply provided with supplies, the dreary journey from the boundary line to the Buffalo range must be attended with great danger

22. Holloway, ed., *A Narrative*, 37–38; Campbell Ledgerbook, April 1832, Campbell Papers, MLA.

23. William Sublette to William Ashley, May 12, 1832, Sunder, *Sublette*, 104.

and privation. On June 11 we came in view of the Black hills, and since have never been out of the sight of snow . . . During the last three weeks we have had frost every night, and have frequently encamped by snow banks; yet such a complaint as a cold is unknown among our men."[24]

The most important precautions were those designed to minimize the chance of an Indian raid for horses or scalps. The men rode in double file with "Mr. Sublette always giving all orders and leading the band, and Mr. Campbell as lieutenant bringing up the rear and seeing that all kept their places and the loose animals did not stray."[25] Scouts ranged the landscape all around the column and carefully explored woods or arroyos suitable for ambush. They camped in a hollow square with a river or stream anchoring a side. Horses were hobbled or staked at night in the camp.

The greater number of trappers in the mountains did more than just make for livelier competition for trade. Like any veteran trapper, Campbell could not help but note how sadly diminished the buffalo herds had become: "this noble, and . . . most useful animal has been gradually retiring from the haunts of civilized men; and is not met with any great distance east of the Black hills [Laramie Mountains]."[26] Reaping a fortune in the mountains paradoxically meant destroying the very basis of that wealth: beaver and buffalo. The fur trade era would reach its height that summer. Never again would as many trappers, traders, companies, and Indian bands gather at rendezvous, nor would prices fetch that year's heights. Observant participants such as Campbell understood all too well that the chance to gain riches from the mountains was fleeting and would soon plummet past its peak.

Estimates vary over the number of buffalo on the Great Plains when Lewis and Clark first headed up the Missouri, but the best estimate is probably around forty million. By the early 1830s, those who had spent years in the field had observed a noticeable decline in the buffalo herds. In the preceding three decades, trappers and Indians had wiped out nearly all the mountain buffalo while the proliferation of trading posts on the Missouri, Platte, and Arkansas Rivers had encouraged the plains tribes to decimate the plains herds.[27]

24. Robert Campbell to Hugh Campbell, July 18, 1832, in Charles Eberstadt, ed., *The Rocky Mountain Letters of Robert Campbell*.

25. Kate N. B. Powers, ed. "John Ball: Across the Continent Seventy Years Ago."

26. Robert Campbell to Hugh Campbell, July 18, 1832, in Eberstadt, ed., *Mountain Letters*.

27. E. T. Seton, *Life Histories of Northern Animals: An Account of the Mammals of Manitoba*, vol. 1, 259; F. G. Roe, *The North American Buffalo: A Critical Study of the Species in Its Wild*

Where Laramie Creek flows into the Platte, the caravan encountered yet another potential rival: nineteen men led by A. C. Stephen of the John Gantt and Jefferson Blackwell Company. These men had spent a miserable, fruitless year in the mountains. Fitzpatrick had run into them on his trip east the previous autumn and bought up their meager collection of pelts. They were still encamped where he had left them, awaiting the promised arrival of Blackwell and a supply train. Fitzpatrick informed them that Blackwell was bankrupt and had abandoned them. He then bought up their furs and asked them to join the Rocky Mountain Fur Company. They did so en masse. After caching his furs, Fitzpatrick hurried on to rendezvous to inform his partners of the caravan's progress. Death would stalk him on his solo trek.

Meanwhile, the caravan had its own scares. On the night of July 2, just beyond South Pass, Indians raided their camp. Joe Meek reported that "camp was sudenly aroused at midnight by the simultaneous discharge of guns and arrows, and the frightful whoops and yells with which savages made an attack." The Indians approached "within 50 yads. and fired about 40 shots into camp and some arrows wounded three animals [They] got 5 from Mr. Sublette One from an Independent hunter and 4 which I left out of camp for better feed mine were all poor and sore backed and useless." In the fight, the trappers managed to kill three of the attackers and wound eight or ten more.[28]

The Indians were Gros Ventres, a tribe related to the Arapaho but living along the upper Missouri in alliance with the Blackfeet. The Gros Ventres frequently journeyed south to winter with their Arapaho cousins. They were headed north from just such a visit when they crossed trails with the caravan. Given their mobility, the Gros Ventres were often responsible for attacks attributed to Blackfeet. It would not be the last time Sublette, Campbell, and the others ran into them that summer. Shortly after the raid, yet another party joined the caravan: thirteen free trappers led by Alexander Sinclair.

The caravan hit the Green River and followed it north and then over the divide into Jackson Hole, and finally over the pass south of the Tetons and into Pierre's Hole. It was a lovely place for a rendezvous, with the

---

*State;* D. W. Moodie and A. J. Ray, "Buffalo Migrations in the Canadian Plains"; G. M. Christman, "The Mountain Bison"; Dan Flores, "Bison Ecology and Bison Diplomacy: The Southern Plains from 1800–1850"; Wishart, *Fur Trade,* 33–35.

28. Victor, *River of the West,* 108–9. Young, ed., "Correspondence of Wyeth," vol. 1, 158. William Sublette to W. H. Ashley, September 21, 1832, Sublette Papers, MoHiS; Sunder, *Sublette,* 106–7.

Tetons on the east and lower mountains and hills bounding a grassy valley through which the Pierre's River flowed.[29]

They arrived at rendezvous on July 8. The nearly one hundred men in the caravan joined forces with "120 lodges of Nez Perce and about 80 of the Flatheads a company of trappers of about 90 under Mr. Dripps of the firm Dripps & Fontenelle connected with the American Fur Co. Many independent Hunters and about 100 men of the Rocky Mountain Fur Co. under . . . Milton Sublette and Mr. Fra[eb]."[30] In all, about a thousand people and several thousand horses scattered in camps across the valley. So many horses could rapidly destroy a meadow. To limit the destruction of the grazing lands, each company camped by itself within a short ride of the others.

To their joy, Sublette and Campbell had beaten the American Fur Company supply caravan led by Lucien Fontenelle coming across from Fort Pierre on the Missouri River. The friends immediately spread out their trade goods and reaped the harvest. After the whiskey kegs were tapped, the camps exploded in orgies of drinking, pranks, sex, contests of every kind, boasts, and tale swapping.[31]

Campbell made a handsome profit at Pierre's Hole—$4,325.50 in trading and $560 as Sublette's right-hand man.[32] Yet the frenzy of dealing and celebration was sombered by an increasingly urgent question—what had happened to Fitzpatrick?

They soon found out. Fitzpatrick ran into that Gros Ventre party that later attacked the caravan. The Gros Ventres chased Fitzpatrick up a canyon, where he had to abandon his horse and hide. After the Gros Ventres finally gave up their hunt, a shaken Fitzpatrick headed on foot toward rendezvous. Not daring to fire his rifle, he lived off berries, nuts, and the carcasses of dead animals. A week after Sublette reached rendezvous, Fitzpatrick straggled into camp, nearly dead from exhaustion.[33]

Although relieved that his friend had survived, Campbell's melancholy deepened at Fitzpatrick's haggard appearance and horrifying tale. Throughout that summer, he pondered retiring from the mountains. In a letter to Hugh, he revealed that the incessant stresses from personal danger, responsibility for the lives and livelihoods for scores of other

29. Washington Irving, *The Adventures of Captain Bonneville.*
30. Young, "Two Expeditions," 159.
31. For Joe Meek's vivid description, see Victor, *River of the West,* 110–11.
32. Campbell Notebook, Campbell Papers, MLA.
33. William Ellison, ed., *The Life and Adventures of George Nidever,* 24–25.

men, and the burden of having invested every penny he owned in an enterprise plagued by a thousand gambles was wearing him down:

> A year has nearly elapsed since we parted and the Fates,—my wayward disposition,—or both combined, have placed us at a distance of some thousand miles from each other. You, in the enjoyment of peace and security; while I, with a small band of hardy trappers, am in the midst of our old enemies the Black Feet Indians—who if they had the chance would take pleasure in "dancing my scalp." Be that as it may, yours is an enviable lot, when compared with mine. You can retire to rest, without apprehensions of midnight alarms; and can walk forth during the day without fear of assasin:—whilst I am compelled to recline on the "green sward," with Heavens for a canopy; my arms by my side—and a strong guard keeping watch over our lives and property. Such are our different situations, and such must they remain for at least another year, when I fervently hope to be enabled to quit forever, a pursuit which has little besides danger and privation connected with it.[34]

Ironically, while penning these lines, Campbell would confront the greatest danger of more than a decade in the wilderness. As he scratched away with his pen, he wrote, "I was . . . interrupted . . . by the cry of 'Black Feet!' "[35]

A rider had galloped into camp with word that Indians were attacking a camp of about sixty trappers who had departed the previous day and were about eight miles south up the valley. The trappers included those of Milton Sublette, Wyeth, and Sinclair. They spotted a caravan moving down into the valley from the east and assumed it was Fontenelle's party. But a hard look through Sublette's spyglass revealed the men to be Indians who "rushed down like a torrent into the valley, flourishing their weapons, and fluttering their gay blankets and feathers in the wind."[36]

It was the same party of Gros Ventres that had earlier plagued Fitzpatrick and the caravan. Treachery—on the part of the white trappers—precipitated the battle. The Gros Ventre chief approached with his hand raised in peace. Antoine Godin and a Flathead Indian volunteered to ride out and speak with him. But Godin, whose father was killed by Blackfeet, wanted vengeance. As he took the chief's hand the Flathead jammed his gun muzzle against the chief's side and fired. With cries

34. Robert Campbell to Hugh Campbell, Lewis Fork, July 18, 1832, in Eberstadt, ed., *Rocky Mountain Letters.*
35. Ibid.
36. Victor, *River of the West,* 111–12.

of horror and anger the Gros Ventres took cover in a swampy grove of cottonwoods and willows, where the men opened fire and the women erected barricades of fallen trees and blankets. It was then that Milton Sublette sent off the express to seek help from Sublette and Campbell.[37]

As they rode to the rescue, the partners verbally made out their wills and each appointed the other the sole executor. When the forty or fifty reinforcements rode up, Milton and his men were under cover debating what to do. William Sublette took command and harangued the men, arguing that now was the time to determine whether trappers or "Blackfeet" would rule the mountains. He also appealed to their thirst for vengeance: "and now boys, here are the Black Feet who have killed so many of your companions;—who have probably been prowling around us several days, waiting a favorable chance of attacking us, when they believed us unprepared . . . Some of us may fall; but we die in a good cause, for whose life and property will be secure if the foe be encouraged by refusing their challenge?"[38]

The Sublette brothers, Campbell, and a score of whites and Flathead galloped up to the thicket and tied their horses. They split into two groups, with Milton leading his men along the creek and William, Robert, and their followers creeping through the thick brush directly toward the Gros Ventres. Firing and war whoops broke out. A bullet killed Sinclair; another bullet plowed into Phelps's thigh and he crawled away in agony. The trappers were outnumbered, but feared that if they retreated the Gros Ventres would swarm out and overwhelm them.

Campbell and Sublette fought side by side:

> We continued to keep up a steady fire, never rising higher than our knee to take aim . . . Sublette and myself had a pair of flint lock pistols. In the lodge which was screened by buffalo skins, one of the Indians peered through a hole. Sublette fired and plugged him right in the eye . . . While . . . taking aim at a rascal who was peeping out between the lodge skins, a bullet whistled by so near my leg, as to induce the belief that I was wounded. I soon found it was a false alarm, and am since grateful that my legs are not larger.[39]

Sublette was not so lucky. A bullet smashed through his left arm, breaking the bone and passing through his shoulder blade. Campbell

37. Robert Campbell to Hugh Campbell, July 19, 1832, in Eberstadt, ed., *Rocky Mountain Letters.*
38. Holloway, ed., *A Narrative,* 39.
39. Victor, *River of the West,* 112.

helped him down to the creek and dressed the wound. With the help of another trapper he fashioned a rude litter and carried Sublette to camp. Meanwhile other Flathead, Nez Perce, and trappers joined in the attack on the Gros Ventres. But the reinforcements could not break through. The firing continued sporadically until dark.[40]

It was a victory of sorts for the trappers and their Indian allies. During the night the Gros Ventres gathered their dead and wounded and hurried away. When the trappers gingerly entered the grove the next morning they found twenty-seven dead horses. The Gros Ventres would later admit that seventeen of their people were killed. Six whites, a half-breed, and seven Nez Perces were also killed and about a dozen among the allies were wounded.[41] A week later, the same Gros Ventre party killed three trappers who had entered Jackson's Hole.

The carnage and danger weighed heavily on Robert's mind. He poured out his experiences and feelings during the Pierre's Hole fight in a long letter to Hugh in which he confessed, "In giving these details . . . I fear I shall only add to your antipathy of the mode of life that necessity and choice have caused me to adopt. To confess the truth I am sick of it."[42]

Campbell and Sublette tarried two weeks in camp while Sublette's wound healed enough for travel. The delay proved profitable. On July 25, 1832, Sublette and Fitzpatrick signed an agreement that acknowledged the Rocky Mountain Fur Company owed Sublette $46,751.13, promised to pay him fifty cents a pound to transport their pelts back to St. Louis, and authorized him to sell their pelts either there or in eastern markets and to deduct their debt and transportation costs from the final sale. If the fur sale failed to extinguish the various debts, the Rocky Mountain Fur Company promised to pay Sublette 8 percent annual interest on what they owed him. Finally, the firm authorized Sublette to supply the next summer's rendezvous.[43]

On July 30 Campbell and Sublette headed back toward the settlements. The return trip was largely uneventful. On October 3, they reached St. Louis with 11,246 pounds of beaver pelts in 169 packs, along with various other furs and castoreum. They sold the muskrat skins in St. Louis for twenty cents each and the castoreum for $1,204.06. The beaver plews were packed in hogsheads that contained anywhere

40. Ibid. From here I'll entwine Robert Campbell's letter to Hugh and his Narrative dictated to Fayel, 39–40.
41. Victor, *River of the West*, 117.
42. Robert Campbell to Hugh Campbell, July 19, 1832, Campbell Papers, MLA.
43. Agreement, July 25, 1832, Sublette Papers, MoHiS.

from 375 to 449 skins, and forwarded to eastern agents who would sell them only if they got $4.25 a pound or better. In all, three hogsheads were shipped to Louisville merchants and sixteen hogsheads to F. A. Tracy in New York. When all the furs and castoreum had been sold off by the following year, Sublette and Campbell showed $58,305.75 on their books. However, even that was not enough to eliminate the Rocky Mountain Fur Company's debt to them. After they tallied up the costs of transportation, insurance, cleaning, packing, and dealers' commissions to the bill, the Rocky Mountain Fur Company still owed them a considerable sum.[44]

Having successfully marketed that mountain of furs, the partners then holed up at Sublette's Sulphur Springs home to work through the details of what they hoped was one last campaign in the Rockies—the one that they dreamed would make them rich. An urgency surrounded their planning. It was increasingly evident to mountain veterans that the goose that laid the golden eggs was slowly being strangled. Nearly a thousand white men were now in the Rockies, trapping out the beaver streams and, together with the Indians, wiping the buffalo from the plains. The worsening scarcity might well raise beaver prices to the point where American and European gentlemen found alternative materials for their hats, such as the Chinese silk that had been introduced by London hatters. If so, a small army of men would be thrown out of jobs, including Campbell and Sublette.

Ironically, these changes were occurring when, after a decade of hard struggle, the partners had finally made good money from the fur trade. That wealth had to be sustained and expanded, which in turn depended on the partners' ability to find and exploit opportunities in other fields. But to do so they first had to reap enough capital from the profession they knew best—trapping and trading beaver pelts. The profits would then be invested in new ventures.

The plan they finally worked out was audacious. The partners would square off with the biggest rival of all—the American Fur Company. They would not only lead trading parties against the American Fur Company in the Rockies but also erect a trading post alongside each rival post on the Missouri River. It was truly a David versus Goliath gamble. The giant reaped annual profits of two hundred thousand dollars from operations that spanned the Great Lakes, Great Plains, and

44. Leroy R. Hafen, *Broken Hand: The Life of Thomas Fitzpatrick, Mountain Man, Guide, and Indian Agent,* 118–20.

Rockies. To protect their expanding empire, American Fur Company lobbyists in Washington, D.C., padded the incomes of congressmen to offset their opponents' complaints of unfair business tactics and thwart any legislative attempts to promote a more competitive market.

The ambition of Sublette and Campbell was in direct conflict with that of John Jacob Astor. For a quarter century, Astor had systematically attempted to realize his dream of monopolizing the American fur trade from the Atlantic to the Pacific. So far he had crushed all opposition in his way, by fair means or foul. By 1833, he had conquered the fur trade from the Great Lakes to the upper Missouri River. For the last several years he had tried to mesh two hitherto distinct production systems, the upper Missouri buffalo robe trade and the Rocky Mountain beaver fur trade, which joined in the warehouses and markets of St. Louis. In fall 1828, his Upper Missouri Outfit dispatched Etienne Provost into the mountains to gather as many free trappers as possible and bring them to Fort Floyd, Fort Union's predecessor at the Yellowstone River mouth. In spring 1829, Henry Vanderburgh led an American Fur Company caravan to rendezvous. In the four years since, American Fur Company trapping brigades had dogged those of Smith, Sublette, and Jackson, and then of its successor, the Rocky Mountain Fur Company.

While those forays mostly lost money, they succeeded in prying loose the best trapping grounds and spoiling some of the take for the partners. Joe Meek, "the merry mountain man," complained how the American Fur Company brigades

> tampered with the trappers, and ferreted out the secret of the next ren-dezvous; they followed on their trail, making them pilots to the trapping grounds; they sold goods to the Indians, and what was worse, to the hired trappers. In this way grew up that fierce conflict of interests, which made it "as much as his life was worth" for a trapper to suffer himself to be inveigled into the service of a rival company, which about this time or a little later, was at its highest, and which finally ruined the fur-trade for the American companies in the Rocky Mountains.[45]

The partners planned to give the American Fur Company an ample dose of its own poison by invading that empire's heart on the Missouri River, where the giant had a dozen trading posts, several hundred men, and dozens of boats. An enormous and risky investment capitalized the operation. First, the partners had to buy a keelboat, most of which were

45. Victor, *River of the West*, 103–4.

built in Pittsburgh or Louisville, and which cost from two thousand to three thousand dollars. At most they carried thirty tons of cargo. Supply-filled keelboats embarked upriver in the spring, reached the posts during the summer, and brought robes downriver during early autumn. If the partners succeeded in garnering a large amount of robes, they could have their men build at their posts mackinaws that held ten to fifteen tons of cargo, drew fifteen to twenty inches of water, and floated down with the spring snowmelt. Two other types of boats could be constructed upriver to convey additional cargo, although given their limited cargo capacity and instability they played a relatively minor role in the trade. Pirogues were canoes chopped and burned from felled cottonwood trees. Two pirogues were often bound together with planks. Bullboats were constructed of rawhide stretched over willow hoops; a mix of tallow and ashes sealed the seams. A well-built bullboat could carry as much as three tons and drew only a few inches.[46]

Keelboats and mackinaws were the workhorses of the Missouri, and each had its disadvantages. Given the relatively limited cargo space in those boats, it took dozens of keelboats and mackinaws to handle all the freight between St. Louis and the trading posts far up the Missouri. Unable to be poled upstream, mackinaws were good for only one trip down the Missouri. They were usually sold in St. Louis for firewood or transportation down the Mississippi. Fighting the upriver current and sandbars aboard a keelboat from St. Louis to Fort Union took an average of three months. Downriver, of course, was much faster. With a strong downstream current and breeze, a keelboat or mackinaw could travel as far as one hundred miles on a good day. Yet, it was a crap shoot every time a boat nosed into the Missouri River. Snags could rip out boat bottoms and destroy tens of thousands of dollars' worth of goods, robes, and furs.

In 1831, the American Fur Company alleviated these transportation problems. During the preceding year its leaders had debated the wisdom of using steamboats on the upper Missouri. Kenneth McKenzie had first broached the idea, and then convinced Pierre Chouteau, Jr., that it would succeed. They then lobbied Astor and his board in New York. Two other experienced river leaders, Bernard Pratte and J. H. Cabanne, dismissed the scheme as an unworkable boondoggle. After considerable debate among the leaders, Astor finally approved the experiment. That winter the American Fur Company contracted with a Louisville firm to build

46. Leland D. Baldwin, *The Keelboat Age on Western Waters;* Wishart, *Fur Trade,* 84.

a lightweight steamboat optimistically christened the *Yellowstone.* It was 130 feet long and 19 feet wide, had a 6-foot-deep hull, and cost seven thousand dollars.[47]

The *Yellowstone* got as far as Fort Tecumseh on June 19. There it unloaded supplies and loaded robes, furs, and ten thousand pounds of buffalo tongues. On July 15 the *Yellowstone* safely returned to St. Louis. The experiment had been an outstanding success, which would be surpassed the following year. In 1832, the *Yellowstone* left St. Louis on March 26 and reached Fort Union on June 17. In 1833, another steamboat, the *Assiniboine,* joined the *Yellowstone.* The American Fur Company thus tightened their already powerful hold on the upper Missouri just as the partners schemed to invade that empire.[48]

Undaunted by the challenge, on December 1, the partners headed not west but east to purchase trade goods. They journeyed via steamboat to Wheeling, stagecoach to Frederick, the Baltimore and Ohio Railroad to Baltimore, and stagecoach again to Washington. There they checked into the Indian Queen Hotel, a half dozen blocks west of Capitol Hill. From December 14 to 20, they met daily with Ashley, who at once agreed to help underwrite their venture. Ashley's name and letters of introduction would greatly ease their negotiations with the merchant houses. On December 20, 1832, the two old friends and business associates formalized their partnership with a three-year renewable contract for their firm "Sublette and Campbell," for whose fate each partner would assume equal investments, profits, liabilities, and duties.[49]

On December 21, they left for Philadelphia. After checking into the Congress Hall Hotel, they visited the firms of Gill, Campbell, and Company; Siter, Price, and Company; and Ferguson, Jones, and Company. All three firms were eager to sell, but they lacked or could provide only shoddy versions of fusils, skinning knives, Mackinaw blankets, and beads. Gunpowder was abundant, but it sold only for cash on the barrelhead. After considerable haggling, the partners succeeded in either ordering or buying much of what they needed on credit ranging from forty days to eighteen months. Each contract stipulated that the merchants would forward the goods to Pittsburgh where the partners

---

47. Hiram Martin Chittenden, *History of Early Steamboat Navigation on the Missouri River: Life and Adventures of Joseph La Barge;* L. C. Hunter, *Steamboats on the Western Rivers: An Economic and Technological History;* W. E. Lass, *A History of Steamboating on the Upper Missouri River.*
48. Mooney, ed., *Catlin,* 95. Lass, *Steamboating,* 9–11.
49. Sublette and Campbell Contract, December 20, 1832, Sublette Papers, MoHiS.

had engaged Riddle, Forsythe and Company to store and load it onto two keelboats Ashley had bought for them.[50]

Campbell had more than pecuniary motives for traveling east. He had judged correctly that his letter to Hugh detailing his latest hardships capped by the Gros Ventres battle would "only add to your antipathy of the mode of life that necessity and choice have cause me to adopt." He was right. His letter had provoked a blistering reply from Hugh. After blasting Robert for not writing sooner (a rather difficult task at best in the Rockies), Hugh as usual denigrated Robert's remarkable accomplishments:

> What you have done during your late expedition I neither know nor in a certain point of view do I care. If you have made any money it is well—if not, in my opinion it is better. I am disgusted with your late mode of life—because it seems to destroy the finest feelings of our nature. Quit it and come on here—you should never want so long as I can command a dollar. If we cannot live like brothers, life and money making both are worthless. There my dear Robert. You can make both you & myself happy—apart from you I am miserable.[51]

Rather than confront his brother, Campbell hoped to enlist him. Hugh could be one of their most trusted business agents. The partners celebrated Christmas with Hugh and Mary at their Philadelphia home. After considerable coaxing, Hugh grudgingly agreed to help back their enterprise.

Unable to find all they needed in Philadelphia, the partners headed to New York to complete their purchases. There they expanded their inventory with goods on credit from Wolfe, Spies, and Clark, and, even more important, cut another deal with Ashley's broker, Frederick A. Tracy, to market their furs. In doing so, Sublette abandoned his own broker, John C. Halsey, who had poorly managed the marketing of the previous year's fur yield. It was not all Halsey's fault. Beaver plews were fetching only $3.50 a pound, a harbinger of the bad times to come. Even fusils and skinning knives were scarce in New York. Tracy overcame these difficulties, finding them the goods they needed and marketing their furs at the best available prices. By March 8, 1833, he had disposed of not only the 1832 haul but also furs still warehoused from 1831 for a total of $47,612.13, which enabled Sublette to wipe the

50. Sublette and Campbell to William Ashley, December 24, 1832, Campbell Papers, MLA.
    51. Hugh Campbell to Robert Campbell, September 10, 1832, ibid.

slate clean on his own debts and those of his partnership with Jackson to Ashley.[52]

The partners decided to split their efforts. In January, Campbell went to Pittsburgh to supervise the keelboat transportation for their goods while Sublette traveled to New York, Philadelphia, and Washington to drum up more financing and goods. After ensuring that Forsythe and Riddle had found two good keelboats and were caring for the partners' goods, Campbell returned to St. Louis to recruit men for their enterprise. Good clerks and wranglers were even tougher to find than quality trade goods. The St. Louis labor market was drum-tight as a half dozen firms jostled to fill their ranks.

Among those he managed to hire was Charles Larpenteur, who appeared with a letter of recommendation from Benjamin O'Fallon, the brother of John who had signed up Campbell as a clerk in 1822. Memories stretching back a decade must have briefly filled Campbell's mind as he interviewed the aspiring young man. Like Campbell, Larpenteur was a foreigner, and only three years younger. He had been born in France, emigrated to America in 1828, and had served as a clerk at a Prairie du Chien trading post on the Mississippi River and then under Benjamin O'Fallon in St. Louis. Larpenteur would spend decades in the robe trade, later writing a memoir entitled, "Forty Years a Fur Trader on the Upper Missouri." In it, he had nothing but praise for Robert Campbell: "very much of a gentleman . . . Mr. Campbell was kind to me and always did his best to make my situation pleasant."[53] Campbell first tried to discourage Larpenteur by recounting all the trade's hardships. But when Larpenteur remained enthusiastic, Campbell agreed to hire him on as a second clerk.

Meanwhile, Sublette cut last-minute deals and decisions back east. During his talks with Ashley in Washington, Sublette decided to take one big keelboat rather than two smaller ones and found a legal loophole in the Indian trade laws that allowed him to take wine into Indian country. It was not all work for Sublette. At a soiree filled with Hugh's high-society friends one evening, he boasted to some admiring ladies that he and Campbell were the "lords of the Western Country . . . Both devilish clever fellows and candidates for matrimony But it was necessary we

52. Clokey, *Ashley*, 191; Sublette and Campbell to Ashley, December 31, 1832, Campbell Papers, MLA; Sublette to Robert Campbell, January 11, 1833, ibid.

53. Paul Hedren, ed., *Forty Years a Fur Trader on the Upper Missouri: The Personal Narrative of Charles Larpenteur*, 13.

should make one trip to the mountains first and; then we wisht [sic] to settle ourselves."[54] Still, Sublette's heart remained rooted in the West. In the same letter to Campbell describing his boisterous encounter with the Philadelphia ladies, he admitted his longing for "the land that flows with Milk & Honey." Campbell's feelings for the wilderness were much more ambivalent.

Reaching Pittsburgh on February 20, Sublette abandoned his idea of taking one big keelboat since none was to be had. Instead he bought two smaller ones and embarked with them and their crews for St. Louis, reaching there on March 4. Together the partners made final preparations for what would be a two-pronged business offensive in the West. Campbell would lead the supply caravan to rendezvous while Sublette headed by keelboat up the Missouri River to garner buffalo robes. They would meet at the juncture of the Yellowstone and Missouri Rivers. There they would establish a trading post in the heart of the American Fur Company empire. Campbell would winter at the post while Sublette returned to St. Louis with that year's furs and robes.

On April 9, Campbell embarked overland with forty-five men. Like most mountain leaders, he ruled his men by example rather than command. All along Campbell "treated us like himself wherever we put up."[55] They reached a camp five miles west of Lexington where they would await Sublette. There he bought mules and supplied each man with three, one for riding and the others for packing. He then organized his men into messes, each with a leader.

Sublette remained in St. Louis awaiting their trade license. He received it from Indian Superintendent William Clark on April 15, 1833. The license was generous, allowing Sublette and Campbell to trade at thirty-three places up the Missouri and across the central and northern Rockies for eighteen months. Sublette then headed up the Missouri with the two keelboats packed with trade goods, sixty-eight men, and one hundred kegs of liquor. At Lexington, Sublette transferred goods to Campbell's camp west of town.

The partners did not separate until May 7, with Campbell heading west across the plains with fifteen thousand dollars' worth of goods and Sublette upriver aboard one keelboat, having sent the empty one back to St. Louis. Perhaps no previous keelboat's crew had enjoyed an easier time up the Missouri. Sublette had arranged for a tow behind the steamboat

54. William Sublette to Robert Campbell, February 22, 1833, William Sublette to Robert Campbell, February 3, 1833, Campbell Papers, MLA.
55. Hedren, ed., *Narrative of Larpenteur*, 15–16.

*Otto*. Word of the partners' ambitious plans had preceded them across the West. At each American Fur Company post, Sublette left a trader and goods. He arrived at the Yellowstone River mouth on August 29 to await his partner.

Campbell led a typically motley caravan crew of youths burning for adventure, half American, half foreign, including ten Germans not long off the boat, and grogshop misfits, leavened by mountain veterans. Louis Vasquez was Robert's second in command and, as such, brought up the column's rear. Edmund T. Christy had entered into a one-year partnership with the Rocky Mountain Fur Company and was heading west to lead a trapping brigade. Perhaps most remarkable of all was the Scotsman William Drummond Stewart, who would soon inherit a lordship. He had forked over five hundred dollars to Sublette and Campbell to convey him to the mountains and would later write two novels based on his western adventures.[56]

The caravan experienced the usual drudgeries. The mules were typically stubborn, "kicking off their packs and running away . . . This kind of kicking up lasted three or four days in full blast; it finally subsided, yet there would be a runaway almost every day." Those pack animals had good reason to protest through kicks, bites, escapes, and general balkiness. Each carried around two hundred pounds of supplies. After a nearly two-thousand-mile journey to rendezvous and back, the mules' backs were raw and most were lame.[57]

The fare—mostly bacon and hard tack—was monotonous, but filling enough. Fuel was ever more scarce and the caravan had to go without fires at times or use sunflower stalks at others. Even after they reached the middle and high plains there was little sign and no sight of buffalo for days at a time.[58]

And, of course, there was the vital need to keep a constant vigil for Indian raiders. A week from Lexington, Campbell organized and enforced a very strict night guard. Every twenty minutes each guard called out "All's well." If a post was silent the guards' officer would immediately creep over and find out what happened. Guards asleep at their post were fined five dollars and three days' marching afoot.[59]

56. Mae Reed Porter and Odessa Davenport, *Scotsman in Buckskin: Sir William Drummond Stewart and the Rocky Mountain Fur Trade* (New York: Hastings House Publishers, 1963).
57. Hedren, ed., *Narrative of Larpenteur*, 10.
58. Ibid., 18–19, 20–21.
59. Ibid., 19–20.

While the caravan plodded west, Fitzpatrick was increasingly worried that the partners would not send them supplies. On June 4, he wrote a letter to Campbell that detailed their brigade's operations of the previous winter and requested supplies, including some good books to read. In all, the rival fur companies had spent an antagonistic winter in the mountains and passions were raging. After apologizing for not writing sooner, Fitzpatrick explained that his sixty-man party had spent the last year trapping the Salmon River region and then crossing over the divide into the Three Forks region. There Vanderburgh and 112 men caught up with them. Blackfeet dogged the trappers, killing Vanderburgh and wounding Bridger.[60]

Fitzpatrick then dispatched Henry Fraeb and ten men east, all the way to St. Louis if need be. Fraeb ran into Campbell at Laramie Creek on the North Platte River and together they journeyed to that year's rendezvous where Horse Creek flows into the Green River. They arrived on July 5, 1833. Campbell had won the race to that year's rendezvous, beating by three days Lucien Fontenelle, who led an American Fur Company caravan overland from Fort Pierre. Fontenelle complained that Campbell had "made much of a boast about" his trading prowess, carried ample amounts of liquor with which to corrupt the Indians, and "spread the report . . . that I would not be out for six weeks after him."[61]

As if rivalry between the two giants were not fierce enough, that year's rendezvous took place only a half dozen miles south of the trading post of Fort Nonsense, erected by Captain Benjamin Bonneville and his company the previous year. Bonneville's own caravan plodded in on July 13. The competition among the companies did not spoil the camaraderie among their men.[62]

Apparently Campbell did not abstain from the debauchery. Larpenteur somewhat disapprovingly recalled, "On the arrival of the trappers and hunters a big drunken spree took place. Our boss, who was a good one, and did not like to be backward in such things, I saw flat on his belly on the green grass, pouring out what he could not hold in."[63] For those who never committed excesses in their youth, it may be hard to reconcile a drunken, puking Robert Campbell with the dignified and prim portrait of him that was painted years later. Those who experienced their share of

---

60. Tom Fitzpatrick to Robert Campbell, June 4, 1833, Campbell Collection, MoHiS.
61. Lucien Fontenelle to William Laidlow, July 31, 1833, quoted in Sunder, *Sublette*, 127.
62. Irving, *Bonneville*, 180–81.
63. Hedren, ed., *Narrative of Larpenteur*, 25.

indulgences, however, might well smile knowingly. The same, of course, goes with the hints that Campbell dallied with many an Indian woman during his years in the mountains.

Given that the men were forced to abstain from sex, sometimes for months on end, it is unsurprising that nothing could divide them more quickly than a comely woman. Shoshone women were especially prized for their beauty and coquettishness, and many a fight exploded over their favors. As always, the trading went fast. Most trappers had no sooner received credit for their pelts than they spent it all on liquor, women, ammunition, and replacements for their worn-out gear.[64]

After selling off most of his goods, Campbell took a small party to raise a cache of pelts in Pierre's Hole. He left Fitzpatrick in charge and the clerk Redmond minding his store. Redmond converted a tent into a saloon where whiskey sold for five dollars a pint and "drinking, yelling, and shooting" was incessant. Redmond drank up too many of his profits and finally passed out dead drunk. Larpenteur was the only sober, trustworthy man left at rendezvous, so Fitzpatrick appointed him to take Redmond's place. The new bartender winced at the "great quarrels and fights outside, but I must say the men were all very civil to me."[65]

Not all was fun and games. That year's rendezvous did not pass without a frightening assault, this time not by Indians but by a rabid wolf. The beast launched several night attacks, biting twelve men at Fontenelle's camp; two of the victims succumbed to madness. Campbell's camp did not escape. One night the wolf raged through camp, biting three men and the bull in the cattle herd.[66]

The mad wolf aside, it had been a successful rendezvous for the three chief rivals. In all, 160 packs worth sixty thousand dollars were brought to rendezvous. Campbell's party gathered 30 from free trappers and 62 packs from the Rocky Mountain Fur Company. The American Fur Company collected the bulk of the others, about 55 packs in all. Bonneville's men accounted for 22 1/2 packs. Sir William Drummond Stewart later observed that "1833 was the last good year, for with 1834 came the spoilers—the idlers, the missionaries, the hard seekers after money."[67] The year was so good for the American Fur Company that the Rocky Mountain Fur Company finally agreed to split the country

64. Irving, *Bonneville*, 182, 183, 181.

65. Hedren, ed., *Narrative of Larpenteur*, 27–28.

66. For various accounts, see William Drummond Stewart, *Edward Warren*, 157; Victor, *River of the West*, 143; Hedren, ed., *Narrative of Larpenteur*, 30–31.

67. Gowans, *Rendezvous*, 1151. Stewart quoted in Porter and Davenport, *Scotsman*, 112.

with them; for the next year, the American Fur Company would take the Flathead, Snake River, and Great Salt Lake regions while the Rocky Mountain Fur Company would trap the Green, Three Forks, and Yellowstone watersheds.

A week after leaving, Campbell returned with his ten packs from his cache and immediately made preparations to break camp. On July 24, he led his caravan from rendezvous toward the Yellowstone's mouth. Joining him were Tom Fitzpatrick with about twenty men, Milton Sublette, and Nathaniel Wyeth. It must have been a somewhat awkward expedition, for Wyeth had underbid Campbell to supply the Rocky Mountain Fur Company with $3,000 worth of supplies at the next year's rendezvous, for which he would be paid $6,521 with furs worth $4 a pound. Thus did Wyeth stand to more than double his investment while the Rocky Mountain Fur Company found a much lower-cost supplier of goods and buyer of their furs than Sublette and Campbell. The deal was contingent on Wyeth's firm and the Rocky Mountain Fur Company staying in business beyond November 1833, and Wyeth's ability to find eastern backers. Each party sealed its contract with a $500 bond to be forfeited to the other if it defaulted. Milton Sublette would journey east with Wyeth to select the goods.[68]

Although Wyeth would later dismiss the mountaineers as "a great majority of scoundrels," he reserved kind words for Campbell: "For efficiency of goods, men, animals, and arms, I do not believe the fur business has afforded a better example or discipline." Wyeth did not allow his admiration for Campbell's managerial skills to cloud his appreciation that he could profit from the trade war erupting between the partners and the American Fur Company: "Mr Sublette and Mr. Campbell have come up the Missouri and established a trading fort at each location of the posts of the Am[erican] Fur Co. with a view to a strong opposition. Good luck to their quarrels!"[69] The following year at rendezvous, Wyeth would include Sublette and Campbell among that "majority of scoundrels."

Danger stalked their journey. In the Wind River valley, a scout who had been sent ahead to find a good encampment returned with three trappers who had departed earlier from rendezvous. The previous night, one of the trappers had been badly wounded by Indians with both a musket ball and an arrow. They stayed for two days before the man was

68. Agreement, August 14, 1833, Sublette Papers, MoHiS.
69. Wyeth to F. Ermatinger, July 18, 1833, in Young, "Two Expeditions," 69–70.

well enough to travel and then set off again. Game was so scarce that "we had to live for two days on such berries and roots."[70]

The havoc wreaked by the mad wolf continued to haunt them. The bull that had been bitten went mad on the Bighorn River and had to be killed. Next affected was a New Yorker named Holmes, who went crazy, refused to cross streams, and finally dashed away naked into the forest. He was never seen again.[71]

At the Bighorn River, Fitzpatrick and his brigade turned east into the mountains for the autumn trapping while Campbell sent his men to hunt buffalo. The slaughtered animals were skinned and their hides used to construct a flotilla of bullboats. He then split his own party in two. He headed downriver with the beaver packs while Louis Vasquez led a land party that herded the exhausted pack animals and cattle.[72]

On the land party's fifth day on the march, a party of Indians appeared on the Bighorn River's opposite shore; there they waved weapons and shouted. Vasquez ordered his men to take cover and secure the livestock. The Indians turned out to be Crows who were inviting them over to a feast and then a trade. The Crow guided them to the American Fur Company's Fort Cass, commanded by Samuel Tullock, a day away on the Yellowstone River two miles below where the Bighorn River meets it. From there they followed the Yellowstone to the Missouri, where the party rejoined Campbell on September 3.[73]

Ironically, Campbell was actually looking for the Crows that had briefly terrified the land party. As he drifted down the Bighorn, he penned a letter to Hugh that summarized his actions and challenges: "our party is traversing a country frequented by bands of Indians, whose friendship can only be depended on, when our vigilence and strength sets hostility at defiance."[74] Even the "friendliest" of Indians viewed the white intruders with mixed feelings. They valued the white man's goods while remaining resentful, contemptuous, and fearful of the trespassers. To prevent those barely concealed animosities from exploding into hostility, the trappers had to supply generous gifts and fair trading, display cultural sensitivity, and, occasionally, act as go-betweens in disputes between tribes.

70. Hedren, ed., *Narrative of Larpenteur*, 32.
71. Ibid., 33–34.
72. Ibid., 34–35.
73. Ibid., 35–38.
74. Robert Campbell to Hugh Campbell, July 20, 1833, in Eberstadt, ed., *Rocky Mountain Letters*.

At that summer's rendezvous, the Shoshone (Snake) band led by Chief Iron Wristband requested that Campbell undertake just such a diplomatic mission:

> We had a smoke and talk . . . in the course of which I discovered that my new friend wished to employ me in the capacity of ambassador extraordinary . . . on a mission to the Crow Indians . . . It seems that a misunderstanding had arisen between the Snakes and Crows—not so serious as to lead to immediate open hostilities,—yet sufficient to render it doubtful whether they could meet as friends. To ascertain the views of the Crows; and if hostile, to deliver a suitable defiance, were to be the objects of my mission.

To talk Campbell into undertaking the mission, the chief recounted that eight years earlier, the Shoshone and Crow had been implacable enemies but William Ashley had negotiated a friendship between those tribes. Could Campbell do no less? A challenge was offered that only a coward would avoid. Furthermore, the elaborate etiquette among the Indians required that Campbell return Iron Wristband's hospitality. Most important, of course, in convincing Campbell to undertake the mission was the common interest that all three parties—American, Shoshone, and Crow—shared in maintaining peace among them. The perennial war with the Blackfeet made any excursion into the fur-rich northern Rockies a dangerous and draining enterprise. The Americans needed every ally they could muster against the Blackfeet. Even worse, the refusal to honor Iron Wristband's request might well convert that strategic ally into an enemy and render the upper Snake River basin and adjacent regions as dangerous as Blackfeet territory. Finally, even the Crow could turn against the Americans if they viewed the intruders as weak-willed and too narrowly focused on immediate profits.

Campbell readily agreed to accept the diplomatic mission, not just because it was good business to do so, but also from his deep admiration for the Shoshone chief: "I have seldom seen stronger proofs of political cunning, than on this occassion . . . you would see in every sentence, evidence of deep policy, and consummate political skill." Iron Wristband dictated a letter for Campbell to deliver to the Crows that would war against the Blackfeet, and hoped the Crows would join the Shoshone along with the Cheyenne, Utes, Arapahoes, and Navahoes so that "before the snow comes [we] . . . will grind them to death."

Campbell's diplomatic mission nearly failed. While descending the Big Horn, the bullboat he was riding in sank and he almost drowned:

Thrice I went under water and but for an all wise and merciful God I should never have seen the termination of this year. I got safe to shore and succeeded in recovering all but about 4 packs of Beaver and our arms. Besides I lost my saddle bags &c. I recovered again my boat and next day was joined by all the Crow Indians—and here again I must acknowledge my dependence on God who inclined those Indians to treat me kindly and return most of my beaver when they had me completely in their power.[75]

He successfully conveyed Iron Wristband's peace overture to the Crows, who gladly accepted it.

In summing up his experiences to Hugh, Campbell admitted that although the venture was richly successful, the strains all along were enormous: "You have no idea of the anxiety and toil of such a march."[76] Actually, the emotional strain he experienced on the march would soon pale in comparison with the ferocious winter that lay just ahead.

75. Brooks, ed., "Private Journal of Robert Campbell," 117.
76. Robert Campbell to Hugh Campbell, July 20, 1833, in Eberstadt, ed., *Rocky Mountain Letters.*

# Fort William (1833–1834)

**O**n August 30, Campbell's party paddled up to Sublette's camp a few miles below where the Yellowstone flows into the Missouri. Sublette had anchored his keelboat there just a few days earlier. After rejoicing over Campbell's success at rendezvous, the partners plunged into the second phase of their strategy. The men unloaded supplies from the keelboat and stacked them ashore. The furs were packed aboard. Crews were dispatched to nearby cottonwood groves to cut and haul logs. Hunters ranged the surrounding plains after buffalo. The outlines of the post, to be called Fort William, were paced off. A mere two-and-a-half miles would separate Fort William from the rival American Fur Company post of Fort Union, just across from the Yellowstone's mouth.

Amidst all this bustle, Campbell found time to write a letter to his mother describing that year's successes: "I took the part of my company that went by land consisting of 50 men and all including 2 or 3 who went on a trip of pleasure—my journey proved agreeable and sufficiently lucrative in both cases beyond my expectations."[1] Like any son, he undoubtedly hoped his mother would take pride in his accomplishments. He then dutifully reassured her, "I would willfully relinquish the 3 years of my life which I intend passing here for 1 month with you." Nor did he neglect telling his mother of his spiritual concerns: "in this country the Sabbath is kept so far as regards manual labor . . . we have 3 or 4 bibles one of which is mine. I bought it in Londonderry and is my intent to use . . . I hope the precepts you incubated in my youth will yet prove of advantage." Campbell's diplomatic skills clearly extended beyond converting Indians, trappers, and merchants to his aims.

1. Robert Campbell to his Mother, September 11, 1833, Campbell Papers, MLA.

Within days of the partners' reunion, a crisis darkened their enterprise. Sublette fell deathly ill. A pall hung over the camp as Campbell wondered if he might lose his friend. The crisis passed. By September 21, Sublette had recovered sufficiently to embark downstream with "the greater number of our indifferent hands . . . and a few good men amounting in all to Eighteen Men—with these men we entered into a new engagement releasing them on their arrival below."[2] En route, he visited each of the thirteen trading posts—most of which consisted of one man in a hastily erected cabin or dugout—that he had planted during his upriver push earlier that summer.

Windbound for three days at the Mandan village, he had ample time to inspect the operations of agent John Dougherty. There were problems, as he revealed in a letter to Campbell. Living with the Mandans was Jean Baptiste Charbonneau, who had, among other things, accompanied Lewis and Clark and married Sacajawea. The now old Charbonneau had "become quite childish & has to be humored much which makes it verry disagreeable and to turn him off it will offend the Indians as he has much influence."[3] When Dougherty and Charbonneau got into an argument, the old man threatened to pack off and go, which upset the Mandan. Sublette managed to patch over the animosity. As if dealing with cantankerous old Charbonneau was not trouble enough, Dougherty faced an American Fur Company employee who traded goods for the same price, except for ammunition, of which he gave seventy rounds when the partners gave sixty. Kenneth McKenzie, Fort Union's bourgeois, had recently passed through to cement his relationship with the Mandan with generous presents and flowery speeches. All this provoked a nagging fear in each partner that they had bitten off more than they could chew. Indeed, they had. Although Sublette's and Campbell's agents tried to offer the Indians even better prices, they would garner few robes that winter. Most Indians remained loyal to the American Fur Company.

Sublette did have good news to report—he had made peace with both the Mandans and the Yanktonais Sioux. He went on to suggest that Campbell send down supplies to their traders as soon as possible and a mackinaw boat in the spring to pick up the robes garnered by their thirteen agents at different river villages. Campbell received the letter on October 12 and promptly sent down the necessary supplies.

2. Brooks, ed., "Private Journal of Robert Campbell," 3–24.
3. William Sublette to Robert Campbell, September 25, 1833, Sublette Papers, MoHiS.

By November 5, Sublette reached Fort Leavenworth, where he rather hypocritically informed officials of the distillery McKenzie had erected at Fort Union. Wyeth had angrily told the same tale when he passed through several weeks earlier. In Lexington, Sublette arranged with James and Robert Aull and Company, and Mr. Meek of the Steam Mill Company, to send supplies upriver to his posts as early as possible the next spring.

Awaiting him when he returned to St. Louis in mid-November was a letter from Ashley urging him to send all his furs and robes east as soon as possible, so that they could be sold for a good price. Sublette promptly complied.[4] Exhausted by his labors, Sublette rested briefly with Milton at Sulphur Springs, where he got Dr. Benjamin Farrar to care for his brother's festering leg. Most days he would ride the half dozen miles to St. Louis to meet with William Clark, his lawyer Henry Geyer, and various merchants. In December, Sublette headed east for another buying trip and, most important, negotiations in New York with John Jacob Astor.

Campbell, meanwhile, supervised the fort's construction. At a cotton-wood grove, trees were sawn into eighteen-foot-tall, foot-thick pickets, dragged by horse to the site, and then planted three feet deep in a rect-angular palisade that would measure 150 by 130 feet. Blockhouses stood atop opposite corners. Within the fort were eight cabins, storehouses, and a corral. Campbell's quarters "stood back, opposite the front door; it consisted of a double cabine, having two rooms of 18X20 feet, with a passage between them 12 feet wide. There was a store and warehouse 40 feet in length and 18 feet in width; two rooms for the men's quarters 16X18 feet, a carpenter's shop, blacksmith's shop, ice house, and two splendid bastions."[5] The fort's only entrance was a well-guarded gate facing the river. Other logs were used to build the barracks, headquarters, storehouse, and cowshed. Suitable rocks were found and hauled to the fort for chimneys. Coal was gathered from a nearby seam. A well was dug.

The well would have killed a man had it not been for Campbell's quick and brave reaction: "The man who digs was about going down in the Tub and entered it before any one had taken hold of the windlass—his weight of course caused a rapid descent which sent the Handle of the

4. W. H. Ashley to William Sublette, November 8, 1833, Sublette to Ashley, November 1833, ibid.
5. Hedren, ed., *Narrative of Larpenteur*, 49.

windlass with such velocity that the man ran from it. I saw the danger and pumped on it and succeeded in stopping it not however without being much hurt by the handle of the windlass. I nearly fainted but had secured the man from inevitable death as the depth is nearly 23 feet."[6]

During these hectic days Campbell found the time to meet frequently for pleasure and business with his archrival, Kenneth McKenzie. In his long career, he would never face a more brilliant, seasoned, and ruthless opponent. McKenzie had first entered the trade in the 1810s with the Northwest Company, and rapidly rose through its ranks. When the Hudson's Bay Company took over the Northwest Company in 1821, McKenzie headed to St. Louis in search of new opportunities. In 1822, he and Joseph Renville founded the Columbia Fur Company, whose traders operated out of Fort Snelling and Lake Traverse to capture a large portion of the upper Missouri and Mississippi fur trade. In 1827, the American Fur Company's Western Department bought out the Columbia Fur Company, renamed it the Upper Missouri Outfit, and hired McKenzie to head it.

In 1829, McKenzie ascended the Missouri with fifty men and a keelboat packed with supplies to found Fort Union at the Yellowstone River mouth. From there he was charged with capturing the Indian trade all the way west to the Rockies. Within a year McKenzie achieved what nearly all thought was impossible—peace with the Blackfeet. In 1830, he sent Jacob Berger up the Missouri to negotiate a peace treaty. To the astonishment of all, Berger succeeded. The Blackfeet agreed to tolerate a trading post in their land but swore to continue to attack any trapping parties. In 1832, James Kipp erected Fort Piegan at the Marias River mouth; the following year the post was moved a half dozen miles and renamed Fort McKenzie. That same year, McKenzie dispatched an expedition up the Yellowstone to establish Fort Cass at the Bighorn River and capture the Crow trade. With Fort McKenzie and Fort Cass, the Upper Missouri Outfit had taken two giant steps westward to the mountains where its trapping brigades had already penetrated to squeeze, anacondalike, the Rocky Mountain Fur Company.

From his Fort Union headquarters, McKenzie presided over the upper Missouri with its dozen trading posts, hundreds of thousands of dollars' worth of trade goods, and hundreds of men. To his engagés, he was a stern, demanding autocrat who kept them on short rations, gave them a pittance for their labors, and severely punished transgressions.

6. Brooks, ed., "Private Journal of Robert Campbell," December 4, 1833.

To those of higher, equal, or near rank, he was a generous and genial host, sharing fine wines, brandies, delicacies, and conversation with his guests. During the 1830s, a parade of notables traveled far up the Missouri, including aristocrats Prince Maximilian of Wied and James Archibald Hamilton Palmer; artists Karl Bodmer, Alfred Jacob Miller, George Catlin, and John James Audubon; and scientists Thomas Nuttall and John Bradbury; along with the occasional army officer and rivals such as Campbell.

Larpenteur would later work for McKenzie and left this portrait:

> Mr. McKenzie, who played the nabob, went to bed late, and rose later, and as nothing could be served till he was ready, it was nine o'clock before we got to breakfast. . . . When I heard the bell ring for supper I saw them put on their coats, for . . . they were not allowed to go to table in shirtsleeves . . . On entering the eating hall, I found a splendidly set table with two waiters, one a negro. Mr. McKenzie was sitting at the head of the table, extremely well dressed. The victuals consisted of fine fat buffalo meat, with plenty of good fresh butter, cream, and milk for those that chose; but I saw only two biscuits were allowed to each one, as these were placed at each plate. I soon discovered, by the manner in which the clerks took their seats, that mine would come very near the end of the table, for it appeared to go by grade.[7]

Campbell and his men exercised more humble social and culinary practices. Two months after they had started work, they were able to sit down at their own tables within warm cabins. They celebrated Fort William's completion on November 15 in true mountain style, with a feast and accompanying antics.[8]

In all, it was a snug little fort, but like other trading posts it soon reeked like a feedlot. Around the fort rooted domesticated animals, including five cows, chickens, turkeys, and possibly sheep and hogs. Sublette had carted the smaller animals by keelboat up the Missouri. Campbell had driven two bulls and four cows all the way from St. Louis to the mountains and then down to Fort William, although one bull had died of rabies.

Campbell proudly wrote his sister Anne that the "location of my fort is beautiful commanding a view of the Yellowstone and Missouri Rivers and the back country."[9] He did not exaggerate—Fort William's setting was starkly beautiful:

7. Hedren, ed., *Narrative of Larpenteur*, 56–57.
8. Ibid., 43.
9. Robert Campbell to Anne Campbell, September 11, 1833, Campbell Papers, MLA.

the mouth of the Yellowstone there were always great numbers of water fowls . . . wild geese, ducks, muskrats, cranes, pelicans . . . The wolves now came very near to the fort, and prowled around, even in broad daytime . . . Troops of 30 to 40 antelopes now came nearer to the Missouri . . . Little prairie foxes so hungrey and therefore so tame, often visited the environs of the fort. And we found these pretty little animals among circles of turf which were left on the removals of Indians tents.[10]

Buffalo robes rather than beaver pelts sustained the Missouri River and Great Plains trading posts. A yearly cycle governed the robe trade just as it did the pelt trade.[11] In the autumn, each post's bourgeois would trade for any robes dragged in by the Indians and white hunters from their summer hunts. Credit would be advanced for their winter hunts. Most Indians and many whites failed to ever pay off their debts. During negotiations, the companies also gave away numerous gifts to the chiefs, who distributed them among their people. The companies made up these losses by knocking up prices on the goods they traded.

Debts often remained on the books for very good reasons—finding buffalo was no easy task. Buffalo wander in herds varying from hundreds to thousands, driven by the relative abundance of fodder and water, and, in winter, the ferocity of storms and temperatures. A herd will hole up in wooded valleys for forage and shelter during especially severe winters. When hunters spotted a herd, they would try to encircle it and wipe it out or drive it over a cliff. The take from even the most successful of hunts was limited by the number of robes the band could process. Curing robes was hard, labor-intensive work. The average woman cured about twenty robes each winter. Bands generally used three of every four robes for their own needs and traded away the fourth.

With its winter or summer hunt complete, the band headed to the nearest trading post. The traders depended on the Indians for not only robes but also dried meat and tallow. In return, the companies packed a wide variety of trade goods. Each tribe had its own favorite colors or patterns of glass beads, paints, blankets, cloth, ribbons, bells, rings, and bracelets; all eagerly sought awls, nails, gun flints, pipes, guns, gunpowder, axes, hoes, and lead. Although the Indians and whites received about three dollars for each robe, that money was nearly worthless when it was spent. When Campbell set up shop at the Yellowstone mouth, traders marked up prices anywhere from 200 to 2,000 percent for whites and

10. "Maxmillien's Travels," in Reuben Thwaites, ed., *Early Western Travels*, vol. 23, 125.
11. Wishart, *Fur Trade*, 79–114.

Indians alike. By then, the Indians had a good general understanding of the relative value of goods and the prices paid by free trappers. That knowledge and the increased competition kept a relative check on prices. After all, each side had what the other needed.

The traders sorted robes according to their quality. Although they would trade for nearly any robe, they preferred robes skinned from cows and young bulls taken in the winter when their fur was the thickest. Ten robes were pressed into a pack that weighed about one hundred pounds. Sometime in midsummer, the supply boats arrived to deposit goods and take on robe and fur packs. Summer was also a time to lay in a good supply of buffalo meat for the long winter ahead. The rations at most trading posts were supplemented by vegetable gardens and corn, squash, and beans traded from the local horticultural tribe. Some post activities lasted all year round; the men were kept constantly busy cutting and hauling wood, hunting, grazing livestock, and repairing equipment.

Fort Union and Fort William tapped into the labor of three nearby tribes—Assiniboines, Crees, and Gros Ventres. Campbell's men had no sooner settled into their new quarters when bands of those Indians and free trappers began arriving with robes and pelts. Campbell reported that the "trade has scarcely commenced; but we, and our rivals, are electioneering hard for it . . . Intrigue, bribery, and corruption are the order of the day. The Indians feel their importance and maintain it."[12]

He left out the most important ingredient of a successful trade—alcohol. Indians were tough and canny bargainers until the trader rolled out a liquor barrel. Then, with their minds turned to mush, the Indians often gave away not just their robes, but often all the rest of their possessions, including women, for nothing. Larpenteur explained how dependent the trade and Indians had become on alcohol: "Early in the fall trade commenced, principally in jerked buffalo meat and tallow, both mostly traded for liquor. The liquor business, which was always done at night, sometimes kept me up all night turning out drunk Indians, often by dragging them out by arms and legs."[13]

This was a gross violation of federal laws of 1802, 1816, 1822, and 1833 that prohibited selling liquor to the Indians and strictly limited the alcohol that could be taken into their country. The law, however,

12. Edwin Thompson Denig, *Five Indian Tribes of the Upper Missouri: Sioux, Arickaras, Assiniboines, Crees, Crows;* Mooney, ed., *Catlin;* Michael Stephen Kennedy, *The Assiniboines.* Robert Campbell to Hugh Campbell, November 16, 1833, in Eberstadt, ed., *Rocky Mountain Letters.*
13. Hedren, ed., *Narrative of Larpenteur,* 60.

could be evaded by smuggling or with bribes to inspectors and licensors. Sublette had, after all, received a license from Indian Superintendent William Clark to pack alcohol in his overland caravan rendezvous for his "boatmen." Not all inspectors, however, were corrupt. Officials at Fort Leavenworth and elsewhere on the lower Missouri River did confiscate shipments and fine the smugglers. In 1832, they impounded fourteen hundred gallons of alcohol bound for American Fur Company posts that had been approved by Clark. Kenneth McKenzie resolved the uncertain supply by building and operating a distillery at Fort Union. He distilled corn bought from the Mandans and produced an unending stream of crude but effective whiskey.

Most bands would remain loyal customers of the American Fur Company. Not only was McKenzie quick to match any price his rival offered, but the Indians also assumed Campbell's venture would soon disappear and did not want to alienate McKenzie's powerful company. Perhaps most important of all, McKenzie had a competitive edge in liquor: "he gives as much whiskey as the Indians can drink for nothing. Barrel after Barrel he sends all around amongst the Indians and these will not trade otherwise." Finally, McKenzie did not hesitate to use a stick as well as a carrot to keep the Indians at his fort. To maintain the Assiniboine trade, he threatened to "kill their dogs if they come" to Fort William.[14]

While Indians brought in the most robes, pelts, and tallow, free trappers traded their own gleanings at the posts for desperately needed supplies. Campbell tried to recruit free trappers to be engagés with offers of $4.25 a pelt for the first year, and $4.50 a pelt if the man hired on for two years. Most mountain men haughtily spurned the offer to throw away their free trapping life for that of a despised engagé, despite the excellent prices for pelts.

To worsen matters, that autumn was poor for robes. The unusually hot summer had driven the herds far north for relief, and most bands in the region had followed. The returns from that harsh winter would be skimpy—one hundred packs of buffalo robes, five packs of beaver pelts, six packs of wolf skins, and one of rabbits and foxes. Fort Union alone, meanwhile, garnered 430 packs of robes.[15]

Campbell did manage to wean some bands away from Fort Union, and literally captured one trade. After Chief Gauche's Assiniboines

14. Brooks, ed., "Private Journal of Robert Campbell," December 2, 11, 1833.
15. Wishart, *Fur Trade*, 72.

arrived, the "liquor trade started at dark and soon the singing and yelling commenced. The Indians were all locked up in the fort, for fear that some might go to Ft. Union . . . Imagine the noise—upward of 500 Indians with their squaws, all drunk as they could be."[16] When the Indians awoke with splitting hangovers in the harsh morning light, all their robes were safely packed away in the fort's warehouse. They morosely packed up and left.

Gauche and a few others lingered. Campbell was not done yet. Hoping to secure Gauche for the winter trade, he made the chief

> a very impressive speech previous to his departure. So the old bear was invited into Mr. Campbell's room, and after quite a lengthy speech, during which the old fellow made no reply, not even by grunt, he merely said, "Are you a goin to give me some salt before I leave?" This being all the satisfaction Mr. Campbell received for his long speech, he could not refrain from laughing. The old devil got his salt, with some other small presents, and then departed without leaving any signs of his intention to return. Thus ended this trade.[17]

Another band of about sixty Assiniboine visited Fort William after trading at Fort Union. Campbell vividly recorded their arrival and subsequent negotiations: they strode in

> walking abreast, some with spears fantastically ornamented with scarlet cloth, and the feathers of the war eagle, others carrying the war club . . . and all armed with guns, or bows and arrows . . . they commenced a song expressive of their arrival . . . When they got within two hundred yards of us they made a halt and their song ceased; the chief then advanced six paces . . . and at mid distance stopped three or four braves, who ranked next in authority—I accordingly took my interpreter along and went up to them; I gave my hand to the chap, which he grasped firmly, and ejaculated, how! . . . He was a fine looking fellow . . . and possesed the easy manners to an Indian chief, who ranks himself second to none that walks the earth . . . the march was resumed, every gun was discharged in the air, and the song commenced, which ended only when we stopped to form a circle to smoke; here the same respect for rank was observed as in the march—the plebians seated themselves in the outer ring, the braves in an inner one, and the chiefs still nearer the centre. I entered and took my seat vis a vis his greatness, my interpreter sitting to my left. A glance at my motley group was amusing; their dress was plain . . . a buffalo skin . . . no shirts . . . their leggins . . . like their mockasons, were plain—excepting a few who had rings painted around the leggins, one leg red, the other black—recording some feats . . . Long

16. Hedren, ed., *Narrative of Larpenteur*, 44–45.
17. Ibid., 46–47.

fringes hanging on each side . . . a few ornamented with hair . . . They were all painted; some had the face all red except the tip of the nose, others painted with vermillion leaving little spots on the forehead and cheek, which were painted lead colour, a few had their eyes painted white and all the other part red; and others again were painted as black as a negro. These last having been to war, and killed some of the enemy . . . [18]

The council then began. Kinninick was packed into pipes, lighted, and passed. After each had "taken a few ambrossial whiffs in dead silence," Campbell explained why they had come to build the fort and the goods they had to offer. He then presented them with three hundred charges of ammunition, sixty plugs of tobacco, a dozen knives, and an assortment of gewgaws. He promised that these presents were but a taste of what the Assiniboine could enjoy if they returned to trade with many robes. The chief enthusiastically promised to return in the spring.

While the council met, the women set up camp beside the fort. Campbell lauded the Assiniboine village's beauty. Many lodges bore painted animals like wolves or bears. Some sported prostrate warriors with blood flowing from their wounds, signs the owner had killed an enemy. Of these Campbell wrote that a greenhorn might avoid such occupants but the killer "nine times in ten . . . is the most generous and hospitable you meet."

As with other tribes he encountered, Campbell displayed a deep curiosity and appreciation for the spiritual beliefs of the Assiniboine, being "forcibly struck with remarkable similarity which some of their traditions respecting creation, bear to divine revelation. One of their prophets gave me a long history of the formation of things 'animate and inanimate.' "[19]

Among the most memorable of the Indians Campbell met at his fort was the Cree chief, Sonnant (Rattle). Campbell observed that when analyzing

an Indian, you generally try to discover his character from his eye; but the optics of this chief defied scrutiny. They were so embedded between high cheek bones, a hawk nose that exceeds belief, and large shaggy eye brows that no man . . . could tell their colour, without such a look as an Indian brooks not; while my new friend Sonnant could peer into your very soul, without appearing to be looking at you. His forehead was prominent . . .

18. Robert Campbell to Hugh Campbell, December 8, 1833, in Eberstadt, ed., *Rocky Mountain Letters*.
19. Robert Campbell to Hugh Campbell, July 12, 1836, ibid.

that without being much of a phrenologist you would at once attribute to him, resolution, to sustain his purposes; implacable hatred and deadly revenge on those who crossed him. His head surmounted by huge masses of hair, tied in a knot before . . . His full chest and brawny arms, were tattooed with blue stripes, very regularly laid on; and indeed handsome after your eye became familiar with it; although at first sight, you would condemn the taste that could admire such horrible and disgusting ornaments. The easy, dignified, and elastic step of this chief proved that he was "born to command." His apparel was simple, but comfortable. A Buffalo skin enveloped him from head to knee. Leggins of Antelope skin ensconced his legs; and plain mocassins protected his feet . . . he has but one fault which materially lessened his claims on my respect . . . he is a beastly drunkard.[20]

In return for promises of trade, Campbell presented him with tobacco, vermilion, ammunition, and, less willingly, alcohol. Sonnant gulped the offered pint of wine at once,

then became very troublesome for his loquacity. I paced the apartment with some degree of impatience; and to his solicitation for more drink, gave a flat denial . . . The old fellow (for he has seen nearly sixty snows) in great good humour, paced through the room with his hand on his sides (Buffaloe robes have no pockets) observing that he . . . would walk as his father (meaning me) . . . The old rascal had seen enough moons to be my grandfather. His comments . . . were irresistibly comic.

Although Campbell still refused to pour any more wine, Sonnant "departed greatly pleased with his interview; vowing everlasting friendship; which . . . means, as long as I had wine and goods to give, and he had robes and beaver to trade."

Not all passing Indians were friendly. On October 31, some men Campbell had dispatched to the Yellowstone hurried back to the fort. During the night Indians had stolen two of their mules. The accounts his engagés gave of their mishaps often had to be taken with a grain of salt. On December 8, Pierre Walsh straggled to the fort to announce that Indians had stolen his horse. But Campbell later learned that the Indians were on the opposite side of the river. When they fired at Walsh he ran off, leaving his horse behind.

Animosities deepened between the rivals as the Indians began trading. Even "social" visits were fraught with tension as each bourgeois or an underling tried to pry out as much information as possible. Not all

20. Robert Campbell to Hugh Campbell, November 16, 1833, ibid. Although Campbell described Sonnant as "Creek" Indian, he undoubtedly meant to write "Cree."

of these spy ventures were successful. McKenzie's clerk, Abel Chardon, tended to tip the bottle a bit too freely. During one of several visits to Fort William, he "got beastly drunk" and so rowdy that Campbell considered kicking him out of the fort. Eventually Chardon passed out in the hog pen. But Campbell tolerated Chardon's behavior "in consideration of his being Drunk and a clerk to our opponents I determined to bear with him lest it might be construed into malice."[21] As usual Campbell's values and business interests went hand in hand. His tolerance paid off when the following day first Fort Union's doctor McCrever appeared to apologize for their clerk's behavior, followed by Chardon himself, who "said he was ashamed and sorry for his conduct and observed that I treated him as a gentleman and he behaved badly."

Despite the mostly amiable encounters, tensions burned between the rival companies. Conflicts arose to be negotiated. On November 24, Campbell learned that two trappers had stolen a pack of furs that he had cached on the Bighorn River that summer and sold it to McKenzie. Chardon, probably while drunk, revealed the secret. Campbell rode over to Fort Union to confront the thieves before McKenzie. But McKenzie sided with the men. All Campbell could do was threaten to sue. With each having had his say, the rivals then set aside the dispute and dined together.

They found common ground on at least one issue—workers. On October 14, Chardon arrived at Fort William to complain that one of his workers had refused to work. Chardon proposed that they not hire any deserters from each other's posts. Though no written or formal agreement was struck, Campbell did inform Fort Union's leaders when deserters arrived. He had his own troubles with bulky engagés. The worst of these was Duro [Durand], whom Campbell claimed "in all my intercourse I never was so much annoyed by a man. The most barefaced beggary and open effrontery I ever seen." Yet Campbell was forgiving. After Duro went on a spree, Campbell swallowed his anger when the engagé "was very penitent and laid his conduct on his being intoxicated."[22]

An eccentric family to say the least neighbored the two trading posts. The Deschamps numbered five: François, the father, his Assiniboine wife, and their sons, François, Jr., Charles, and Joseph. Among the more inhospitable families in American history, the Deschamps liked to lure solitary

21. Campbell Journal, November 2, 1833.
22. Ibid., November 27, 26, 1833.

trappers and Indians to their home on the Missouri River, befuddle them with alcohol, rob and murder the victims, then dump their bodies. Most of their livelihood, however, depended on more traditional pursuits. The Deschamps trapped, traded, and hunted, and hired out to the forts for various tasks. While so employed they lost no opportunity to rob their boss blind. Campbell bought fifty-one beaver pelts from the Deschamps and paid François, Jr., $500 to interpret and Joseph $510 to hunt for Fort William. He would later regret doing so.

Charm apparently was a part of the Deschamps' modus operandi, which at times led to Grand Guignol scenes between the rival trading posts. Campbell reported on October 28 that "Joseph Dechamp [sic] seduced from the bed and board of Doctor McCrevee his own lawfully purchased wife which he obtained from her father for the sum of 280$ in merchandise . . . The little doctor was outrageous but today the fair damsel accompanied her paramour on a Buffalo hunt and thus left her late spouse time to forget her before they again meet." The incident provoked Campbell to ruminate not on the morality of Joseph Deschamp, but of that of Indian women in general: "This proves the instability of the dear angels—receive them all love and affection and in a week they leave you for something new." It sounds like Robert was speaking from personal experience.

McKenzie was torn between supporting his cuckolded doctor and Joseph, whom he had employed as a spy in the enemy camp. McKenzie did have some scruples. He finally decided that Joseph Deschamp was no longer welcome at Fort Union, a status that complicated the diplomacy over Campbell's missing dog on November 18. When Campbell learned that the dog had somehow shown up at Fort Union, he made the mistake of sending a slightly drunk Joseph Deschamp over to fetch it back. Deschamp had words with Mckenzie, Brazo, and Legrett, and soon fists were flying. A bruised Deschamps returned to complain of his ill treatment, a rather ironic attitude given his own family's reputation for hospitality. Campbell wrote a letter of complaint to McKenzie, who promptly fired back a letter denouncing Deschamp. The dog was sent back the next day.

Campbell would eventually realize the depth of the Deschamps' deceits and petty thefts. By December he was calling them "the greatest rascals in the world." A showdown of sorts came on December 29 when Campbell's interpreter, Francois Deschamp, "became drunk and threatened to leave. I was very near shooting him." This was an astonishing statement from someone as level-headed as Campbell. Deschamp had definitely strained his legendary patience. Instead, Campbell took back all the equipment he had given Deschamp and had him escorted to the gate. Within minutes he was back to reveal that McKenzie had paid him forty dollars not only to spy on Campbell and the fort but also to create as many conflicts as possible. He then apologized profusely. Campbell forgave him and let him stay. Deschamp paid back that generosity by slipping over the wall a few nights later with stolen goods including Campbell's spyglass.

In all, given the ceaseless tension of dealing with rapacious Indians and whites alike, Campbell found the trade "troublesome and unprofitable."[23] By late autumn, he was willing to sell out. On November 12, he received a visit from McKenzie and offered him all the merchandise at 80 percent of costs, the mules and horses for fifty-five dollars each, and a promise to pay the men's wages from September 1 and fulfill their contracts. He also offered to sell out the other posts down the Missouri River.

McKenzie rejected the offer but said he would present a counteroffer the next day. Instead, McKenzie wrote Campbell that their positions were so far apart that they could not be bridged, and thus he would not submit a counteroffer.[24] Negotiations at the Yellowstone River mouth ended there. It was now up to William Sublette a couple thousand miles away to cut a good deal for the partners.

At no time in his life was Campbell more revealing of his feelings and outlook than he was at Fort William. In a September 11 letter to his sister Anne, he explained that the West's allure rested on how much wealth he could wring from it:

> The object in this country . . . is to make money although we account for it under many feelings of excitement, love, adventure, unrestrained indulgence to all of our inclinations without being subject to the shackles of society—true there may have been some effect and probably all act in some part yet the primary object is money. Were it not this, we would all endure no questions ourselves to civilized life and no doubt feel ten times the happiness which we enjoy here.[25]

The work was nearly incessant. Stress and possible danger accompanied virtually every activity, including "social visits" to Fort Union

23. Ibid., December 1, 1833.
24. *Fort Union Letterbook*, 2; quoted in Brooks, ed., "Private Journal of Robert Campbell," 19.
25. Robert Campbell to Anne Campbell, September 11, 1833, Campbell Papers, MLA.

or hunting on the surrounding plains. On the night of November 13, Campbell and his men did find time to marvel at a meteor shower: "falling stars were seen shooting in all directions and 10, 15, and 20 visible at a time. They continued without intermission until morning and became larger, some remaining suspended as it were for two minutes, beautiful and bright."

Twice that autumn, he entertained two visiting dignitaries, Prince Maximilian of Wied and artist Karl Bodmer. He found the prince "fond of enquiry and anxious to possess all the information he could respecting the mountains." Campbell not only answered all the prince's questions but also satisfied his craving for cigars by giving him a handful. Maximilian promised to carry Campbell's business letters down to St. Louis.[26]

As bourgeois, Campbell had a duty for his men's emotional as well as physical well-being. Yet there were limits to what he could provide. On November 9, he wrote, "Poor Mr Janis heard of the Death of his wife and I never saw a man so distracted. Nothing I could say would reconcile him. I let him remain so." Another time, "Pierre Garo asked me privlege to purchase a squaw by doing which he would overrun his account. I allowed him to do so as I am desirous of having him learn to speak the Assiniboine tongue."[27]

Depression plagued Campbell throughout that harsh winter, a malady he failed to conceal from his men. On November 29, he complained,

> I am now at this place Three months and I can safely say more trouble and less pleasure I never experienced in . . . that length of time. What is worse my troubles are but commencing as all the low unprincipled means of annoyance Mr. McKenzie can give he is throwing in my way. I fear much the result of our business and as I have cast my fortunes on this die, all my future happiness depends on the turn. Would to God I was free from it with my loss of time—but reflections are useless. I must only try my best in my present case.[28]

Although many of his men were undoubtedly equally or more depressed, the lot of them gathered before his cabin at four o'clock on Christmas morning and fired three volleys; musicians played the fife and drum. Campbell packed them into his cabin and treated them to wine, flour, coffee, sugar, and dried apples. After dismissing them, he

26. "Maxmilian's Travels," in Thwaites, *Western Travels,* vol. 23, 207.
27. Campbell Journal, December 7, 1833.
28. Ibid., November 29, 1833.

tried to return to sleep but was kept awake by the drunken din outside. Later that day, he threw a dinner for them.

New Year's eve was bitterly frigid—eighteen degrees below zero! Campbell led the men in cutting and hauling wood. A snow storm struck, and the wood cart broke down. Later that day in his smoky cabin, he admitted to his journal that

> I feel a Hell upon earth on account of the uncertainty of all our affairs—the poorest beggar would scarce exchange situations with me at present and I have vowed if an offer arrives that I can leave this country I will do so forever, for even admitting that we made money (which is more than doubtful) I would not undergo the vexations which I now do for all that can be made here. Send out men and you know not but the property they have is stolen, or that they may be killed . . . I can safely say as unhappy a time as this I have never before passed during my life. What is worst our prospects are not good for McKenzie has hired our interpreters and bribed them whilst they were here to betray us. But he must answer for this so soon as I get one to whom I can leave this business in charge.[29]

He then prayed to God to give him the strength to endure and eventually prosper.

While his partner froze on the Yellowstone, William Sublette haggled with American Fur Company executive William Astor, John Jacob's son. Sublette had several powerful cards to play against Astor.[30] Unfortunately, any written details of the negotiations were destroyed along with the American Fur Company records in a disastrous fire.

John Jacob Astor was then an alert and canny but ailing seventy-year-old besieged by family and business burdens. His wife had recently died. His company's quarter-century charter was about to expire. The word from the mountains maintained that beaver were increasingly scarce. He had left for Europe on June 20, 1833, and would not return until April 4, 1834, months after his son had cut a deal with Sublette. As Astor toured European markets, it was clear that silk was elbowing aside beaver felt as the more fashionable component for top hats. Although the buffalo robe trade was slowly expanding, sheepskin remained far more popular in America and Europe alike. The American Fur Company's twenty-five-year charter, granted in 1808, had expired in April 1833. Astor had not renewed it. Perhaps now was the best time to completely shut up shop. From Europe, John Jacob sent William, Chouteau, Pratte,

29. Ibid., December 31, 1833.
30. Porter, *Astor*, 769–79.

and Crooks letters detailing market conditions, the worsening difficulties the American Fur Company faced, and his mounting desire to retire from the business.

More immediately pressing was a set of American Fur Company liquor law violations. Technically, Clark upheld the letter of the law when he signed that April 1833 license for Sublette. He was aware, however, that a bill was being debated in Congress that would establish a Department of Indian Affairs and also, among other things, completely outlaw any liquor in Indian territory regardless of who consumed it. Not only did that bill pass Congress in July 1832, but also, to the surprise of many, it did so with the full support of William Ashley. When the bill first appeared in April, John Jacob Astor wrote Ashley asking him to fight it. While they competed fiercely in markets, Astor assumed that they were natural allies for defeating the bill. No trade item was more profitable than alcohol. If the United States completely outlawed trading liquor to the Indians, the Hudson's Bay Company would use whiskey to divert the furs of northern Indians to themselves.

After the bill was passed but before word reached St. Louis, Clark signed a license for Pierre Chouteau to send one thousand gallons of alcohol up the Missouri for the "medicinal" use of American Fur Company employees. American Fur Company clerk J. P. Cabanne conveyed the shipment upriver. By this time, word had reached St. Louis and government agents up the Missouri. At Fort Leavenworth, zealous officials confiscated Cabanne's whiskey and reported the violation to Washington. Cabanne sputtered in rage but could do nothing to overturn the ruling. Meanwhile, independent trader P. N. Leclerc had also received a liquor license before the new law was promulgated. Learning of the shipment, a still enraged Cabanne illegally boarded Leclerc's boat, found his alcohol, and had his men chain Leclerc and carry him down to Bellevue, where officials promptly confiscated his liquor. Now it was Leclerc's turn to be enraged, but at the American Fur Company rather than the U.S. government. He returned to St. Louis to inform the newspapers that Cabanne had abused him and filed suit against the American Fur Company. Clark dutifully sent word of all these machinations to Indian Commissioner Herring, who promptly opened an investigation against the American Fur Company operations and monopoly on the upper Missouri River.

Worried that all the bad publicity could rally support in Congress against the American Fur Company's monopoly, Ramsay Crooks wrote Kenneth McKenzie at Fort Union, warning him not to fulfill his known plans to build a distillery. McKenzie ignored Crooks and built his still. Then, in fall 1833, both Wyeth and Sublette brought word down to St. Louis of the Fort Union distillery. Clark passed the reports on to Commissioner Herring, who added them to his investigation.

American Fur Company officials tried to stem the damage. In 1834, Chouteau paid Leclerc ninety-two hundred dollars to settle his suit and ordered McKenzie to shut down his still and take a year's vacation in Europe. Given all these related headaches, it seemed a good time for Astor to sell. On June 25, 1834, Astor would split and sell out the American Fur Company, with the Northern (Great Lakes and Mississippi) Department going to Crooks and the Western (Missouri River) Department to Pratte, Chouteau, and Company. In response to these initiatives, Herring ordered the charges against the American Fur Company dropped.

Meanwhile, there was the question of what to do about the upstart company of Sublette and Campbell. It seemed that with the backing of Ashley and other prominent eastern merchants they had an endless source of finance and goods. It was easier and cheaper to simply buy out competitors rather than try to crush them through a bidding war with Indians and trappers.

The deal Astor and Sublette finally cut was for the American Fur Company to purchase Sublette's and Campbell's Missouri River posts in return for staying out of the Rocky Mountain trade for one year and thereafter splitting that territory between the two firms. The territory for Sublette and Campbell "commenced on the Arkansas, at a point South of the Platte, then to the dividing line of the waters emptying into the Missouri; thence we continued that line to the Rocky Mountains, and thence on to the three forks of the Missouri, covering all west and south of that line. To [the American Fur Company] was assigned all the Territory North and East of that line."[31]

After concluding the deal with Astor, Sublette traveled to Philadelphia to celebrate with Hugh. In a letter to Robert, Hugh extolled the agreement: "in no instance have I ever known a settlement conducted with more ability—nor has our friend Mr. Sublette ever shown himself to more advantage than in bringing those men to the terms agreed on . . . with regard to the importance of setting to rest all competition . . . This article itself looks much like a treaty of peace betwixt two sovereign potentates . . . a little resembling the partition of Poland." Hugh went on to express his pleasure that "you have resigned the trade on the

31. Holloway, ed., *A Narrative*, 45.

Missouri. Connected with it, there seems to be much toil, some danger, great uncertainty, & very little nett gain."[32]

With a stroke of the pen and a handshake, the partners' main rival had suddenly shifted from the giant American Fur Company to the honorable, ambitious, and inexperienced Nathaniel Wyeth. Wyeth and Milton Sublette had come east to buy goods. If Wyeth succeeded in getting those goods to rendezvous, Sublette and Campbell would have lost the year's business opportunities in both the Missouri River and Rocky Mountains.

It was essential to beat Wyeth to rendezvous. Once there, Sublette and Campbell had an enormous advantage—they were longtime friends with all Rocky Mountain Fur Company partners, and William and Milton were brothers. It would not be a hard sell to get their friends to switch from Wyeth to Sublette and Campbell. It would actually be to the advantage of Sublette and Campbell to lead Wyeth on, to encourage him to commit as many resources as possible on his gamble as it would likely fail.

Sublette began undermining the contract between Wyeth and the Rocky Mountain Fur Company after his brother joined him in New York. Explaining that he would supplement the three thousand dollars' worth of goods Wyeth was contracted to supply, William talked Milton into helping him select the necessary supplies in New York and Philadelphia. After doing so, Milton went to Boston to help Wyeth garner supplies to fulfill the contract as well as those for his own Columbia River Fishing and Trading Company. Wyeth sent William Sublette an offer through Milton that they join forces in journeying to rendezvous. Milton returned to Philadelphia two days before Sublette left for St. Louis but no deal was then struck. Sublette had already signed most of his deals with Ashley and Tracy; the goods were being packed and sent west. It was only when Wyeth received Sublette's rejection that it began to dawn on him that the success of his enterprise might well depend on beating him to rendezvous. Wyeth hastily closed his deals with eastern merchants and headed west.

Accompanied by Milton, Sublette hurried back to St. Louis, where he obtained from Indian Superintendent Clark a license to build a trading post where the Laramie River joins the Platte River. The brothers agreed that while Sublette headed west with the supply caravan, Milton would

32. Hugh Campbell to Robert Campbell, February 14, 1834, Campbell House Foundation.

travel up the Missouri to take word of the deal with the American Fur Company to Campbell.[33]

As usual, buying and transporting appropriate goods to St. Louis was less difficult than recruiting enough able men and draft animals for the Rockies. The Santa Fe trade was booming, Wyeth and Bonneville were gathering their own expeditions, the U.S. First Dragoons were preparing an expedition onto the plains, and the missionaries Jason and Daniel Lee were heading to Oregon. The price of men, pack animals, and supplies was sky-high.

Wyeth got in the first blow. His caravan set off on April 28 from Independence, ten days before Sublette's. It was a colorful group: seventy men, including Wyeth's second in command, the sea captain Joseph Thing, naturalists Thomas Nuttall and John Kirk Townsend, the Methodist missionary Jason Lee, and Milton Sublette. At the last minute, perhaps plagued by a guilty conscience and fear of a lawsuit, Milton abandoned his promise to his brother to carry word to Campbell and instead accompanied Wyeth's caravan as he had originally agreed to do. Milton's leg pained him so severely, however, that at the Little Vermillion he turned back to St. Louis.

William Sublette meanwhile hurriedly marshaled his men, horses, and supplies at Independence. Finally, on May 5, Sublette started west with thirty-seven men and ninety-five horses. With him was William Marshall Anderson, who was traveling west to regain his health after an attack of yellow fever. Anderson became friends with Sublette and kept a diary of his journey, from which he later wrote a narrative that gives vivid glimpses of the events from spring through autumn of that year.[34] Another member of the caravan was an Arapaho boy whom Tom Fitzpatrick had found starving and abandoned on the Santa Fe Trail in 1831. Calling him Friday after the Daniel Defoe character, Fitzpatrick had adopted him, brought him back to St. Louis, and put him in school. Sublette would return the lad to his adopted father.

Sublette's caravan followed the well-trodden trail west up the Blue River and over the divide to the Platte and then up its braided course. As early as May 12, Sublette passed Wyeth's party during the night. Although Wyeth urged his inexperienced men to pick up their pace, they never regained the lead and at best closed within a few days of Sublette.

33. William Sublette to Robert Campbell, February 14, April 5, 1834, Campbell Papers, MLA.
34. Morgan and Harris, eds., *Rocky Mountain Journals of William Marshall Anderson*, 223.

All along, Anderson was a sensitive observer, describing experiences that most mountain men had long buried or discarded. Anderson

> picked up to-day a human skull, and carried it for many miles. My companions had passed it by, without comment, perhaps without reflection, but I could not help feeling saddened at the sight. I built it up as a living being, as a companion, invested with flesh, vivified with spirit. It told me that, impelled by the love of adventure, he had, years gone by, bade adieu to his kin and country, and sought to behold the wonders of these unknown wilds; that he had once rejoiced in the beauties of nature; that, like me, he had seen with admiration, the glorious uprising and down-going of the sun in this ocean of verdant prairie, and whilst beholding with satisfaction these plains, animated by immense herds of deer and buffalo, he had fallen the victim of an unseen foe.[35]

One can only wonder whether Robert Campbell's first sight of such a mournful relic had inspired similar thoughts. If so, like Anderson, he probably soon became hardened to such encounters and the thoughts they provoked. Anderson reports that he later passed another skull without reflection. What was once a thought-provoking novelty became a trivial commonplace. Incessant danger forced even the most philosophical to concentrate on more pressing needs of comfort and survival.

On May 30, Sublette's caravan reached Laramie Creek. There he halted to plan the outline of a trading post, to be commanded by William Patton and fourteen men. Anderson reported that a "friendly dispute arose between our leader and myself, as to the name. He proposed to call it Fort Anderson, I insisted on baptising it Fort Sublette, and holding the trump card in my hand, (a bottle of champagne) was about to claim the trick. Sublette stood by, cup reversed, still objecting, when Patton offered a compromise which was accepted, and the foam flew, in honor of Fort William, which contained the triad prenames of clerk, leader, and friend."[36]

Fort William was completed later that year. It lay in a narrow valley, enclosed by grassy hills near the west bank of the Laramie River a mile upstream from the Platte River. It was built of upright cottonwood logs in a triangle whose walls rose fifteen feet. Each wall had a watchtower. Inside were flat-roofed cabins which included barracks, a storehouse, and a blacksmith's quarters. A horse pen took up much room inside the

35. Ibid., May 18, 1834.
36. Ibid., May 31, 1833.

fort. A flagpole at whose top fluttered the stars and stripes stood in the fort's center. Those who were superstitious might have believed the fort was cursed. The branches of those cottonwoods that had been chopped down into planks or fuel for Fort William had once held the blanket-wrapped bodies of Sioux Indians. The sacred grove was no more.[37]

Sublette did not tarry long at his new post. On June 1, the caravan headed west once again. Wyeth had closed within several days but could get no closer. At Independence Rock on June 9, Wyeth dispatched a letter to Fitzpatrick urging him not to buy from Sublette and reporting that Milton's festering leg had forced him back to St. Louis. The letter did no good.

On June 18, Sublette's caravan arrived at rendezvous on Ham's Fork, off Black's Fork of the Green River. Sublette had a powerful card to play—the Rocky Mountain Fur Company owed him money. Fitzpatrick promptly dropped his contract with Wyeth and bought from Sublette. In extinguishing its debt to William Sublette, the Rocky Mountain Fur Company could finally escape his control.

Wyeth arrived alone that same evening, having left his caravan on the Big Sandy. Fitzpatrick broke the news to him and handed him a five-hundred-dollar forfeit for breaking their contract. In doing so and spurning Wyeth for Sublette, Fitzpatrick was legally if not exactly ethically correct. He escaped a legal challenge, but the charges of betrayal stuck. Wyeth's caravan did not trudge in until June 20. A bewildered Wyeth expressed his "astonishment the goods which I contracted to bring up to the Rocky Mountain Fur Co. were refused by these honorable gentlemen." To Milton, he later declared that "business is closed forever between us, but you will find that you have only bound yourself over to receive your supplies at such price as may be inflicted and that all you will ever make in the country will go to pay for your goods, you will be kept as you have been a mere slave to catch Beaver for others."[38] In all this, Wyeth was prescient.

While this drama was unfolding, everyone else was wildly blowing off months of repressed tensions. In all, nearly a thousand whites and Indians were scattered in three large camps along Ham's Fork, with the American Fur Company's camp under Lucien Fontenelle and Andrew Drips the farthest downstream, the Rocky Mountain Fur Company in the

37. Frederick Adolphus Wislizenus, "A Journey to the Rocky Mountains in 1839," quoted in ibid., 35–36; Stewart, *Warren*, 94.

38. Ibid., 27–28; Young, "Two Expeditions," 225.

middle, and Wyeth's upstream. Bands of Shoshone, Bannock, Flathead, and Nez Perce pitched their lodges among the three camps.

Wyeth's party was the first to leave. As he pointed his caravan west, Wyeth issued a final warning: "Gentlemen, I will roll a stone into your garden that you will never be able to get out."[39] A month later, on August 6, his caravan reached the juncture of the Portneuf and Snake Rivers. There he built Fort Hall.

On July 10, Bill Sublette headed east with forty packs of beaver that would fetch $12,250 in St. Louis. It was good money, but not as good as in previous years. The Rocky Mountain Fur Company partners increasingly wondered whether it might not be a good idea to get out while money might still be made. After an initially promising beginning, the Rocky Mountain Fur Company's fortunes had quickly soured. The partners collected 169 fur packs from 1830 to 1832, but only 55 from 1832 to 1833, and perhaps 40 to 60 from 1833 to 1834. Meanwhile, in 1833 fur prices in eastern markets dropped to $3.50 from $4.50 a pound the previous year as labor prices rose in the mountains. Experienced brigade leaders commanded $1,500 a year and experienced trappers demanded $9 a pound for pelts. Of course, the Rocky Mountain Fur Company could cover those higher prices by inflating the prices they charged for goods at rendezvous. The trouble was the competition kept prices relatively low. All the firms were buying pelts and selling goods at a loss. The mighty Rocky Mountain Fur Company had driven under upstart firms led by Bonneville, Wyeth, Sinclair, and Gantt and Blackwell.[40] But in turn the Rocky Mountain Fur Company itself was eventually ground down by the American Fur Company's relentless, grueling competition.

On June 20, Henry Fraeb and Jean Gervais were the first partners to bow out when they sold off their shares to the other three partners, who called their new firm the Fitzpatrick, Sublette, and Bridger Company. The new firm lasted little more than five weeks before the competition swallowed it. Yet another enterprise emerged on August 3 when Fitzpatrick, Sublette, and Bridger joined hands with Lucien Fontenelle and Andrew Drips. That merger, named Fontenelle, Fitzpatrick, and Company, was wholly controlled by the American Fur Company, which was now one step away from monopolizing the Rocky Mountain fur trade. The new American Fur Company subsidiary would receive its supplies from and

39. Ibid., 138–39.
40. Wishart, *Fur Trade*, 146–47; Gowans, *Rendezvous*, 118.

sell its furs to its parent firm. Sublette and Campbell had been effectively squeezed from the mountains.

During these momentous events of 1834, Campbell was still high up the Missouri River. On June 24, he received word of the sale when the American Fur Company steamboat, the *Assiniboine,* reached Fort Union. On board was a messenger sent by Sublette who brought "the boundary treaty, and the conditions of sale, of our merchandise at the fort, to the American Fur Company . . . I then turned over the goods to the American Fur Company, and I sent a party of our trappers across the country from the Yellowstone, with our furs, to our new fort . . . Having closed up our business at the mouth of the Yellowstone, I then came down to St. Louis," where he arrived on August 7, 1834.[41] Campbell's western wanderings were not yet spent.

When word of the Rocky Mountain Fur Company's death reached St. Louis, Sublette and Campbell decided to shut down their last western operation, Fort William, and concentrate on outfitting fur and robe companies from St. Louis. With the American Fur Company firmly in control of the fur trade, Fort William stood only to lose money. Not only had the American Fur Company monopolized the mountain trade, but St. Vrain and Company had boasted openly of its plan to plant their own post near Fort William and drive it from the plains, using the same strategy Sublette and Campbell had tried against the American Fur Company. It was a good time to sell Fort William, if the partners could find a buyer. Fitzpatrick and Fontenelle had returned to St. Louis to organize a supply caravan for the next rendezvous. When Sublette and Campbell offered them Fort William, they eagerly snatched it up. Campbell agreed to ride out to Fort William in spring 1835 and transfer it to the new owners.

Before he did so, he had both business and family concerns to attend. In January 1835, he traveled to make the rounds of eastern merchants for their proposed St. Louis store and to visit Hugh and Mary. Goods were abundant and he soon filled his orders. Resting at his brother's home in Philadelphia, he caught up on his family's fate in Ireland. The previous year his mother had fought an illness that took her to death's door, then recovered; his "careless brother" Andrew struggled to manage the estate, tolerate his "scolding wife & squalling weans," and stay away from the bottle; while his sister Ann spurned a proposal from a wealthy bachelor.[42]

41. Holloway, ed., *A Narrative,* 45.
42. Hugh Campbell to Robert Campbell, May 14, 1834, Campbell House.

Ever since arriving in America, Campbell had tried to help out his family when he could, remitting part of his meager earnings to his childhood home. In February he sent Andrew a letter along with fifty pounds sterling to help him keep his head above water. In a letter from Ann thanking Robert on Andrew's behalf for the money, she ended by saying, "You are daily the object of our prayers. May the hearer of prayers bring you back safe from the wilderness and preserve you at all times and in all places is the sincere petition of your loving Mother and grateful sister."[43]

After Campbell returned to St. Louis, Hugh wrote to give his usual advice: "Should you enter the business in St. Louis, the only prospect of doing well is in selling wholesale—for at this moment I do not believe that the retail is either more expensive or less profitable . . . owing to the great competition which now exists there . . . The first year I would not wish to sell more than half the quantity of goods you calculate on being your average sales. The second year the sales may be moderately increased—and not until the third year ought you to calculate on extending fully your business to its legitimate extent."[44]

The advice was sound. But before Campbell could execute it, he had to shut down Fort William. Accompanied by only two men, he reached Fort William in May. He sent his men to the nearby Cheyenne and Oglala Sioux bands to encourage them to come to Fort William for trade. After fifteen days at Fort William, he traded goods to the bands, receiving several packs of buffalo robes in return. He then headed back east with Andrew Sublette and fifteen other men.

Over the years the deep-flowing upper Platte River had tempted many mountain men to run it down to the Missouri. Nearly all such ventures ran aground in the Platte's middle reaches, where the river fanned out to "an inch deep and mile wide." Although he had doubtless heard many such a remorseful tale, Campbell succumbed:

> I built a boat at this post and started down the North Platte, with buffalo robes, while a party by land, with mules, carried the beaver skins. The boat had a fine state of water till I reached Scotts Bluffs. There the quicksands rendered navigation impossible . . . I constructed then at Scotts Bluffs, two Bull boats, fitting in each three full skins, sewed together like a crate. I then procured some plum bushes, that made the ribs. We loaded the robes on

43. Ann Campbell to Robert Campbell, June 26, 1835, Ann Campbell to Robert Campbell, January 15, 1835, Robert Campbell to Andrew Campbell, February 10, 1835, ibid.
44. Hugh Campbell to Robert Campbell, July 4, 1835, ibid.

these two boats, and brought the Mackinaw boat along . . . Just below the forks of the Platte there was an Arikara village. We were on the North side. The Indians were hostile. I took a dozen men and went on a little island, where I prepared for defense. The Indians came across, but not with their guns. I held a talk with them by signs, gave them tobacco, and told them to go back, that my mules would be frightened. I traveled on the north side as fast as the mules would carry us. It was a beautiful moonlight night and we camped without building any fires. We took different trails, and went on till we reached the Pawnee Loupes village on the loupes Fork of the Platte. There I learned that Gen. Dodge was going with a regiment of Rangers—a U.S. regiment, merged into the first U.S. dragoons. He was going up the Platte. This news gave us confidence. I crossed the Missouri at Omaha, and came down to St. Joe.[45]

Safely back in St. Louis, Campbell and Sublette were pleased that their robes, for the first time, sold for more than beaver pelts. The partners had retired from the beaver trade at just the right time. New York fur prices plummeted in the late 1830s to about $2.50 by 1840, a result of the increased popularity of silk, the use of South American nutria pelts for felt, and the depleted supply of American beaver. The last Rocky Mountain rendezvous occurred in 1840, and by all accounts it was a depressing affair, a mere shadow in numbers, extravagance, and fun of those a decade earlier. Meanwhile, money could still be made selling at rendezvous no matter what price beaver was fetching; it simply meant charging the destitute trappers and Indians even more pelts for the supplies upon which their lives depended. Sublette and Campbell invested in that year's caravan led by Fontenelle and Drips. But the partners were trying to squeeze into the robe trade. By 1839, robes had risen in value to six dollars each, compared to three dollars in the early 1820s. In 1840, ninety thousand robes came down the Missouri from various posts.[46]

Although it was his easiest trading venture yet, Campbell returned from the plains so sick and exhausted that he wrote another will. He recuperated at Sublette's Sulphur Springs plantation, joining not only William but also Milton, whose festering leg had finally been amputated in January.

Sulphur Springs would be a wonderful refuge for Campbell and Sublette over the next decade. The house and slave cabins at Sulphur

45. Holloway, ed., *A Narrative*, 6.
46. Wishart, *Fur Trade*, 109.

Springs were being finished that very summer when Campbell rode exhausted into the yard. The plantation nestled within the River des Peres's shallow valley a half dozen miles west on the Old Manchester Road from downtown St. Louis. Woods still blanketed much of the 779 acres. As the woods were gradually cleared, the trees were sawn into firewood and sold in St. Louis. In the fields, Sublette grew mostly corn, and also oats, cabbage, potatoes, timothy, and various fruit trees. Horses, sheep, and cattle grazed pastures; pigs rooted in their pen. Sublette even collected such exotics as buffalo, cranes, swans, and deer. In his spare time, he studied the latest scientific farming methods, subscribing to the *Cultivator,* buying hybrid seeds and animal stock, exchanging ideas via correspondence with Sir William Drummond Stewart in Scotland, and displaying the results at the St. Louis County Agricultural Fair. Sublette farmed for enjoyment rather than income; Sulphur Springs's fields and pastures rarely made money. Beneath the thin soil, however, lay a coal vein two to five feet thick, which he mined. Coal rather than agricultural sales supported his plantation. Ice was sawed from the ponds in winter and stacked in the icehouse; the surplus ice was sold in the summer.

Sulphur Springs's most important source of income was its mineral waters. In 1835, Sublette sent samples to Hugh Campbell, who had them analyzed. Hugh excitedly forwarded to Sublette the report that the spring held the same mineral content as White Sulphur Springs, Virginia. Sublette erected guest houses beside his spring and promoted it as a resort. In 1838, he organized the St. Louis Jockey Club, and laid out a horse track and ninepins alley, both of which were illegal within the city limits.

Sulphur Springs became a lively, idyllic retreat from the congested, polluted, expanding nearby city. While health seekers bathed in the mineral waters, Sublette, with Campbell often at his side, entertained a mingled parade of mountain men, merchants, politicians, industrialists, lawyers, bankers, farmers, relatives, professors from nearby Kemper College, artists such as Alfred Jacob Miller, dilettantes such as Sir William Drummond Stewart, and various supplicants. One can imagine Campbell and Sublette, drinks in hand, discussing business strategies in the parlor, or hosting friends or investors with cards, dinner, or songs around the piano, and plying them with whiskey and cigars. Sulphur Springs also became a refuge for Sublette's siblings. His sister Sophronia would flee to Sulphur Springs from a bad marriage in 1840, and his brother Andrew retired there from the mountains in 1841.

A mere two decades after Sublette began work on his dream home, St. Louis devoured Sulphur Springs. The plantation was sold after Sublette's death, and the land repeatedly subdivided, the trees cleared, streets laid out, homes and businesses erected, the spring and stream buried, the air polluted with coal smoke.[47] All that was in the future. In the summer of 1835, three grizzled, wounded mountain men passed quiet days and nights with their memories and hopes.

Learning of his brother's dangerous trip and illness, Hugh Campbell demanded that he "never attempt such a thing again. It is madness and say what you will about the advantages of experience and watchfulness I cannot believe in the prudence of traveling through such a country with only a couple of companions."[48] Hugh's wife, Mary, freely expressed with the deepest love and piety her fears and hopes for Campbell:

> owing to the desponding state of mind I was in when you left or the fact that this journey was to be your last to the mountains and your luck might change . . . I became superstitious and had a presentiment that you would give the Indians your scalp as your friend Smith has done . . . I thank your Almighty Protector that your danger was only in our imaginations and that you have accomplished your lonely, hazardous journey without accident or even "hair breadth 'scapes" enough to make it interest to you. You have much, much cause to be thankful to him who has been with you in all your wanderings . . . I have a claim on you, and you know how fond I am of exercising my authority over all my kin.[49]

She went on to describe the couple's visit to St. Louis earlier that summer when Campbell was still up the Platte River. She extolled Sublette's hospitality, but admitted that Hugh "left St. Louis this time liking it little better than he did before—he has not an exalted opinion of the hospitality of St. Louis but his visits have been made under very unpleasant circumstances." Hugh would eventually overcome his dislike for St. Louis. In 1859, he and his wife would move there so that he could join Campbell's company. But that was twenty-four years in the future. In 1835, it would be Robert Campbell who would move, briefly, to Philadelphia. That sojourn would change his life, for it was there that he met the woman of his dreams.

47. Sunder, *Sublette*, 175, 177–93.
48. Hugh Campbell to Robert Campbell, July 25, 1835, Campbell House.
49. Mary Campbell to Robert Campbell, July 27, 1835, ibid.

# Chapter 5

# A Home and Family of His Own (1835–1845)

**S**till weak, Campbell embarked for Philadelphia in October for a surprise visit to Hugh and his family. His appearance on November 5, 1835, shocked Hugh, who wrote Sublette that he has been "quite sick and weak ever since his arrival . . . and likely to be confined to his room for some days longer."[1] How was he to be nursed back to health? Hugh wisely adopted the policy of avoiding doctors and medicines at all costs. He knew all too well that his era's doctors could not help but violate their hippocratic oath to first do no harm. At best they had but a rudimentary understanding of diseases and treatments.

Hugh understood that the best tonic for his brother would be Sublette's presence:

> Mary is a pretty good nurse—but after all I fear he will never believe he can have any nurse to be compared with you . . . if you will only contrive to come on & take lodgings with him, I think you can contrive to make the time pass agreeably until my return . . . He is constantly talking of you and of your noble & disinterested conduct during his late dreadful illness. I know not when I was more amused than to hear of the partnership he wished to establish while suffering under the attack. He firmly believed you have divided the pain and thought it queer that you should be moving about while he was laying prostrate. Perhaps there are few whims more rational— for your feelings, wishes, tastes, and dangers have been so much in common of late years, that a community in suffering might readily be considered as a natural consequence . . . I know his health having become very bad he required all the civilities of an invalid.

While Campbell wintered at his brother's home, Hugh visited Ireland. He wrote to relate the mysterious disappearance of Andrew's son

1. Hugh Campbell to William Sublette, November 6, 1835, Campbell Papers, MLA.

on the moors, the purchase of a cork leg for Milton Sublette, and how "bothersome" were all the inquiries over Robert: "I have told every symtom of your late illness more than twenty times."[2]

Campbell got his wish. In December he and Sublette exchanged contracts that would renew their partnership on January 1, 1836, for another three-year term. Each invested $9,717.10 for a merchant business in St. Louis. Either partner could withdraw from the partnership at any time after paying off any liabilities. The partners had taken yet another major step in the transition from a dangerous life in the West to a staid but hopefully profitable mercantile business in St. Louis.[3]

As Campbell recovered, Sublette struggled to wring payments from debtors and pay off creditors in St. Louis. The burden was an enormous strain on Sublette, who admitted, "Times are worse here than you have ever seen. There is not one debt I believe we are owing in St. Louis but what I have paid and I have not received one Dollar from one of our customers . . . nor is there much prospect as many are writing that they cant raise money before Spring . . . they have not money in the Country [with which] to pay and it is getting scarce every day."[4]

The biggest deadbeat was a firm that remained popularly known as the American Fur Company, although it held a mere fraction of its namesake's power, wealth, and geographic expanse. That debtor's official business name was Pratte, Chouteau Jr., and Company. When Astor sold out in 1834, Pratte and Chouteau bought the American Fur Company's Upper Missouri Outfit of the Western Department. In doing so, they took over that firm's debt to Sublette and Campbell for the "partition of Poland" agreement. Pratte and Chouteau were financially strapped and pleaded for understanding from the partners. Having a financial grip on their greatest rival had no practical value for Sublette and Campbell. The partners had little choice but to grant their rivals an extension on their payment. Such truces were fleeting.

For the next three decades, Campbell, first with Sublette and later with a succession of other partners, would compete against the new monopoly with all the ferocity he had mustered when that Upper Missouri Outfit was still a branch of the American Fur Company. From now on, however, he would struggle against the American Fur Company from the comfort of his St. Louis headquarters rather than a wretched trading

2. Hugh Campbell to Robert Campbell, December 13, 1835, Campbell House.
3. William Sublette and Robert Campbell Contract, January 1, 1836, Campbell Papers, MLA.
4. William Sublette to Robert Campbell, January 14, 1836, ibid.

post far up the Missouri River. His strategy would involve financially backing a succession of upstart companies that squared off with the monopoly. In doing so, he would play the role that Ashley did for Sublette, Campbell, and other entrepreneurs.

The partners kept the pressure on Pratte and Chouteau. Not only did they desperately need the money, but they also hoped to weaken their rival with every possible means. In a January 12, 1836, meeting, Sublette had warned the rivals that the partners would once again head to rendezvous if the American Fur Company did not pay up. Chouteau asked for more time. Given the circle of debt in which most St. Louis–based entrepreneurs existed, Chouteau could not pay the partners until Lucien Fontenelle paid what he owed him. In early February, however, Pratte and Chouteau did manage to scrape up some money to retire some of their debt, but again asked for Sublette's patience until Fontenelle's return. The partners were anxious for Fontenelle's safe return on two counts; he owed money not only to Pratte and Chouteau but also to Sublette and Campbell for buying Fort William.[5]

Although the down payment enabled the partners to pay off some of their own creditors, it did not fulfill the contract. Legally, the partners could send a caravan to rendezvous or even head up the Missouri River again with keelboats packed with trade goods. The stickler was time. A decision on whether to buy a year's worth of mountain and river trade goods had to be made as soon as possible. Campbell would have to mount a hasty buying expedition in Philadelphia, New York, and other eastern cities, then convey those goods to St. Louis. Further complicating their decision was the necessity of debating what to do over such a chasm of distance and time between them. It took weeks for letters to circulate between Sublette in St. Louis and Campbell in Philadelphia. Pratte and Chouteau relieved some of the pressure when they paid off the rest of their debt on February 26. Now only Fontenelle's debts remained, to the partners and the new American Fur Company alike.

Although Fontenelle's fur- and robe-laden caravan reached St. Louis the following day, he kept Sublette and Chouteau waiting while he enjoyed a whiskey-soaked spree with his men. As Sublette angrily put it, Fontenelle refused to "leave off Frolicking fer two days to arainge them." One of Fontenelle's partners, Tom Fitzpatrick, returned to St. Louis around the same time. Sublette urged Fitzpatrick to get Fontenelle to pay up or else pay off his partner's debt himself. Fitzpatrick failed to

5. William Sublette to Robert Campbell, January 12, February 9, 1836, ibid.

get a drunken Fontenelle to settle with Sublette. Disgusted, Fitzpatrick simply dissolved his own partnership with Fontenelle. Even after he sobered up, Fontenelle refused to honor his debt and instead slipped out of St. Louis on a steamboat bound for New Orleans.[6]

Even though he was still sickly, Campbell returned to St. Louis in March. By then it was too late to organize an expedition to rendezvous. Campbell was not well enough to lead one, anyway: he could not shake his illness, which may have included malaria. William Drummond Stewart wrote Campbell that he was "sorry to hear that you had resumed your shaking habits & would strongly recommend some other religion. Take a dose of morphine when you first feel the chill & one of quinine every two hours—this cured me."[7] It is not known whether Campbell took Drummond's advice, but the fever and shaking would gradually disappear.

One essential task for the partners was to find a permanent store for their business. During the previous three years and throughout most of 1836 they were forced to make do with storing their goods in rented space in a warehouse. Construction could barely keep up with St. Louis's bustling, expanding economy. Prime real estate and buildings sold at astronomical levels. The previous summer the partners had bid for a store vacated by Kyle and Edgar Company, but lost out. In January 1836, Captain Holt asked $20,000 for his building. Although he was mighty tempted to bid, Sublette deferred such a momentous decision until Campbell returned. By then someone else had bought it. It was not until September that the partners found the prime business location for which they had searched so long. They paid $12,823 for the brick building that occupied a lot 160 feet deep by 38 wide at 7 Main Street. It proved to be an excellent location. Credit was just a stroll away. The St. Louis branch of the United States Bank had been across the street before President Jackson shut it down. A new bank, the Commercial Bank of Cincinnati, had moved into the vacant building on June 15, 1836.[8]

Throughout these months, Campbell lived at the National Hotel. While his health gradually improved, it was now Sublette's turn to collapse. The stress and lingering illnesses forced him to retreat back to his Sulphur Springs home in November. The burden of sustaining and expanding their business now fell squarely on Campbell's shoulders. As

6. William Sublette to Robert Campbell, February 27, 29, 1836, ibid. Alan C. Trottman, "Lucien Fontenelle," in Hafen, ed., *Trappers of the West*, 138; Sunder, *Sublette*, 152.

7. W. D. Stewart to Robert Campbell, April 30, 1836, Campbell Collection, MoSHi.

8. Sublette to Campbell, January 12, 1836, Campbell Papers, MLA; *Missouri Republican* (St. Louis), September 6, 1836.

a merchant he not only had to manage the store but also make at least one and sometimes more yearly business trips east.

Like Campbell, most merchants would make an annual buying trip to eastern cities such as Philadelphia, New York, Baltimore, and Boston, scour those markets for a month or six weeks, and return with tens of thousands of dollars' worth of goods. Among Campbell's most consistent source of goods was the Philadelphia firm of Siter, Price and Company, but he naturally tried to buy from both the lowest-priced and the most reliable sources—which, of course, often failed to coincide.

As Campbell knew all too well, buying trips were expensive, costing as much as four hundred dollars when various steamboat, railroad, and stagecoach tickets, food, lodging, and incidental expenses were tallied. Although such expeditions could be undertaken any time, they were most common during the summer, when transportation was the easiest. Low autumn or icy winter river water beached boats. The extension of railroads to the upper Mississippi valley during the late 1840s made buying trips relatively easy year-round. Shortages of some goods throughout the year could be filled through correspondence and freighting subcontractors.[9]

Goods were usually bought on six months' credit, with the bill due in a year. New entrepreneurs established credit with letters of introduction from prominent St. Louis citizens and maintained it by paying up on time. During the 1830s, credit rating bureaus emerged to investigate an aspiring borrower's claims. Once a merchant's operations became profitable he could begin to pay cash for goods; by eliminating interest rate payments he could save up to 25 percent on the cost he paid for goods. That gave him an immense financial advantage over rivals still dependent on credit, but meant taking huge risks in carrying bags of coin and paper money across the country.[10] Campbell and Sublette had already achieved this degree of financial autonomy, but their problems with getting debtors to pay up and goods to arrive on time made for a

9. Atherton, *Pioneer Merchant*, 56. For contemporary accounts see Charles Keemle, ed., *St. Louis City Directory for 1836–37* (St. Louis: Charles Keemle, 1836); Alphonso Wetmore, *Gazeteer of the State of Missouri;* James Hall, *The West: Its Commerce and Navigation;* John Beauchamp Jones (alias Luke Shortfield), *The West: Its Commerce and Navigation; A Review of the Trade and Commerce of St. Louis, for the Year 1849, as Compiled for and Published in the* Missouri *Republican; Annual Review, History of St. Louis, Commercial Statistics, Improvements of the Year, and Account of Leading Manufactures, ect., from the Missouri Republican, January 10, 1854;* J. N. Taylor and M. O. Crooks, *Sketch Book of St. Louis;* John Beauchamp Jones, *Life and Adventures of a Country Merchant.*

10. Atherton, *Pioneer Merchant*, 83.

nerve-racking life. The constant stress combined with the foul hygiene of the era's cities to lay the partners up with assorted illnesses for weeks and sometimes months at a time.

The cost of freighting goods from Philadelphia or Baltimore to St. Louis raised prices by around 25 percent. Some prices were even higher. Saddles, for example, cost twelve to fourteen dollars in St. Louis compared to five dollars on the East Coast. Transportation was also risky. From 1822 to 1827 alone, snags destroyed $1,362,500 worth of boats and cargo on the Ohio and Mississippi Rivers. Efforts to clear those obstructions reduced property losses to $381,000 from 1828 to 1832. Distance from wholesalers, higher prices from freighting, and less competition caused the average Missouri store to stock $7,370 worth of goods yearly compared to $5,485 for Pennsylvania and $3,500 for New York or Massachusetts stores. In Missouri, there was an average of 340 inhabitants per store, compared to 260 per store in Pennsylvania.[11] Missouri's relatively fewer merchants gave Sublette and Campbell an advantage that was diluted by the weaker buying power of the state's households and retailers. Missouri was a much poorer state than those of the Northeast. And the need to keep large stocks on hand raised costs along with risks of loss from fire or theft.

During the 1830s New York caught up to Philadelphia as the nation's leading wholesale center and slowly surpassed it during the 1840s. New York's harbor was closer to Europe and more ice-free than Philadelphia's. That advantage was offset by New York's fierce rivalry with Boston for that region's trade. The opening of the Erie Canal in 1825 allowed emigrants to pour into the Great Lakes region and New York wholesalers to supply them. Goods destined for St. Louis were unloaded at Erie and then transported by wagon to Pittsburgh. Even then Philadelphia remained the most important wholesale market for St. Louis since the transportation route linking those cities was the most direct from any eastern entrepôt and long-standing business relationships were not easily severed. Railroads from Chicago to Mississippi River cities in the 1850s, however, reduced the costs of goods from New York via the Great Lakes. The rate war between the Great Lakes and Ohio River routes to St. Louis caused freight costs to plummet to as much as 10 percent of prices before the railroads. Campbell and other wealthy merchants cut costs further by investing in their own steamboats and railroads. All along, Baltimore and, to a lesser extent, Boston were important secondary

---

11. For this and the next paragraph, see ibid., 25, 31, 67–68, 100.

suppliers to western merchants, but their shares diminished as New York's grew. New Orleans also remained an outlet mostly for bulky commodities such as grain and lumber carried down by flatboat by small-scale entrepreneurs. Goods in New Orleans tended to be more expensive and less varied than those in East Coast cities. Over the decades, Campbell constantly adapted to changing business opportunities and costs, spreading his bets as appropriate.

Like Sublette and Campbell, the most successful merchants were in partnerships that combined wholesale and retail business. Partnerships split the financial risks and workload. One partner could head east on a buying trip or collect debts in the countryside while the other tended the store. The wealthiest merchants tended to center their business in one large store in St. Louis or another expanding big city and then establish branches elsewhere.

Campbell found that retailing was the simplest if not the easiest part of their expanding business. Like other merchants, Sublette and Campbell hired a clerk for $150 a year, but usually handled the negotiations, buying, and accounting themselves. Clerks often used their positions to learn the trade and then open their own store, with or without their former employer's blessing. Campbell would lose some good clerks over the years that way. The store was usually open from dawn to well into the night, and sometimes as much as eighteen hours a day when trading was brisk. Merchants often rented display space for their goods in local hotels and took out advertisements in newspapers; Sublette and Campbell did advertize and probably set up displays elsewhere as well.

Sublette and Campbell competed with more than just other merchants in fixed sites like themselves. Itinerant peddlers worked from boats tied up at towns and farms along rivers, or from wagons rumbling across the countryside. Few peddlers got rich; what they saved in overhead they often lost through greater risks of being on water or road and in the minuscule stock they carried.

The most successful merchants, such as Campbell would later become, diversified their enterprises as widely as possible, investing in railroads, steamboats, manufacturing, real estate, insurance, and banking, of which the latter was by far the most important. Sublette and Campbell were already quasi-bankers. Like other financiers, they dispensed credit free for the first six months and with interest rates ranging from 6 to 10 percent thereafter. Most sales were made on credit, payable in kind or coin. Debtors were expected to pay up twice yearly, in June and January. Sublette and Campbell, like their fellow merchants, often resorted to newspaper advertisements to shame recalcitrant debtors into paying up. Those merchants who became wealthy tended to concentrate their business on banking and investing in their later years. These were the paths by which Campbell rose from rags to riches.

The shift into banking was quite natural for Sublette and Campbell. The biggest problem they faced was the shortage of hard money. No circulating national currency existed before the Civil War. Payments in "money" could be made from a melange of American, Mexican, Spanish, British, and other nations' coins along with paper certificates issued by various state-chartered banks or corporations. To survive in that cutthroat unregulated market world, merchants had to become experts at playing the currency market, trading certificates of fluctuating values, ferreting out inside information on which banks were going to discount their paper money or go bankrupt, and keeping creditors at bay while collecting payments from debtors. Campbell would eventually excel at these skills and strategies.

Like Campbell, most merchants were relatively well educated for that time period and tended to be Presbyterians.[12] Merchant leaders played important social as well as economic roles. John Jones, himself a prominent Arrow Rock, Missouri, merchant, described his profession as including the roles of a

> counselor without license, and yet invariably consulted, not only in matters of business, but in domestic affairs. Parents ask his opinion before giving their consent to their daughters' marriages; and he is always invited to the weddings. He furnishes the nuptial garments for both bride and groom, and his taste is both consulted and adopted. Every item of news, not only local, but from a distance,—as he is frequently the postmaster, and the only subscriber to the newspaper—has general dissemination from his establishment, as from a common center; and thither all resort, at least once a week, both for goods and for intelligence.[13]

Although his hundreds of surviving letters are largely mute on social issues and gossip, Campbell would have undoubtedly dispensed news on politics, business, and styles to his customers. Every store, whether in a large city or tiny hamlet, played such a role—it made good business as well as social sense. Did Campbell ever play cupid? If so such ventures are lost to history. But as he rose into the elite class, he would attend ever more society weddings.

12. Ibid., 24.
13. Jones, *Western Merchant*, preface.

The new wholesale-retail business of Sublette and Campbell took off despite the fierce competition from their rivals, with all benefiting from what proved to be a short-lived economic boom: "Business has been pretty good throughout the fall and all the old established houses which had their goods here in season have done well. We have, however, had a great influx of new establishments, thus will find some difficulty. Money is considerable scarce but we can only feel a promise when compelled to mix midwestern cities or eastern cities."[14]

Although most of their business was transacted in St. Louis, they continued to help underwrite the ventures of their old trapping companions such as Tom Fitzpatrick, Andrew Sublette, Jim Bridger, and Louis Vasquez. Payment for merchandise was usually in furs.

As if the pressure of surviving in a Darwinian business world when his partner was ill was not heavy enough, Campbell was distracted from his usual single-minded pursuit of business—he had fallen in love!

Virginia Kyle was a vivacious fourteen-year-old North Carolina native attending school in Philadelphia and a cousin of Mary Campbell. Campbell first met Virginia in November 1835 while he was convalescing at Hugh's home, and he was naturally smitten by the pretty girl who helped nurse him back to health. Virginia in turn was starstruck by the famous mountain man and wealthy entrepreneur who regaled her with adventure stories. For Christmas, he gave her the "Heath's Beauty Book for 1836," which was filled with love poems and pictures of lovely women.[15] But Campbell was unable to celebrate Christmas with Virginia, and reluctantly returned to his partnership in St. Louis.

What followed was an extraordinary "Romeo and Juliet" courtship that lasted years. Divided from Virginia by nearly half a continent and with seventeen years' difference in age, Campbell faced seemingly unbridgeable chasms in his quest. Younger, perhaps wittier and more handsome swains had ready access to the teenage girl's fair hand. At best, Campbell could use the excuse of buying trips back east to spend a fleeting month or two near her each year. As if distance, age differences, and limited time were not hindrances enough, the beau faced the united opposition of Sublette, Hugh, and Virginia's mother, Eleanor! Sublette and Hugh secretly conspired to undermine his love for Virginia by continually urging him to forget her and search for a more suitable mate. Eleanor simply forbade any marriage until the girl reached her

14. William Sublette to Hugh Campbell, November 1836, Sublette Collection, MoHiS.
15. Campbell House Foundation display.

eighteenth birthday, and even then managed to stall it for another year. Undeterred, Campbell overcame each of these obstacles with the unwavering earnestness and depth of his love and good character.

We gain extraordinary insights into his feelings through an exchange of letters between his closest loved ones, Hugh and Sublette. As always, Hugh's letters are highly articulate, intelligent, calculating, and revealing of his need to manipulate and control those he loved. Sublette's letters are even more interesting for they reveal an indifference to females, affection for Robert, and compassion at odds with the macho mountain man image.

Upon returning to Sublette in December 1836, Campbell revealed his love for Virginia. The obsession disturbed Sublette, who worried that it would

> . . . render him unhappy through life unless it should prove different from what it is at present he made some advances toward this young lady which was rather rejected and you are well aware what his feelings were in this respect if you know him as well as I think I doe he has converst with me frequently on the matter, and appears to have lost all hopes and declares he will never adress another nor can I as yet prevail on him to try the experiment again with the same. I have chided him, scoalded him telling him he is to blame, to make some allowance she is young and undecided as yet in her own opinions . . . I scoalded him for not letting you know something about it which he wisht he had of done, Robert is not aware that I drop you these fleu lines.[16]

An alarmed Hugh quickly replied that

> the attachment he formed while in this city during last winter preys upon his mind and depresses his Spirits—I am truly grieved at this State of Affairs;—and confess that I feel deeply mortified that he should allow such a trifle to give him a moment's pain. While he was here during the summer, I was told of his attachment, but never spoke to him on the subject . . . because I believed that a brief absence and a little reflection would effectually cure him. The fact is, my dear Sublette, I have been in love (and I confess it with shame) a dozen times before my marriage—yes, ardently, romantically, passionately in love! Sometimes, perhaps it was reciprocated—sometimes not;—but in no case did my affection long survive the test of absence & sound reflection.[17]

Hugh explained how the "attachment" developed:

16. William Sublette to Hugh Campbell, November 21, 1836, "Glimpses of the Past: Correspondence of Robert Campbell, 1834–1845."
17. Hugh Campbell to William Sublette, December 5, 1836, ibid.

Robert, it is said resembles me closely in his temper & disposition. It seems that during Robert's indisposition at my house—& more especially during his slow recovery, he was much in the company of Virginia Kyle. He was a decided favorite with all our household & of course there was much of that playful intimacy which exists between members of the same family. All of them treated him as a brother;—and I believe he mistook his familiarity on the part of Virga. for love . . . I did not feel uneasy about the result until lately.

Of Virginia, Hugh described her as

tall for her years & good looking;—without having any pretensions to being a beauty. Her manners are like those of all school girls, when they get clear of the restraint of their teachers—affable and lively. I have not discovered anything like talent or genius in her conversation but she seems to have a better capacity for learning than her sister. It has been the misfortune of both sisters to have had too much latitude allowed them in their intercourse with society;—and of course to be allowed to think themselves young ladies when they were only girls. The elder sister (Ellen) has been four times regularly courted and twice engaged. Virg. has also been courted two or three times. The consequence is that both of these young ladies are more of coquettes than is agreeable to me. They talk of beaux until I am sick of the subject;—or rather untill I put a decided stop to the subject. The foregoing is a brief but correct outline of her character;—but it is likely poor Robert would think it a caricature . . .

The affair and his inability to end it exasperated Hugh:

I esteem her mother most highly—and I esteem both the young ladies,—yet I confess that I do not approve of the conduct of Virginia towards Robert. I do not blame her for rejecting him (if she has done so) but I do not approve of either her or her sister speaking of it,—or of him. On one occassion they have done so in my presence & in my house—but they shall not do so again . . .

And, of his brother's choice for marriage, Hugh claimed that

I care not who may be Robert's choice in some respects . . . I would not have suffered dictation even from a parent in my own case . . . yet I assure you that I think he could have made, & can make a much wiser connection;—and with much better prospects of matrimonial happiness . . . She is too gay & frivolous . . . After all I hope that Robert will forget her & laugh at the whole affair before many months elapse. My pride makes me wish this sincerely.

He then ends his letter with an intriguingly suggestive aside: "It is a pity that either [of you] would ever get married—for you get along wonderfully."

Just how close were Campbell and Sublette? Was their relationship more than simply a hearty male bond forged through shared adventure, laughter, and ambition? Sublette and Hugh justified their attempts to stymie Campbell's courtship of Virginia by arguing that the two were wrong for each other. In that judgment, Hugh and Sublette would be proven profoundly mistaken. And their words to each other are laden with a passionate jealousy that Campbell was slipping beyond their control. Their attitude cannot help but make one wonder. Given the muted allusions to his liaisons with Indian girls and his rather prolific fathering of thirteen children, Campbell was undoubtedly attracted solely to women. As for Sublette, who knows? As will be seen, he would confess to Hugh that his interest in women was largely confined to their wealth. Perhaps Sublette merely had a low sex drive. Or perhaps he was driven in different directions than most people. Such questions are important to raise but impossible to answer. Without documentation it does not pay to speculate further.

In his reply, Sublette admitted that the argument he used to dissuade Campbell from the relationship, "that a wife two easy courted was scarce worth having," had failed. He had not realized that

> Robert could be over come by and blinded by love at his age . . . I am well aware Robert's situation at that time was one that was rather inclined to lead him astray. Just recovering from a long spell of sickness when a man's mind is rather week and not other wise engaged in business the least kindness or attention shown him at that time and especially by a female was inclined to make the more lasting impression.[18]

Sublette then mentions his own tantalizing aside: "But as I think this is not more than the second or third time he has been in love and probably a long absence may over come it, not a short one." Who were those two or three other infatuations? How did Campbell meet and woo them? What were they like? Who broke off the courtships? Once again a shard of history raises unanswerable questions.

He then reveals his own view of love: "I am not capable of judging for I must candidly confess which you may think strange for a man of my age to say I was never seriously in love in my life nor would I permit myself to be for I never was in a situation to get married as that which I could wish . . . ." Sublette had a purely pecuniary interest in marriage: "It is a pity we both could not get married to wives of fifty thousand [dollars]

18. William Sublette to Hugh Campbell, January 1, 1837, ibid.

each as I have more need of her money than love . . . I don't want her too smart for she might out general me and perceive my weaknesses and not be so affectionate in case I should spend the money."

In December 1836, Campbell again headed east for business, family, and, most important, to press his courtship of Virginia. Hugh was conducting business in New York when he arrived at Philadelphia. Upon returning home, Hugh found his brother Robert

> in very low spirits, but did not hint a word that I knew the cause. Soon afterwards he went to Baltimore. On his return here I dined with him one day & afterwards went up to his room where I came out in very plain terms. We had half an hours talk on the subject, in the course of which he spoke in the usual desponding terms, of disappointed love;—and I . . . treated the whole affair as one of those common occurances which happen to every person—approved of his being in love—said not a word against the object of his passion—but condemned his plan of allowing the matter to prey on his mind, or depress his spirits . . . Since then (about three weeks ago) . . . I am happy to discover that . . . He is now as gay & lively as I have ever seen him, & seems to mix as agreeably with society as he ever did. Robert has repeatedly met Virginia Kyle at my house. Both seem to be quite at their ease;—and in due time, I think it likely the attachment on his part will be forgotten.[19]

Hugh went on to clarify that

> you understood me to say that Virginia was a coquette. I did not intend to convey that impression exactly, but merely that, like many young ladies, she was fond of admiration;—and of being enabled to count the number of her beaux. This is a common feeling with the sex. It is amongst the first of their thoughts on emerging from childhood. I must not attribute to her any mischeveous motive, in her conversation with Robert. On the contrary I believe she is sincerely sorry for the past—and almost afraid to look me in the face;—for she knows that I am aware of all.

What Hugh observed was correct—Campbell was in ever-higher spirits. The reason for the startling change, however, was the opposite of what Hugh thought and hoped. Campbell's love for Virginia was slowly being reciprocated. Virginia had an intelligence and blossoming maturity greater than Hugh surmised. She awakened gradually to the deep dependability, honesty, kindness, and enterprise in Campbell lacking in the far younger, livelier, and perhaps more handsome men who had courted her.

19. Hugh Campbell to William Sublette, January 20, 1837, ibid.

As Campbell pined for Virginia, the perennial national and Missouri debate over economic policy reached a fever pitch. The latest shifts in that tug-of-war would directly affect the fortunes of Sublette and Campbell.

From the nation's founding, Americans have engaged in an endless conflict over the government's "proper" role in the economy. On one side are those who echo Thomas Jefferson's belief that the best government is that which governs least, leaving markets and profit-seekers alone no matter what the result. On the other side are those who, like Alexander Hamilton, argue that self-interest often conflicts with national prosperity, and that the government should regulate market excesses and guide the nation's economic development.

During the late 1820s and throughout the 1830s, the debate reached a crescendo in Missouri and across the United States. Democrat Andrew Jackson picked up Jefferson's banner of minimal government by denouncing the U.S. Bank, tariffs, government-supported internal improvements, and public schools. Whig Henry Clay promoted his "American system," which echoed Hamilton's belief that government should work with business to develop the economy by nurturing industry with tariffs, internal improvements, and an educated workforce. "Locofocoism" was the label stuck by Whigs on all those who mindlessly disparaged government investments of all types, whether it be in building roads, bridges, or schoolhouses, draining sewage from streets, clearing sandbars and sawyers from rivers, or providing clean water to homes. The Whigs maintained that locofocos preferred to mire Missouri in poverty, disease, and ignorance rather than sully their Darwinian market and minimalist government idealism. Locofocos retorted that the least government was the best government, the "market" solved all problems, and that anything else was unconstitutional and immoral.[20]

Ironically, Jacksonianism provided at least one golden opportunity for Sublette and Campbell—they would become directors of a newly created Missouri state bank. Ever since the banking debacles of the early 1820s, Missouri had gone without a bank of its own. The void had been partially filled in 1829 when the Second Bank of the United States opened

20. James Neal Primm, *Economic Policy in the Development of a Western State, 1820–1860*, 90–91, 98–99; Charles F. Holt, *The Role of State Government in the Nineteenth Century American Economy, 1820–1902: A Quantitative Study*; Carter Goodrich, *Government Promotion of American Canals and Railroads, 1800–1890*; Richard P. McCormick, *The Second American Party System: Party Formation in the Jacksonian Era*; Arthur M. Schlesinger, *The Age of Jackson*; John Ashworth, *"Agrarians and Aristocrats": Party Political Ideology in the United States, 1837–1846*.

a branch in St. Louis. Uncertainty over that bank, however, had festered following Jackson's first presidential message to Congress in 1829, in which he vehemently denounced the Second Bank as corrupt and swore he would not renew its charter. Jackson made good on his promise. When Congress passed a bill rechartering the Second Bank, Jackson gleefully vetoed it on July 10, 1832. He ordered the secretary of the treasury to make all future deposits in the banks of his political cronies. In 1836, after the charter expired, Pennsylvania issued the Second Bank a charter, but the bank finally went bankrupt in 1841.[21]

The closing of the Second Bank's St. Louis branch in 1835 was a financial disaster for Missouri, but would eventually bring more wealth and power to Sublette and Campbell. The Commercial Bank of Cincinnati gladly took over the deposits for the St. Louis and Illinois branches. As a result, hard money deposited by Missourians was whisked away to be invested in Cincinnati and elsewhere; that hard money was replaced by paper money of dubious and declining values issued by various Illinois banks. Missouri's economic development remained stunted and distorted by the want of a sound banking and currency system.

Throughout the mid-1830s, as the crisis over the U.S. Bank was followed by the resentment over the Commercial Bank of Cincinnati, ever more prominent businessmen and legislators called for the creation of a Missouri State Bank as allowed by the state constitution. Between 1835 and 1837, an unlikely coalition of opponents managed to shoot down attempts to pass state bank bills. A state bank was opposed by more emotional Jacksonian Democrats because they hated all banks, by more legalistic Democrats because they believed state or national banks to be unconstitutional, and by Whigs because they feared it would undermine the United States Bank. Mainstream Democrats, however, favored a state bank because it both jibed with their belief in "state's rights" and met the demands and donations of well-heeled, pro-bank businessmen.

Yet another reason arose for creating a state bank. The U.S. Bank's sound fiscal management of the national economy, the tariff, and public land sales had resulted in a government budget surplus of $41,468,859 in 1836. Jackson hoped to distribute that money along with the U.S. Bank's assets in loans to his political allies through the state banks. Without a

21. Leonard C. Helderman, *National and State Banks: A Study of their Origins*; Bray Hammond, *Banks and Politics in America from the Revolution to the Civil War*; James Roger Sharp, *The Jacksonians versus the Banks: Politics in the States after the Panic of 1837*; William G. Shade, *Banks or No Banks: The Money Issues in Western Politics, 1832–1865*.

state bank of their own, Missouri's Democratic Party leaders would miss out on all that loot.[22]

The bank controversy dominated the 1836 election. The Democrats ran and won on a pro-bank stance. When the new legislature convened on November 22, 1836, Governor Lilburn Boggs asked for the creation of a state bank. Representative James B. Bowlin, a friend of Sublette's, led the campaign in the Missouri legislature. On February 2, 1837, Governor Boggs signed two bank bills.

One bill incorporated the State Bank of Missouri to be capitalized with $5 million in fifty thousand shares of one hundred dollars each. The governor was authorized to use state funds to subscribe up to half of the bank's shares. The bank's headquarters would be at St. Louis and its first of five branches at Fayette. Legislators would choose the six state directors and the president for two-year terms; private shareholders would annually vote for the six private directors. All directors had to be citizens of Missouri and the United States. The presence of any five directors constituted a quorum. Each branch had a president and four directors appointed by the legislature and four elected by shareholders.

The bank was empowered to issue notes, receive public and private deposits, and deal in bills of exchange, drafts, and checks. Bank notes were payable on demand in gold or silver. In addition, the bank would serve as fiscal agent for Missouri's government by negotiating loans and transferring funds without charge. Although the bank could loan money to the state, it was not required to do so. Interest rates were fixed at 8 percent on commercial loans after six months, 6 percent on commercial paper after three months and 7 percent after six months, and 8 percent on farm and real estate loans, with 20 percent to be repaid each year. If the bank ever suspended specie payments, the governor could revoke its charter. The Missouri Bank was essentially a joint public-private financial venture. The 1820 state constitution allowed it monopoly rights over banking. It had taken seventeen years for Missouri's legislature to fulfill the opportunity granted by the constitution.

The other bill the governor signed on February 2 named the state directors for the State Bank of Missouri board. William Sublette was appointed, along with Robert's old employer John O'Fallon, Samuel Rayburn, Edward Walsh, Edward Dobbins, Hugh O'Neal, and president John Smith. On February 6, a bill was passed allowing any money received from Jackson's distribution of the U.S. Bank and government

22. John Ray Cable, *The Bank of the State of Missouri,* 129.

budget surplus to be deposited in the State Bank of Missouri. Another bill passed on February 6 required all other banks to leave the state immediately, except for the Commercial Bank of Cincinnati, which was allowed until June 1 to close its operations.

Sublette had no sooner taken his position on the board when the Missouri Bank faced a crisis. Jackson's inept economic policies helped cause the 1837 financial "Panic," which hit Missouri hard. Scores of older businesses failed, and few of the newly chartered corporations survived. The depression lingered until 1843. The Missouri Bank weathered the financial crisis by pursuing a hard-money policy of only accepting specie for repayments on loans, and set a good example by paying specie to its own creditors. Deposits dropped steadily over the following months, leading to even tougher measures in 1838. The tight money policy angered many of Missouri's businessmen, who were forced to borrow from financially insecure banks in Illinois and other states, or pay higher interest rates on loans from private loans, insurance companies, or the St. Louis Gas and Light Company.[23] Sublette and Campbell faced a worsening crisis as more of their debtors pleaded for more time to make repayments.

Campbell found an escape from all his frustrations over business and love. In 1837, the First Presbyterian Church opened at Fourth and St. Charles Streets. Campbell rented a pew for forty-two dollars a year and attended every Sunday he spent in St. Louis. More than religious services took place at the church. Debating societies also rented the church to present the age's great issues. Campbell undoubtedly attended many of those gatherings as well. But for a man as devout as Campbell, his church was an island of faith, community, and compassion in treacherous seas.[24]

In the winter of 1837, Campbell once again headed east for business, family, and romance. He was most successful in the latter pursuit. After nearly three years of courting Virginia, he finally won her hand. They announced their engagement shortly after Christmas. His joy dissipated before the icy reaction of their families. The stress, coming atop a faltering business, deeply wounded Campbell. To Sublette, he explained what happened:

> I wrote her mother immediately after we were engaged and Virginia wrote her at the same time—but she refuses to consent to Virginia marrying any person until she is 18 years of age. She is this day 16 so it will defer our

23. Dorothy B. Dorsey, "The Panic and Depression of 1837–1843 in Missouri."
24. Campbell Account Book, Campbell Papers, MLA.

marriage yet two years . . . she thinks it wrong . . . to form any engagement so early . . . I have written Mrs. Kyle two days ago requiring a more explicit sanction but I do not expect to get any more confirmation . . . Virginia writes her today Saying she will acquiesce in her mother's decision but that when She is 18 then She will be mine let who may oppose it . . . Virginia is as unchangeable as her mother though soft and pliant. She has a very great reverence for her Mother's opinions, but when the time arrives at which her mother can no longer object on the score of age she will then shew by conduct that her mother ought not to interfere . . . Two years is a very long engagement and such as I thought I would never form. During my sickness Virginia came to see me every day sometimes twice a day and sat by my bedside for hours—they were the happiest I ever enjoyed . . . [25]

Although unaware of the critical letters that had passed between Sublette and Hugh, Campbell clearly sensed that his love for Virginia had provoked a barely concealed smoldering jealousy in his partner. He sought to reassure Sublette that his love for Virginia enhanced rather than diminished their own relationship:

Are you not a little tired of being my confidant in these love affairs—fear not I will not trouble you with many such letters but to tell the truth my happiness would be incomplete if I did not share it with you My Dear Sublette—You have always been my exclusive confidant—whatever pleases me or Vexes me it gives me pleasure to communicate to you—My joys are heightened my sorrows alleviated. I know you will be pleased with Virginia when you See her and when she is mine I will shew her to you with pride.

Campbell's frustration is certainly understandable. There must have been many times during what became a five-year courtship when he longed for the uninhibited ease of mountain romance. There an Indian girl's "hymeneal" (to use Jim Beckwourth's quaint expression) affections could be won with a handful of beads, or she could simply be bought from her father for a horse or two. Ironically, even if Virginia had been of age when they met, Campbell's courting of her would have demanded patience and subtlety. In the dozen years that he had struggled in the wilderness, the American mating ritual had grown steadily more chaste. At one time, one of three brides who appeared before the wedding altar was heavy with child. Of course, most of those sexual romps had transpired in the hay of a country barn. Campbell's ardor was restrained by not only the setting of a city townhouse filled with eavesdropping and disapproving relatives but also the newly emerged standards of

25. Robert Campbell to William Sublette, January 25, 1838, "Glimpses of the Past."

romance, which confined affection to hand-holding and chaste pecks on the cheek. A woman in a "rushed marriage" was now forever condemned to exist "under a cloud." Men as well as women now "saved" themselves for marriage. Teenage brides, in the family way or not, were no longer common; girls now delayed marriage until their twenties. As the social historian Erastus Worthington had noted in 1827, "the sexes had learned to cultivate the proper degree of delicacy in their intercourse."[26]

What provoked such an abrupt about-face in sexual attitudes? Industrialization and urbanization straitjacketed behavior as never before. What one did with one's time and where one did it was now strictly prescribed. Ever more refined and restrained mores accompanied the steady expansion and incomes of the upper and middle classes alike. Greater literacy and mass publishing brought into the hands of anxious readers books and pamphlets such as Robert Dale Owen's "Moral Physiology" (1831), Dr. Charles Knowlton's "The Fruits of Philosophy" (1832), and Sylvester Graham's "Lecture to Young Men on Chastity" (1832) that both reflected and reinforced existing social forces. Society now demanded abstinence before marriage and restraint afterwards. Women were once thought to have sex drives as powerful as those of men; now that was denied, and anyone with such urges was advised to divert those energies into more pedestrian pursuits.

Although the years of restraint made him miserable, Campbell had no choice but to await the consummation of his love for Virginia. Instead he devoted himself to Sublette and Campbell. While their mercantile business remained their central concern, they invested in a range of other enterprises. They amassed a real estate empire throughout the upper Mississippi River valley. They served as loan agents for several banks, including the Farmers and Mechanics Bank of Philadelphia and the Bank of Mineral Point, Wisconsin. They also invested in the St. Louis Insurance Company, the St. Louis Hotel Company, and the Marine Insurance Company, when the legislature chartered all three institutions in 1837, with Bowlin once again sponsoring the enabling acts.[27]

These ventures left Sublette and Campbell grossly overextended. Their income was falling ever shorter of their commitments. To their customers, the partners sent out scores of letters politely requesting

26. Quoted in Jack Larkin, *The Reshaping of Everyday Life, 1790–1840*, 199, 193–95, 199–201; see also Page Smith, *The Shaping of America: A People's History of the Young Republic*, 382–84, 370–72.

27. Sunder, *Sublette*, 167.

full or partial payment of their debts. More often than not the replies were either silence or regrets. Of one customer, Campbell noted, "we have no hopes of collecting the amount of John Duram. He has not answered our letters . . ." Their business teetered at bankruptcy's brink. Sublette admitted to Campbell, "I have not received one dollar from one of our customers since my first letter to you nor is there much prospect as many are writing us that they can't raise money before spring . . . money . . . is getting scarcer every day." A month later, he wrote, "Such times has scarcely been known in St. Louis the pressure for money . . . as the Country Merchants are generally much behind their payments and goods cannot now be obtained East without funds."[28]

To their distributors, the partners warned that "goods are scarce and . . . you Country Merchants must shorten your Credit or all fail. The farmers must pay up as far as they can and their whole dependence are on the Country Merchants and they are very Backward in paying up. But we hope as New Years Day has come around that all those that are Indebeted to us will try and pay all they can or we cant get our money we must have." By fall 1840, the partners owed the State Bank of Missouri $7,128, while Sublette had borrowed from it another $2,074.[29]

Meanwhile, the partners' nemesis, the American Fur Company, underwent a business reorganization and consolidation of territory. In 1838, the American Fur Company's official name changed from Pratte, Chouteau, and Company to Pierre Chouteau, Jr., and Company. That year Bernard Pratte fulfilled his long-standing political ambition when he won a Missouri General Assembly seat and dropped out of the partnership. Even then, Pierre Chouteau owned only about half of his company's $500,000 worth of shares. John Sarpy, Joseph Sire, and John Sanford each held about $80,000 of the rest but were content to let Chouteau run the firm. For the next twenty-seven years, Pierre Chouteau, Jr., and Company would reign supreme over the upper Missouri River as its predecessors had since 1827, when the American Fur Company took over. During those coming decades, Campbell would engage in a near ceaseless and largely futile but often profitable struggle to break Chouteau's monopoly, which would continue to be commonly called the American Fur Company.

28. Robert Campbell to [Hugh?] Campbell, May 21, 1837, Campbell Papers, William Sublette to Robert Campbell, January 14, 1838, Sublette and Campbell to W. W. Wright, January 29, 1839, MLA.
29. Sublette and Campbell to Solomon Sublette, January 7, 1838, ibid. Sunder, *Sublette*, 164–65.

Also in 1838, Chouteau and Company cut a deal with Bent, St. Vrain, and Company to split the West between them. Chouteau and Company would exploit all that territory north of the Platte River, including Sublette and Campbell's old Fort William (now officially Fort John, with Fort Laramie its popular name), while Bent, St. Vrain, and Company took all to the south.

The division of the spoils boosted Chouteau's profits. His trading posts up the Missouri and Platte brought 45,000 robes down to St. Louis in 1839 and 67,000 in 1840 out of about 100,000 that moved through the city's warehouses each year. By 1842, Chouteau had increased his capital investment in the upper Missouri from $36,000 to $60,000, his employees from 90 to 130, and his posts from 14 to 18.[30]

The partners and all other ambitious entrepreneurs now faced twin powerful monopolies controlling the robe and fur trade on the northern and southern plains. Given their experience, knowledge, and connections with the trappers and Indians of the region, Sublette and Campbell naturally eyed the northern plains far more closely than the southern plains. For now, the partners could only watch and wait for an opening.

While their archrival acquired ever more power, Sublette became increasingly interested in politics. In December 1838, he attended a Democratic Party meeting at the St. Louis courthouse to plot strategy for the next year's election. He helped organize the annual January 8 dinner at the National Hotel, which was attended by 200 prominent Democrats. Friends nominated Sublette for state senator. Sublette excitedly wrote Hugh of the possibility. Ever the killjoy, Hugh declared "politics a farce. My firm conviction is that a man of business should have nothing to do with the legislation of the country. Excuse this plain language but I beg you to do all you can to withdraw from this contest."[31]

Spurning Hugh's advice, Sublette continued his run. He and Campbell received a jolt when they learned that William Ashley had died on March 26 while he prepared to run as the Whig candidate for governor. Ashley had named Campbell and Sublette among the six executors of his estate. The partners mourned Ashley's death; he had been not only a financial and political patron, but a friend and father figure as well.

Still very sick, Campbell returned amidst all these events on April 12. The mingled grief and stress over Ashley's death, his delayed

30. John E. Sunder, *The Fur Trade on the Upper Missouri, 1840–1865*, 3–8, 17, 31.
31. Hugh Campbell to William Sublette, February 24, 1838, Sublette Collection, MoHiS.

engagement, and their faltering business laid him up for weeks at Sulphur Springs. He finally reemerged in St. Louis and gradually resumed his duties. On June 12, Campbell again embarked on a buying trip to the East Coast. Yet he sold few goods upon his return. The economy continued to sputter along. Beaver prices steadily dropped. The coin shortage inevitably blocked any business expansion. Only land and financial speculation kept the demand for goods and services alive.

The Democratic Party's platform threatened to deepen the depression and stunt economic development. In February 1839, with words that sound eerily familiar, the Democrats declared their opposition "to a National Bank, to protective tariffs, to constructive Internal Improvements, upon the principle that the people can better appropriate their own means than have it dragged from them by taxation, and then appropriated by Congress contrary to the spirit and letter of the Constitution . . . It is against every tendency to consolidation of the States—it is in favor of the States being maintained in all their legitimate rights."[32]

Sublette went along with these ideas, although his level of conviction cannot be determined. Campbell privately rejected the Democratic Party platform; he was a closet Whig when it came to economic policy. He recognized that a tariff nurtured American industries that not only expanded and distributed national wealth but also raised desperately needed federal revenues. The revenues could be used to improve the nation's transportation and communication infrastructure, which in turn boosted economic efficiency, opportunities, and wealth. The resulting government revenues could be invested in further improvements. Campbell also supported a national bank that would maintain a sound national currency, which was essential for sound economic development. He understood that the economy developed more rapidly, efficiently, and equitably when public and private investments worked together to nurture a diverse range of manufacturing, commerce, and transportation enterprises. Despite his beliefs, Campbell remained loyal to the Democratic Party throughout his life. Indeed, for four decades Campbell was one of the Democratic Party's power brokers.

What explains the discrepancy between Campbell's economic beliefs and political loyalties? Hard-nosed realism determined which party would bear his loyalty. Campbell supported the Democrats because it was politically expedient to do so—after all, the party dominated Missouri. To be a Democrat was to belong to a club whose members

32. Primm, *Economic Policy*, 40.

helped enrich and empower each other; the higher one's standing in the party, the greater the benefits and opportunities to enhance one's wealth, status, and power. But the Democratic Party could accommodate Campbell's economic positions. The 1839 platform aside, the party generally provided a large tent for its leaders and followers alike. The economic views of moderate Democrats differed little from those of Whigs.

Sublette contributed little to the partnership that tenuous summer as he devoted more time, energy, and money to his election campaign. His investment did not pan out; when the election returns were published on August 13, Sublette had garnered only 1,177 votes to Whig opponent John Darby's 1,895. Although Sublette vowed never to run again, he did continue to serve the Democratic Party through committees, after-dinner speeches, convention delegations, and campaign contributions, and the general public through city council, school board, and state militia "colonel" appointments.[33]

Fortunately for the partners, business began to pick up that autumn. But even though goods were selling better, they still had trouble collecting debts. In desperation they turned to their old mountain companion, William Drummond Stewart. The Scottish lord was able to advance them only four hundred dollars.[34]

In December, Campbell was once more in Philadelphia for another buying and courting trip. He would not return to St. Louis until March 1839. Despite his efforts, Mrs. Kyle continued to stonewall any marriage before Virginia's eighteenth birthday. While pleased at her daughter's happiness with Campbell, she warned her

> never marry a man if you do not respect or esteem him more highly than any other nor if you have a secret reason (provided it is a good one) for not marrying him, which must be the case with yourself, or you never would have acted so strangely, you know you never have communicated with me on the subject, but if there is any one event which could occur tha would please me, it would be to see you married to Mr. R. C.[35]

The mother's allusions to "secret reasons for not marrying" and Virginia's acting "strangely" are intriguing. What rumors or innuendos were whispered about Robert Campbell that may have caused Virginia to doubt her commitment to him? Just how did Virginia act "strangely"? Apparently, Virginia never revealed just what was troubling her. Lacking

33. Sunder, *Sublette*, 170–73.
34. Sublette to Campbell, January 20, 1839, Campbell Papers, MLA.
35. Lucy Kyle to Virginia Kyle, September 26, 1840, Campbell House.

hard proof of any "secret reasons," Lucy concluded her letter by essentially approving a future marriage to Campbell. Unfortunately, any answers to such mysterious questions have been buried with Campbell and the others.

In December, shortly after he returned to St. Louis, an honor was bestowed upon Campbell that alleviated some of the lingering gloom from his relationship with Virginia. The legislature elected him to the State Bank of Missouri's board of directors. Unfortunately, it was at the cost of Sublette's seat. The legislature kicked Sublette off the bank board, perhaps because his campaign had alienated too many representatives from both sides of the aisle. The legislature then promptly elected Campbell. More than anything, the appointment revealed that Campbell had finally been accepted in Missouri's uppermost tier of society.

Although with their positions on the board Sublette and Campbell had little trouble getting credit, they prudently limited their borrowing for the sake of liability and propriety. As of October 20, 1840, Sublette and Campbell had borrowed $12,020 from the state bank and Sublette himself owed $2,074. From that peak, the partners would slowly pay off their bank loans. Given their constant buying, selling, and extensions of credit, the partners rarely had much money on hand. Their deposits in the State Bank of Missouri never exceeded $1,500.[36]

The state bank continued to hemorrhage. On November 12, 1839, the board announced it would no longer accept deposit notes of non-specie-paying banks from neighboring states such as Illinois and Kentucky. The declaration immediately depreciated the value of those notes, hundreds of thousands of dollars of which were held by Missourians and by the state bank itself. Merchants protested by withdrawing their money from the bank and depositing it with corporations such as the St. Louis Gas and Light Company, Perpetual Insurance Company, or Mutual Insurance Company, which were conducting some banking functions. The only banking function they did not and could not do by law was to create money. The withdrawals caused the State Bank of Missouri's deposits to plunge from $1.75 million in 1839 to $332,000 in 1840.[37]

If Campbell was pleased over his election to the bank board, he was ecstatic over another vote in his favor early in the new year. On February 4, 1841, Mrs. Kyle finally gave in and approved her daughter's engagement. To Campbell she wrote,

36. Cable, *Bank of Missouri*, 209; Sunder, *Sublette*, 163–66.
37. James Neal Primm, *Lion of the Valley: Saint Louis, Missouri*, 142.

Three years ago I promised you, when Virginia would arrive at the age of 18 I would give you my most "cordial consent to your marriage," I now give it even more willingly than I would have done then, she is now fully capable of judging for herself and knowing her own mind . . . And now Mr. Campbell I have given you my free and full consent to marry my daughter, I have nothing to ask nothing to fear, had I not the most implicit confidence in you, you would have never gained my permission.[38]

Shortly after receiving Mrs. Kyle's letter, he hurried to Raleigh, North Carolina, to join his fiancée. On February 25, 1841, Robert Campbell and Virginia Jane Kyle were married. Then thirty-seven, Campbell was easily old enough to be the nineteen-year-old Virginia's father. Yet their mutual understanding and affection had deepened steadily during their five-year courtship. Predictably, they honeymooned at Hugh's home in Philadelphia. Hugh's feelings on Campbell's latest defiance of his advice can only be imagined.

Campbell then triumphantly took his bride to St. Louis. They stayed at the Planter's House on Fourth Street a few blocks from the partners' business. Their suite cost $13.75 a week.[39] What the Planter's House may have lacked in outward elegance it made up for in service and cuisine. It even pleased Charles Dickens, whose "American Notes" lambasted Americans and their beloved nation on every page. Shortly after the newlyweds moved in, Dickens stayed at the Planter's House, which was

> built like an English hospital with long passages and bare walls and skylights above the room doors for the free circulation of the air. There were a great many boarders in it; and as many lights sparkled and glistened from the windows down into the street below, when we drove up, as if it had been illuminated on some occasion of rejoicing. It is an excellent house, and the proprietors have the most bountiful notions of providing the creature comforts. Dining alone with my wife in her own room one day, we counted fourteen dishes on the table at once.[40]

Did Robert and Charles ever tip their hats to each other in the hall or exchange pleasantries? Dickens's works were well known to Americans by that time and his visit to St. Louis must have caused a stir. Alas, if they did meet, neither bothered to record the experience.

Campbell may have rued that his business ventures did not match the happiness of his marriage or status of his bank board position. Getting

38. Lucy Kyle to Robert Campbell, February 1, 1841, Campbell House.
39. Campbell Account Book, Campbell Papers, MLA.
40. Charles Dickens, *American Notes for General Circulation*, 155.

debtors to pay up remained as difficult and unappealing a task as pulling teeth, and often was unsuccessful. When a debtor refused to pay, Sublette and Campbell did not hesitate to sue. In 1842, the partners won twenty of twenty-nine lawsuits against debtors in Missouri and three of five in Illinois. These legal victories often proved to be Pyrrhic. The suits cost the partners lost time, money, and energy. Some debtors simply filed for bankruptcy and the partners got nothing. Others paid with hard-to-sell land rather than cash. Friends and even relatives were not immune from the partners' lawsuits. Sublette and Campbell sued their old Rocky Mountain comrades, Henry Fraeb and Edmund Christy, in 1839, and Andrew Sublette and Louis Vasquez in 1842, for collection of debts; although the partners won both cases they received no payments in the first case and seventy-seven acres of land in the second. They sued the Bank of Mineral Point, Wisconsin, after it collapsed in 1841. Once again they won, but probably received no payment. Of one particularly costly transaction, the partners lamented that "our situation in that whole affair has been unpleasant and we have endeavored to act in it with as much delicacy to each party as was possible . . . Col Crick owes us between $700 and $800 which we cannot get from him although we have frequently written him."[41]

The same 1840 election that affected the bank board also gave the partners a possible opening in the Missouri River trade. Over the years, Chouteau had managed to pack the Office of Indian Affairs with allies who turned a blind eye to his liquor trade and monopoly on the upper Missouri. When an Indian agent could not be bought, he was intimidated into keeping his mouth shut about the American Fur Company's machinations. The most important ally was Joshua Pilcher. Chouteau had used his power to help Pilcher take the upper Missouri agency from 1837 to 1838, and the superintendency at St. Louis in 1839. Pilcher was all but Chouteau's official partner; he bought his agency's supplies from the American Fur Company and awarded Chouteau the contracts to handle the annual annuities to the Indians even if competitors underbid him. Pilcher defended his favoritism by arguing that Chouteau ran the only steamboats on the Missouri and thus was the most efficient operator. Chouteau, of course, did nothing to disillusion the Indians from their belief that the annuities were gifts from him rather than America's taxpayers.

41. Sublette and Campbell to Boone and Hamilton, October 13, 1841, Campbell Papers, MLA; Sunder, *Sublette*, 157–60.

To replace Pilcher on the Indian superintendency, Campbell and Sublette quietly backed John Dougherty, the former clerk at their Mandan post and now a Whig member of the Missouri General Assembly. Dougherty had led the fight in the assembly against a Chouteau-backed bill that would have incorporated the American Fur Company in Missouri, giving it even more political power. On February 1, 1841, the bill lost in a tie vote of forty-four to forty-four. The American Fur Company targeted Dougherty as its number one enemy in the assembly.

The partners' hopes that Dougherty would replace Pilcher were dashed when Whig President William Henry Harrison died a month after taking office and thus never fulfilled his promise to sweep out the dead political wood from the previous administration. His successor, John Tyler, was not disposed to rock the political boat. Dougherty's was one of a half dozen names floated to replace Pilcher. Chouteau wielded all his power to keep Pilcher in the position. On September 13, 1841, President Tyler finally agreed on the compromise choice of David Dawson Mitchell, who, like Pilcher and Dougherty, was an experienced fur trader and negotiator with Indians.

Mitchell's appointment did not bring the hoped for opening on the Missouri River. Although Mitchell was not in Chouteau's pocket, he was not eager to take on the American Fur Company. Even if he had curbed some of the company's excesses, its sheer economic power made it seem likely it would preserve its monopoly. Since the 1834 "partition" with Sublette and Campbell, Chouteau had not faced any significant competition on the Missouri. Each year some independent traders pooled their money, wits, and goods, ascended the Missouri, and set up one or more trading posts. Sublette and Campbell were among those who helped outfit such ventures. They rarely turned a profit. Whenever the outsiders arrived on the upper Missouri, the nearby American Fur Company trading posts would simply undersell and crush them.

Sublette and Campbell faced mounting debts and blocked opportunities amidst a lingering national depression. Sublette was exhausted from the stress of all his economic and political ventures. He decided to call it quits. On January 15, 1842, Campbell and Sublette chose to end their partnership. Campbell bought out Sublette's share for $6,656.82; the two split their store evenly and each continued to work out of his half. Campbell also retained "Sublette and Campbell" as his business name for another two years until the old accounts were closed.[42]

42. Article of Dissolution, January 15, 1842, Sublette Collection, MoHiS.

It was a good time to retire. Sublette's civic activities and political aspirations allowed him little time to devote to the partnership; his various agricultural, livestock, coal, ice, and resort ventures at Sulphur Springs gave him an alternative source of income. The worsening economy made debt recovery ever more difficult. The partnership itself teetered at bankruptcy's brink. Sublette may have decided to abandon what seemed to be a sinking ship.

Still, the partners had weathered similar financial crises in the past. Given the unusually tight relationship between the two men, one can only speculate as to whether Campbell's decision to marry had anything to do with the dissolution of their partnership. Probably not. The dissolution was reached amicably enough, and Sublette remained friends with Robert, frequently stopping in on Virginia when Campbell was on business in Jefferson City or the East Coast. Sublette would continue to travel around the region trying to collect debts owed to their old partnership, whose name both men continued to use when the occasion demanded. And the old partners would sometimes join for other business deals. Though their official partnership had ended, they remained close business partners in all other ways.

Upon dissolving the partnership, Campbell embarked east on a buying trip. He left full of anxiety at leaving not only his new wife but also the child growing within her. He returned with three thousand dollars' worth of goods, just in time for an economic meltdown and the birth of his first child. That summer of 1842, a huge speculative financial and real estate bubble burst in the Mississippi and Ohio valleys. Campbell wrote Sublette, who was trying to collect debts in western Missouri, that "I never felt so much anxiety about money even in our worst necessities as I do at present."[43]

Conditions got so bad that on June 3,

> a number of persons collected together last night with a view of Mobbing the brokers on account of the depreciation in value of city and county notes but they separated without doing any harm—it is feared there will be a Mob tonight but I dont think any harm will be done—the Brokers require a little regulating for if ever a community was swindled by Brokers it is the citizens of St. Louis—I dislike to see Mobs but some times they do good and a little fright might be of service.[44]

A week later Campbell wrote Sublette with more bad news: "Shawneetown Bank will not resume—this must depreciate the money and

---

43. Robert Campbell to William Sublette, May 12, 1842, ibid.
44. Robert Campbell to Bill Sublette, June 4, 1842, "Glimpses of the Past."

if you have any I would recommend you to change it for Kentucky or
Indiana Money, or for specie as high as 3 to 5 per cent . . . I think the
Shawneetown money will be good, but if she does not then resume her
money must go down."[45]

During these financially desperate times, the Campbell family stayed
at Sublette's farm. Campbell's first child, James Alexander, was born
on May 14, 1842. Mrs. Kyle had arrived four days earlier to help the
new family. Mary wrote to Virginia, "It is too amusing to think of
Robert nursing a babe. I would give anything to see him playing with
the little rascal." Mrs. Kyle would later send a book on child-rearing
and her own advice to her daughter: "I believe all wise parents agree
that it is right to commence with children when very young to teach
them implicit obedience. I now feel most sensibly my deficiency in
governing my children when they were young, particularly your sister.
You by nature was more easily managed."[46] Mrs. Kyle's admission of her
motherly failings to Virginia is refreshingly honest. Clearly the mother
and daughter had an intimate, open relationship.

Their closeness and the gift of an advice book was not at all uncom-
mon. By the mid-1840s, a host of advice books, magazines, pamphlets,
and novels were available to help young wives and mothers. The production of America's printing presses had increased tenfold from 1820
to 1850. A publishing world once centered almost exclusively on men
shifted its output increasingly toward the interests of women. Along
with self-help books, fiction was increasingly popular. A mere 109 novels
were published during the entire 1820s; in 1840 alone, over a thousand
novels and short stories were published. By 1860, the woman's magazine
"Godey's Lady's Book" alone enjoyed a circulation of 150,000.[47] The
supply and demand for advice books reflected the population's growing

45. Robert Campbell to Bill Sublette, June 10, 1842, ibid.
46. Mary Campbell to Virginia Campbell, July 11, 1842, Lucy Kyle to Virginia Campbell, March 14, 1844, Campbell House.
47. Mary P. Ryan, *The Empire of the Mother: American Writing about Domesticity, 1830–
1860,* 13, 34, 116. Among the leading works of that era, see Lydia Maria Child, *The Frugal
Housewife;* Catherine Maria Sedgwick, *Home;* Timothy Shay Arthur, *The Mother;* Catherine
Beecher, *The Duty of American Women to their Country;* Lydia Maria Child, *The Mother's
Book;* Lydia Maria Child, *Good Wives;* Horace Mann, *Lectures on Education;* William Andrus
Alcott, *The Young Husband;* William Andrus Alcott, *The Physiology of Marriage.*
For contemporary studies of women in that era, see Francis Trollope, ed., *Domestic
Manners of Americans;* Nancy Cott, *Bonds of Womanhood: "Women's Sphere" in New England,
1780–1835;* Nina Baym, *Women's Fiction: A Guide to Novels by and about Women in America,
1820–1870;* Carl N. Degler, *At Odds: Women and the Family in America from the Revolution
to the Present.*

affluence and literacy, the social dislocations of industrialization and urbanization, and new techniques for mass producing books.

Those books at once reflected and shaped a "cult of domesticity" that had recently emerged in the popular culture. Although that cult centered around the hearth and cradle, contrary to prevailing images of that era, women were "neither victims nor puppets" but had achieved "dignity, self-esteem, and even power." While a woman's role was to assist her husband and raise her children, relations between husbands and wives were becoming more egalitarian. The days were rapidly fading when Herman Humphrey could unequivocally state: "Every family is a state or empire . . . governed by its patriarchal head with whose prerogative no power on earth has a right to intervene."[48]

Nationwide, in family matters, patriarchal dictatorship was giving way to partnership. Marriage was increasingly seen less as an economic bridge between two families and more as a companionship of mutual enrichment. Husbands and wives consulted carefully with each other; the wife gave as well as took advice. Sex was viewed as natural, healthy in moderation, and to be mutually enjoyed. Husbands were admonished to hurry straight home to their loved ones after work rather than join friends at the local tavern. In most cases he needed little persuading. Industrialization and urbanization devoured the traditional independence a man enjoyed in his field or workshop. As increasing numbers of men became factory or office drones, they depended on their wives to restore to them the humanity and companionship lost in an increasingly harsh, uncertain, impersonal, and regimented world. Every one of their surviving letters reveal that Robert and Virginia personified this loving partnership ideal.

Likewise, children were not to be brutally crushed and remolded by fathers as in the old days, but gently and lovingly nurtured to bring out their better nature by their mothers. Relations between a mother and child were not a battle of wills but a joyful union to be cherished. Discipline was invoked through moral persuasion rather than beatings. The child-rearing literature of the era had a surprisingly sophisticated understanding of psychological development. Learning was understood to begin early in the child's first year. "Early impressions" were thought to be lasting. Mothers were exhorted to shower their children with affection and avoid inflicting or exposing them to any trauma. Lydia Sigourney encouraged mothers that if the child "looks up in the midst of play, a

48. Ryan, *Empire of the Mother*, 2, 23.

smile should always be ready for him, that he may feel protected and happy in an atmosphere of love."[49] The father's role, meanwhile, shifted from that of stern disciplinarian to kindly playmate. Here too, Robert and Virginia would epitomize the new standards of child-rearing—perhaps too successfully.

These practices kept children emotionally tied to their parents. In the old days, most children welcomed the chance to flee into the world from a tyrannical father. By the mid–nineteenth century, an ever greater number of children preferred to remain bound to the family hearth. By the 1860s, as many as 40 percent of children were still living at home in their late twenties.[50] Indeed, the three surviving Campbell sons would remain welded to their boyhood home for the rest of their lives, never striking out on their own in career or marriage.

The birth of his first son helped divert Campbell's mind from a sour business climate—he sold little that summer. It was Sublette's debt collection trip across western Missouri that sustained Campbell. The several thousand dollars Sublette brought back to St. Louis that September was enough to keep their own creditors at bay and allowed Campbell to purchase more goods.

One bright spot amidst the financial gloom was the visit of President Martin Van Buren during his trip to St. Louis from June 21 to 24. Campbell hoped to work into his busy schedule a meeting with the president: "Mr Van Buren arrived here to day and was welcomed by the largest crowd I ever saw in St. Louis he is at the Planters House and dined to day at the Ladies Ordinary . . . I have not yet called on him but think I will very soon."[51]

That September, desperate to stay afloat, Campbell and Sublette sought twelve thousand dollars from William Drummond Stewart. Sublette's letter to Drummond gives a succinct account of the far-flung ventures of Campbell and Sublette, along with the general business climate. After giving an in-depth account of their mountain operations, Sublette played up a business opportunity that wanted only the proper investment:

> There is now the greatest opening I have ever seen, as peltries of all discription is plenty and cheap—for want of goods—the Santa ferans [Santa Fe traders] was fortunate in getting in and got their goods on from the East but

49. Quoted in ibid., 52.
50. Ibid., 60.
51. Robert Campbell to Bill Sublette, June 24, 1842, "Glimpses of the Past."

with in fifty miles of Independence the Steam Boat Sank and made entire loss of eighty thousand dollars worth—one third this fall's outfit. So you see now how it goes,—the prettiest opening in the Indian trade that a man could wish and if I had of had the wherewith you would have seen me on the head waters of the Platte this winter . . . I got back from Independence the first of September and found . . . many old houses had failed in St. Louis and business completely prostrated. Such times I have never seen . . . Sublette & Campbell had as much or more than they could doe to get on without Giving a way real estate as it will not now fetch more than 1/4 its value— by the by we have considerable of borrowing money which is impossible to do allmost here at this time . . . Sublette & Campbell wishes to borrow of you about $8000. and myself about $4000. making in all about $12,000, which we would like to draw on for in 2 drafts of 60 days each. Sublette & Campbell for their part will secure you by mortgages on Real Estate and so will W.L. Sublette Paying you interest for same for such time as you may think propper to Lend us. We have never had any property mortagaged nor doe we wish to Borrow money in St. Louis particularly at present as it is allmost impossible as all the Illinois Banks has gone down and Missouri is not Loaning nor has she for one year past. We have large out standing amts. and can only collect by suit and to sacrifice real estate as it will scarcely fetch any thing. I dislike the Idea. We hope you will be kind enough to assist us as this amt. will answer our demands . . . Probably we may draw on you for some five or six thousand before we can hear from you in return. I hope you are in funds and if we doe draw please meet it as it will be a favour. If you have funds to invest now is your time in Missouri for I would wish no handsomer fortune than I could make out of fifty or one hundred thousand dollars.[52]

Stewart promptly sent them the money.

Once again a timely influx of cash pulled them from bankruptcy. Yet business continued to stagnate. Campbell wrote Hugh that "business is worse by far than I have ever known it in St. Louis—and I am selling nothing at present and no money is coming from the country . . . How long matters will continue so is impossible to say." Despite his dismal financial straits, Campbell had not forgotten his Irish roots. In October 1842, he agreed to buy uniforms for "a military company called the Montgomery Guard" formed among Irish Americans.[53]

In letters to Sublette written in November and December of that year, Campbell revealed his in-depth understanding of economics, politics,

52. William Sublette to W. D. Stewart, September 1842, ibid.

53. Robert Campbell to Hugh Campbell, October 24, 1842, Letterbook, MoHiS. Robert Campbell to H. and A. Campbell Co., October 22, 1842, Campbell Papers, MLA.

and policy. The financial crash was largely attributed to unregulated speculation encouraged by the Democratic Party's Darwinian market philosophy. Campbell hoped that a coalition of hard-money Democrats and Whigs could be forged to push through laws regulating the financial industry: "I hope you will recommend such Democrats as will sustain our principles, and if such cannot be had let us have (in preference to traitors of our own party) good Whigs—but I think that we can get good sound men of our own party capable of managing it." Campbell was to be disappointed. The laissez-faire adherents prevailed. A month later he expressed his regret that Missouri's legislature failed to pass a hard-money policy for the State Bank of Missouri.[54]

Yet, thanks to the persistent lobbying of Campbell and other hard-money advocates, the legislature shifted its views. On January 3, 1843, the legislators not only renewed Campbell's appointment on the state bank board by a vote of 127 to 1, but also added William Sublette to its ranks. Later that year the legislature passed two "bills of pains and penalties" that tried simultaneously to strengthen the bank's power, curb the power of corporations to act like banks, and firm the foundation of the money supply. One law repealed all charters to firms that performed banking functions and authorized the attorney general to investigate the activities of St. Louis Gas and Light, Mutual Insurance, and Perpetual Insurance corporations. Another bill forbade any corporation, money broker, or exchange dealer from changing any note or currency of less than ten dollars after January 1, 1844. Any firm that violated that law was liable to a five-hundred-dollar fine and forfeit of its charter.

Despite his busy schedule, Campbell always found time to help a friend in need. With the beaver trade exhausted, Tom Fitzpatrick was out of work. Campbell asked Hugh to help Fitzpatrick lobby for a possible Indian agency that would open if the appropriate bill passed Congress. Hugh gave Tom little chance of success: "Fitzpatrick arrived here and called on me . . . He seems to be an excellent man, but not much accustomed to 'paddle his own canoe' in this scheming political world. After perusing your letters and conversing some time with him, I came to the conclusion that his journey eastward would prove useless—or at any chance for an appointment was desperate . . . I never saw a more retiring or less egotistical person."[55] Despite his misgivings, Hugh agreed

54. Robert Campbell to Bill Sublette, November 22, 1842, Robert Campbell to Bill Sublette, December 20, 1842, "Glimpses of the Past."
55. Hugh Campbell to Robert Campbell, January 31, 1843, Campbell House.

to travel with Fitzpatrick to Washington to help him lobby for a position. The bill did not pass Congress.

More than friendship was involved in the effort to find the "retiring" Fitzpatrick a job. The American Fur Company's various incarnations had succeeded because they had mastered a virtuous cycle of political and economic power. The more profit the giant reaped from the field, the more money it had with which to lobby Congress for favorable treatment in laws or to place allies as agents. This in turn swelled the bottom line, which allowed the company to devote even more money to political payoffs. Campbell understood that the chance of beating the American Fur Company in the field was unlikely as long as he could not beat them in Washington.

While one mountain comrade headed east, another headed west. Since dissolving their partnership and losing his election, William Sublette had dabbled at various pursuits, including a half-hearted courtship of Frances Hereford, the daughter of Dr. Thomas Hereford, who managed his Sulphur Springs resort. Yet all along, he remained reluctant to follow his friend into matrimony. Instead, in April 1843, he escaped any possible "tender trap" by agreeing to guide William Drummond Stewart on one last adventure before settling down. The expedition ground temporarily to a halt just outside of Independence for want of supplies. While waiting there, Sublette learned that his sister Sophronia had died on April 20 and was buried at Sulphur Springs. For Sublette the expedition would end as morosely as it began.

Campbell ended up selling the "excursion" most of its supplies and animals. In a letter to Sublette at the expedition's camp outside of Independence, Campbell advised that many draft animals and other supplies should be taken from those in the area who owed money to the partners: "I feel the strong necessity of prompt action on our part in making collections—and I trust for the short time that you remain that you will do your part."[56]

Now it was Campbell's turn to act as love adviser. Taking advantage of the expedition's delay, on May 5, he wrote Sublette a long letter in which he expressed "from the Most brotherly love and the best of Motives . . . that you will never be happy until you are Married . . . And

56. Robert Campbell to William Sublette, May 5, 1843, in "Glimpses of the Past." For the expedition's preparations, see also William Sublette to William Stewart, September 1842, Robert Campbell to William Sublette, November 22, 1842, December 11, 15, 20, May 5, 13, 17, 1843, ibid.

from my knowledge of the female sex have no hesitation in saying you will never do better [than Frances Hereford], if you would hunt the world over." Campbell admitted that "I would prefer marrying her and enjoying her society to that of all the Sir Wm Stewarts and Mountaineers and Buffalows that this world ever produced, for one is all a fleeting show and soon vanishes, the other is real, and lasting—it certainly makes a man more happy, and much more respectable in society."[57]

The letter is remarkable in several respects. It reveals the deep divisions in values, motivations, and passions between the two men, differences that neither partner may have understood despite their long, powerful friendship. For Campbell, a dozen years in the mountains were simply a means to the end of a loving family, financial security, and social respectability. In contrast, Sublette was happiest when surrounded by "all the Sir Wm Stewarts and Mountaineers and Buffalows." Although a half dozen years earlier they had discussed Campbell's love for Virginia, their talks apparently never extended to Sublette's feelings about women, love, marriage, and related concerns. When one of them had a problem, the other would offer a "solution" based on his own values. Campbell seems to have believed Sublette merely bashful and innocent about the opposite sex; thus he urged his friend to not pass up a lifetime opportunity. Sublette, however, was simply disinterested in marriage, unless the prospective bride had a large estate. Thus did even the best of friends talk past each other and remain strangers in vital areas.

In the letter, Campbell's feeling for Hereford seem to have gone beyond simply believing she was the best possible match for his friend. Following their intimate tête-à-tête, Campbell concluded that Frances Hereford had "as much grace as any lady in my knowing" and that "he would prefer marrying her and enjoying her society." It is no wonder that he asked Sublette to destroy his letter. As happens in nearly all long-term relationships, while Campbell's love for Virginia was as deep as ever, its essence had changed from passion to a partnership in raising children and rising ever higher in "society." Campbell's closeness to Frances seems to have reawakened the romantic fantasies that he had once felt so powerfully for his wife.

Finally, and ironically, Campbell would change his stellar opinion of Hereford after William died. The widow quickly remarried; she wed Sublette's brother Andrew. The newlyweds accused Campbell of mismanaging William Sublette's will to his own financial advantage, the

57. Robert Campbell to Bill Sublette, May 5, 1843, ibid.

only recorded time anyone ever accused him of a shady deal. Campbell then must have greatly regretted his advice to Sublette to abandon the mountains for Hereford.

Of course, only a fraction of Campbell's time was spent acting as love adviser and supplier to Sublette. In addition to managing his widespread business interests from his headquarters, debt collection was always an unpleasant but essential burden. In June, he had to "go up the Mississippi and visit some of our hard customers in that section of the country."[58]

He also helped equip John C. Fremont's expedition when the vainglorious "pathfinder" dumped wholesale merchandisers Peter Sarpy and Pierre Chouteau after a disagreement over the expedition's supplies and personnel:

> Mr. Sarpy did not wish him to take Fitzpatrick along, he wanted also to have the hiring of all the men and the purchasing and furnishing of every thing and that Fremont should have nothing to say in the matter. Fremont was greatly provoked with this movement of Sarpy and determined to give up the expedition rather than submit to such dictation, so, he came to me and I got for him the Groceries and furnished the dry goods and all that he required, he has hired his men and is equiping them at my store.[59]

Campbell would later comfort Jessie Fremont, who grew increasingly nervous as weeks and months passed with her husband absent. After tracing their probable route on a map, he reassured her, "They may have a tedious journey but I assure not a dangerous one." This calmed Fremont, who wrote to a friend, "If you knew Mr. Campbell you would feel as quiet as I do—for he is an honest man."[60]

Virginia, meanwhile, "left on friday last . . . she will remain some two or three weeks in Ohio and then proceed to Philadelphia where I hope to join her in July and if I can procure a House (in St. Louis) to suit me I think of commencing Housekeeping in the Fall . . . Since Virginia left I have returned to my old room and am now quietly settled at the store."[61] Later that summer, Campbell assuaged his loneliness when he joined his pregnant wife in Philadelphia to buy merchandise for the business and furniture for a future home, and to visit relatives. They returned in September to allow her to rest before the baby was due. On October 9,

58. Robert Campbell to William Sublette, May 17, 1843, ibid.
59. Robert Campbell to William Sublette, May 5, 1843, ibid.
60. Jessie Fremont to Adelaide Talbot, St. Louis, February 1, 1844, in Pamela Herr and Mary Lee Spence, eds., *The Letters of Jessie Benton Fremont*.
61. Robert Campbell to William Sublette, May 17, 1843, "Glimpses of the Past."

1843, he experienced some joy amidst the business depression when his second son, Hugh, was born.

The following month, Campbell was happy to learn that Sublette had returned safely to Sulphur Springs by November 2. The "excursion" had been a pale imitation of the "old days" at best, a disaster at worst, with ample doses of mirth, exaltation, drudgery, misery, and tragedy. In mid-May, about sixty-two men, half of them "gentlemen," had finally headed west across the plains. The supply carts frequently broke down or mired in the mud. Several men deserted when the pleasure trip proved to be too arduous. High up the Platte River, Stewart's companion, fifteen-year-old François Clement, accidentally shot himself in the chest, died a miserable death, and was buried in a shallow, unmarked grave. There were a half dozen Indian scares as horse raiders skulked periodically behind the caravan, but they were not attacked. Game was scarce, and food supplies dwindled. The summer was unseasonably cold and rainy. Hordes of mosquitos mercilessly assailed them. The various miseries caused tempers to flare, fights to break out. Stewart became "overbearing," and some "threatened to shoot him if he persisted in his tyrannical course." In South Pass, Stewart sent out riders to invite trappers and Indians to a rendezvous on the Piney Fork of the Green River. A mangy pack of mountain men and Indians from Fort Bridger and a band of Shoshone joined them the second week of August for several days of horse races and drunken orgies. On August 18, Stewart and Sublette turned their party east. A snow and ice storm walloped them on the Platte. For Sublette and Stewart, it had been a melancholy last trip west. The misadventure worsened rather than alleviated Sublette's tuberculosis and money problems.[62]

Sublette and Stewart did not tarry long at Sulphur Springs. Stewart headed down the Mississippi River to winter at New Orleans. There he got word that his elder brother had died without an heir. He promptly returned to Scotland to manage his estate. Sublette meanwhile determined to make one last try for elected office and submitted his name for nomination. Then in January he headed downriver to New Orleans to collect debts. Despite Campbell's encouragement, Sublette seemed determined to sidestep that yawning marriage with Frances.

As always, Campbell preferred to indulge in politics from behind the scenes. He remained active in promoting the hard-money position within the Democratic Party. He wrote Sublette that

62. Sunder, *Sublette*, quote, 211, account, 197–216.

politics are much as when you left—the Softs had a meeting on the 8th [January] and selected delegates to Jefferson city in opposition to the [hard] selection at Machester. Dr. Nutt, one of your colleagues was placed on their ticket—you were not. I saw Hudson a few evenings ago and he said that the two committees should Ballot to see which should go to Jeff city to the Convention—I told him no for they had Doc. Nutt on their committee who I understood was with the Softs and it would give them the advantage—I told him further that he knew the Soft Committee would not be allowed a seat in the Convention.[63]

He began canvassing potential supporters in St. Louis and elsewhere.

In early March, Campbell and Sublette were among seventy prominent Democrats who signed a petition calling on the St. Louis city government to throw a party honoring former president Andrew Jackson. The city rejected the petition. The signatories threw their own party on March 15 at a warehouse with a pig roast, a German band, and speeches by aspiring candidates. The convention broke up in a shouting match between hard- and soft-money advocates. The warehouse's owner, Colonel J. B. Brant, angrily ordered them all to leave his premises.

Why would hard-money Democrats want to honor Jackson, the destroyer of the Bank of the United States? Politics explain the seeming anomaly. Jackson's economic policies were a disaster for the United States and hurt hards and softs alike. But image in politics often overshadows reality. Jackson was a popular western hero. In honoring Jackson, the hards hoped to associate that image with themselves and thus to bring voters who worshiped him to support their own candidates. Also, economic policies aside, nearly all westerners shared a hard-line position against Mexico and Britain over territorial disputes in the West. The annexation of Texas was perhaps the most heated issue in the 1844 elections.

Amidst all this political commotion, Sublette finally tied the knot with Frances Hereford on March 21. The marriage would last little more than a year and was attended by some controversy—Hereford and Sublette's brother Solomon had courted throughout William's measly efforts. When William finally proposed, Frances reluctantly chose financial security over love.[64]

The split over financial policy plagued the Democratic Party's formal nominating convention, which opened on April 1. To the joy

63. Robert Campbell to William Sublette, January 19, 1844, "Glimpses of the Past."
64. Sunder, *Sublette*, 226.

of Campbell and Sublette, the hard-money faction's choice to run for governor, John C. Edwards, won the nomination, and wrote most of the party's platform. A week later, the softs organized their own convention and vowed to counter the hard candidates with candidates of their own. Campbell and Sublette helped organize a hard rally on April 20 at the Concert Hall.

While the partners helped the hards win a majority in the state party, they were disappointed by the decision made by the national party. At the Democratic Party convention in Baltimore in early June, soft-money candidate James K. Polk won the presidential nomination over Martin Van Buren, the choice of the hard-money faction. The Missouri Democratic Party largely unified behind their national candidate. In better news, Sublette ended up serving in public office after all when the party tapped him to serve as a presidential elector in the Seventh District.

Campbell did what he could to promote a hard-money, state trade surplus policy on the state bank's board of directors. He remained in the minority on the board: most of the board members spurned his advice, instead heeding the pressures applied by, and perhaps accepting the "donations" from, well-heeled speculators. He tried to finesse the central bank's loose money policy by encouraging branch president J. J. Lowry "to set an example which public opinion will compel the Mother Bank and Branches to follow . . . it is certainly better that Gold should be paid out to our citizens, than that it should be sent off to the eastern cities as has been done (on four different occasions) heretofore."[65]

At times, Campbell must have wondered who was more stubborn, the bank's board or his debtors. Many of those who had borrowed money from him were as ornery and balky as Missouri mules in repaying him. Yet he always remained civil no matter how exasperating the situation. Nonetheless, an iron determination underlay his good manners. His handling of a certain John Groom was typical. He firmly rejected Groom's attempt to settle a debt with a section of land. Campbell pointed out that the land was in a "poor location" that would "cost us money." He went on to insist that "your desire that we should not proceed to collect our debt would not benefit you . . . I think it will be better for both of us to have it close as soon as possible as the Judgements are increasing in amount by the interest accruing on them . . . if you are willing to make a respectable payment on our claim we are willing to wait a reasonable

65. Robert Campbell to J. J. Lowry, March 27, 1844, Campbell Papers, MLA.

length of time but if nothing is paid by you we must proceed . . . It is not our desire to injure you."[66]

As the November election neared, Campbell spent more of his time trying to influence politics. In mid-October, he was on the Resolutions Committee that helped to organize another Democratic Party rally at Brant's warehouse. When the votes were tallied, Democratic candidate James Polk won. Campbell was more enthusiastic about

> the welcome news of Benton's reelection and of Judge Atchinson—all Demo-crats here were rejoiced and the more so as it was accomplished without the aid of the Softs and with but two Whigs—I am glad to see the party lines drawn so closely—I wrote Benton by this morning's mail and Bowlin also . . . if the legislature wish to complete the ruin of the institutions they have but to Elect Softs . . . Previous to the Election two Years ago Collier told me that there must be Democrats and Bank Directors sent to the Legislature to appease the country members or we might lose the Bank charter and accordingly [Thomas] Hudson and Kennett were sent—the one came back Our Bank Attorney and the other the President—both joined the Softs and endeavoured to break down the Democratic party . . . I was much pleased to find that our community could thus at once drive out the Spurious circulation from amongst us, but those who expected to benefit by . . . money being kept in circulation opposed it.[67]

The new legislature reelected both Campbell and Sublette to the state bank's board of directors. But the most exciting and rewarding news he received that November was the birth of yet another son, Robert Jr.

Political campaigning spilled over into 1845. Sublette continued to lobby Missouri's elite to be named as the nominee for nearly any elected or appointed public office. He allowed his name to be submitted as a possible candidate for Indian superintendent. Campbell did what he could to promote his friend's candidacy. On May 22, Campbell and a committee of seventy-five leading St. Louis citizens signed and sent a petition to President Polk requesting that he appoint Sublette as super-intendent. Polk ignored the petition.

Campbell talked Sublette into joining him on that summer's buying trip back east. Perhaps they could lobby the president and congressmen for a job for Sublette when they reached Washington. Before leaving, Campbell moved his family into his first house, at the corner of Elm and Fifth Street. He had little time to savor his latest triumph.

66. Robert Campbell to John Groom, June 19, 1844, ibid.
67. Robert Campbell to William Sublette, November 24, 1844, ibid.

That year's buying trip east was the most involved yet. Campbell carried with him three thousand dollars for purchases of merchandise and possibly securities and stocks. He was accompanied by William and Frances Sublette, her sister Mary, and a slave. On July 14, they embarked on the *Swiftsure, No. 3* for Cincinnati. On July 16, the party stayed overnight in Cincinnati while Campbell visited his cousin, Robert Buchanan. The following day, they boarded the *Uncle Ben.* Although Sublette seemed healthy enough when their voyage started, he became gravely sick. On July 22, he drew up a will in which he named Campbell and his brother Andrew as his estate's executors. They disembarked at Pittsburgh and settled into the Exchange Hotel. Dr. William Addison attended Sublette but could do nothing. Campbell's best friend of nearly two decades died on July 23, 1845.[68]

The following day, Campbell purchased a lead-lined coffin for Sublette and placed it, along with Frances, Mary, and the slave, aboard a steamboat. After seeing them off, a grief-stricken Campbell then continued on east. He undoubtedly assumed Sublette would have approved his choice of putting business before sentiment.[69]

68. Sunder, *Sublette*, 228–30.
69. Robert Campbell to Robert Buchannan, July 24, 1845, "Glimpses of the Past."

*A pastel portrait, probably created from a photograph, of Robert Campbell during his mature years. All known images of him are in similar poses. Campbell House Foundation, Inc., St. Louis.*

*Aghalane, built in 1786, the birthplace of Robert Campbell, was located in Plumbridge, County Tyrone, Ireland. This typical stone country house has been moved from its original location to the Ulster-American Folk Park, Camphill, Omagh, County Tyrone, and has been restored to its eighteenth-century appearance. Campbell House Foundation, Inc., St. Louis.*

*Robert Campbell's house in St. Louis, now the Campbell House Museum. Campbell House Foundation, Inc., St. Louis.*

*Oil portrait of Virginia Jane Kyle Campbell, by an unknown artist, dates from approximately 1882. Virginia Campbell is seen in what is assumed to be a posthumous portrait against the background of her drawing room as it appeared in the later years of her life. Campbell House Foundation, Inc., St. Louis.*

*An 1895 oil portrait of James Alexander Campbell (1860–1890), Robert Campbell's son, by Jules LeFebvre. This likeness, by a leading French portraitist, shows James with his pet dogs at the time of his unexpected death in Paris in 1890. Campbell House Foundation, Inc., St. Louis.*

*Photograph, circa 1890, of Hugh Campbell (1847–1931), son of Robert and Virginia Campbell, who kept the family household together following the death of his parents. St. Louis Mercantile Library.*

*Campbell family burial plot, Bellefontaine Cemetery. Individual graves are not marked; the central stone obelisk records the birth and death dates of Robert, Virginia, and their children. Campbell House Foundation, Inc., St. Louis.*

158

*Oil portrait of Hugh Campbell (1797–1879), Robert Campbell's older brother and lifelong mentor and confidant, by Samuel Bell Waugh, 1848. Campbell House Foundation, Inc., St. Louis.*

*Oil portrait of Mary Kyle Campbell (1810–1901) by Samuel Bell Waugh, 1848. Mary was not only Virginia Campbell's sister-in-law but also her cousin. It was at Hugh's and Mary's Philadelphia home that Robert and Virginia first met in 1835. Campbell House Foundation, Inc., St. Louis.*

BELLVUE.
Mr DOUGHERTY'S AGENCY

*Artist Karl Bodmer's illustrations document the travels of Prince Maximilian of Wied-Neuwiess in the American West between 1832 and 1834. Campbell had the opportunity to meet the Prince and Bodmer during their travels and even entertained them in October of 1833. Campbell wrote in his personal journal on October 30 concerning the prince: "Baron Brandsburgh [Prince Maximilian] started in a Mackinaw Boat and halted at our landing to bid me goodbye. I gave him a letter of introduction to Mr. Dougherty at the Gros Vents as he intends passing the winter there. He is remarkable agreeable and I much regret his leaving." This illustration by Bodmer shows one of the small trading posts on the Missouri River that was operated under the direction of John Dougherty, an agent of Sublette and Campbell. Joslyn Art Museum, Omaha, Nebraska.*

# Chapter 6

# Wealth, Power, and Tragedy (1846–1859)

The year 1846 was a turning point for Robert Campbell and the nation.[1] Campbell's character, business acumen, and connections would be rewarded with two public trusts, one of which would prove to be especially lucrative. Also that year, after nearly two decades of struggle, his business finally took off; it would amass ever greater wealth thereafter. However, unlike so many others, Campbell's sense of morality forbade him from simply accumulating more money for the money's sake alone. Rather than hoard his wealth, he devoted much to charity and public works. That year he headed the St. Louis Hibernian Benevolent Society's finance committee, which, among other things, distributed money to the needy and helped organize a Grand Ball whose proceeds were sent as relief for the poor in Ireland.

Yet all of Campbell's business and charitable accomplishments that year were overshadowed by two events in the West: the nation's acquisition of the Oregon Territory from Britain and of the Southwest from Mexico. By year's end, America's western frontier stretched all the way to the Pacific Ocean. The United States won their new territory from Britain through diplomacy and from Mexico through war, codified by treaty in 1848. Campbell would contribute his talents to the Mexican War and reap some of its fruits. Those victories would give him and other enterprising men vast new realms from which to extract wealth. The national leap to the Pacific represented a much more assertive stance in American foreign policy.[2]

---

1. Bernard Devoto, *The Year of Decision: 1846.*
2. Norman A. Graebner, *Empire on the Pacific: A Study in Continental Expansion;* David Pletcher, *The Diplomacy of Annexation: Texas, Mexico, and the Mexican War;* Robert W. Johannsen, *To the Halls of Montezuma: The War with Mexico in the American Imagination.*

Shortly after fighting broke out between American and Mexican troops in disputed territory near the Rio Grande River on April 23, President James Polk asked Congress for a war declaration. Congress declared war on May 11, 1846. The Polk administration had decided on a strategy it hoped would decisively win the war. General Zachary Taylor's army in Texas would march deep into Mexico to capture Monterrey, while another army under Stephen Watts Kearny at Fort Leavenworth would march west along the Santa Fe Trail to capture first New Mexico and then California. Each state would raise its own volunteer regiments and send them to bolster the regular forces under Taylor and Kearny.

As the Santa Fe Trail's terminus, Missouri would make a vital contribution to Kearny's campaign, and Campbell would play an important role in organizing St. Louis for war. Governor John C. Edwards named him inspector general and a colonel in the state militia. On May 24, 1846, Campbell received from Missouri Militia Adjutant General G. A. Parsons orders to "raise forthwith, in the county and city of St. Louis, four hundred volunteers of mounted men. You will receive no man who is in years apparently over forty-five or under eighteen, or who is not in physical strength and vigor; nor the horse of any volunteer not apparently sound and effective, with the necessary horse and furniture equipments . . . These volunteers are destined for the frontier, and they will immediately proceed with all possible dispatch to Fort Leavenworth."[3]

Campbell served those duties with the same organization, energy, intelligence, and civility that he displayed in business. Within a week he had recruited four hundred Laclede Rangers and a hundred-man artillery company. On May 30, Colonel Campbell reviewed his troops in Lucas Park. That evening he hosted a banquet for his officers at the Planter's Hotel. He then sent his troops to Jefferson Barracks just south of St. Louis, where they awaited transportation up the Missouri River. As always, Campbell was modest over his accomplishment, attributing it to the volunteers "who so promptly responded to the Call."[4]

Throughout late May and June, steamboats conveyed troops and supplies up the Missouri to Westport. From there the troops marched west along the Santa Fe Trail. Kearny's 1,600-man army included his 300

3. G. A. Parsons to Robert Campbell, May 24, 1846, Campbell House.

4. Robert Campbell to Terry, June 15, 1846, Campbell Papers, MLA; see also Campbell to Edwards, May 14, 1846, Campbell to Edwards, May 16, 1846, Campbell to Edwards, May 18, 1846, Campbell to Edwards, May 19, 1848, Campbell to Edwards, May 21, 1846, Campbell to Parsons, May 26, 1846, Campbell to Young, June 8, 1846, Campbell to Parsons, June 10, 1846, ibid.

regular dragoons, the 860 Missouri volunteers, the artillery's 250 troops, and 190 teamsters. Tom Fitzpatrick was appointed to guide Kearny's Army of the West to Santa Fe and beyond. On August 18, the army marched into Santa Fe without firing a shot. A courier was sent galloping back along the trail with the word that New Mexico was now American! Campbell and other merchants were thrilled by their feat, as well as by the lower business costs that would follow the elimination of Mexican tariffs and corruption.

Having organized and dispatched the troops, Campbell reoccupied himself with family and business. He had more than patriotism to celebrate during that year's Independence Day—his first daughter, Lucy Ann, was born on July 4. Two days later he would receive an unexpected gift—a champion to back against the American Fur Company.

Although beaver had played out, money could still be wrung from the West through buffalo robes. Yet Campbell had hesitated to commit himself too deeply to the trade, largely because of the American Fur Company's monopoly up the Missouri and across the northern Rockies. Another obstacle was the fluctuating supply and demand for the robes: "Buffalo Robes are Commanding a good price this season but that will have no effect on next year's prices and it will not be safe therefore to make any Calculation on more than a moderate price. Beaver is very low and not likely to do better."[5]

Then, seemingly out of nowhere, a new firm arose to challenge the American Fur Company. On July 6, 1846, former American Fur Company employees Alexander Harvey, Charles Primeau, Anthony R. Bouis, and Joseph Picotte received a license to erect trading posts by the Bad River near Fort Pierre for the Sioux trade and the Marias River near Fort Benton for the Blackfeet trade. With his finances in order, Campbell could throw his full support behind Harvey, Primeau, and Company, also known as the St. Louis Fur or Union Fur Company. He equipped them with fifty thousand dollars' worth of trade goods, chartered the steamboat *Clermont No. 2* to carry them up the Missouri, and promised to market the robes brought downriver on the return trip.[6]

Why had the opposition arisen, and just what kind of characters was Campbell backing? Harvey was the company's firebrand, a feared frontier bully and murderer.[7] His temper was as vile as his body was

5. Robert Campbell to Harry Preuion and Co., n.d. 1846, ibid.
6. Sunder, *Fur Trade*, 93.
7. See Hedren, ed., *Narrative of Larpenteur*, 142–46, 188–90, 194–96.

immense, powerful, and tireless. For eight years Harvey traded for the American Fur Company up and down the Missouri. In 1839 Chouteau fired him following complaints from other employees over his violent outbursts. In the middle of winter, Harvey trudged from Fort McKenzie to St. Louis to plead his case in person to Chouteau. Amazed at Harvey's endurance, Chouteau set aside his misgivings and rehired him. Upriver again, Harvey caught and savagely beat one by one the half dozen men who had dared speak against him, and killed one Isadore Sandoval who resisted. Then, in January 1844 at Fort McKenzie, he murdered a Blackfeet who had stolen a cow. When the Piegan Blackfeet killed a trader in retaliation, Harvey and Francis Chardon, the fort's bourgeois, plotted vengeance. In February when the Piegan came in to trade, the two men opened fire with rifles and a cannon, killing three and wounding two. They succeeded in driving off the Blackfeet and their business. When the American Fur Company's Alexander Culbertson arrived with a supply keelboat in August, a confrontation arose with Harvey. Culbertson ordered his men to beat Harvey, then paid him off and fired him.

Harvey once again swore revenge, this time against the entire American Fur Company. He appeared before St. Louis Indian Superintendent Thomas Harvey (no relation) and accused the American Fur Company of a wholesale violation of the liquor law. Other opposition leaders filed their own complaints. The superintendent opened an investigation. Chouteau fired François Chardon as a sacrificial lamb, but the investigation continued. Agent Andrew Drips was fired for not reporting the liquor violations. On June 5, 1846, District Attorney Thomas Gantt filed charges against Pierre Chouteau, Jr., and Company in the United States Circuit Court of the District of Missouri for carrying forty-three hundred gallons of alcohol worth twenty-five thousand dollars into Indian territory and distributing it in violation of the Indian Intercourse Law of 1834. Four American Fur Company bourgeoises, Chardon, Culbertson, James Kipp, and Honore Picotte, were charged with distributing the alcohol. These charges were the greatest challenge the American Fur Company had ever faced on the Missouri. In the end, the charges were dropped.

Meanwhile, upon being supplied by Campbell, Harvey led his partners and forty-six men upriver aboard the *Clermont No. 2*. Men and goods were deposited at Medicine Creek, and Fort Bouis (Fort Defiance) was built. Harvey continued upriver with the rest of his men and landed just below Fort Union, not far from the ruins of Robert's Fort William. The *Clermont No. 2* then steamed downriver, reaching St. Louis on September 20. Harvey set his men to work constructing mackinaws and rebuilding the old fort. He then split his command into thirds. One stayed at the rebuilt fort to compete with Fort Union for the Assiniboine trade. He sent the other party up the Yellowstone into the Crow country to garner their furs. He ascended the Missouri with another party until they arrived above the Marias River. There he set his men to work constructing Fort Robert Campbell, from which he hoped to wrest the Blackfeet trade away from Fort McKenzie downstream. He would spend most of his life's remainder at the fort until his death in 1854.

Chouteau met this threat by deploying a new, shallow draft steamboat, the *Martha*, captained by the Missouri River's most experienced pilot, Joseph La Barge. He also ordered his bourgeois to slash trade good prices below anything the opposition offered to the Indians. Finally, he sent a party up the Missouri to build Fort Clay (Benton) just below Fort Robert Campbell and compete directly for the Blackfeet trade.

For the next half dozen years, relations with the upper Missouri tribes remained stable, enabling Campbell's robe business to prosper. For years leading up to 1846, however, tensions had worsened with the central plains tribes. Over the decades, the parade of trappers, traders, and immigrants along the Santa Fe and Platte river trails had decimated or scared away the buffalo and inadvertently infected those tribes with diseases such as cholera and smallpox. Although warriors from all the tribes had run off horses or picked off stray whites, no general war had yet broken out. The passage of Kearny's Army of the West during the summer of 1846 had certainly intimidated those Indians who had witnessed or heard of it.

For years Campbell and others had lobbied Washington to create an Indian agency for the region to ease tensions and distribute annuities. On August 3, 1846, the U.S. Senate finally acted when it created the Indian Agency for the Upper Arkansas and Platte region and named Tom Fitzpatrick to head it. Fitzpatrick was then guiding Kearny's Army of the West toward Santa Fe. The War Department sent his commission to his old friend and business associate Robert Campbell to forward to him. The news elated Campbell. After forwarding the commission to Fitzpatrick at Santa Fe, he wrote the commissioner of Indian Affairs that "I can speak myself from an acquaintance with him of twenty years duration, and a better [man] could not be found for the situation."[8]

8. Robert Campbell to Indian Commissioner, September 12, 1846, Office of Indian Affairs, Letters Received, Upper Platte, c-2579/1846.

Where was Fitzpatrick? After occupying Santa Fe, Kearny, Fitz-patrick, and the dragoons headed for California by the Gila River route. On October 6, they encountered Kit Carson and eight others bringing word from Fremont in California that the province was in American hands. Kearny sent Fitzpatrick to carry that message to Washington while he pressed on to California. Fitzpatrick reached St. Louis in mid-November for a brief joyful reunion with Campbell before hurrying on to the nation's capital to accept the commission, which formally began on December 1, 1846. Having an old companion like Fitzpatrick as Indian agent meant not only a greater chance for peace on the plains but also a favorable outlook for Campbell's business ventures as well.

That December, Campbell received the year's second and far more lucrative honor when he was elected president of the State Bank of Missouri. As president, he received an annual salary of three thousand dollars and presided over a small staff. When he became president, the St. Louis–based bank had five branches—Fayette, Lexington, Jackson, Palmyra, and Springfield.[9] Campbell's position was lucrative not for his modest salary, but for the inside information it provided on business conditions in Missouri and the Midwest.

No president of the State Bank of Missouri exceeded Campbell in his management skills. During his first two years in office, he increased the bank's deposits from $980,000 in 1846 to $1,359,000 in 1848. Profits in 1848 ranged from 13 1/2 percent at the St. Louis headquarters directly under his control to 8 1/2 percent at the Springfield branch. The bank's circulation was below the official policy of two dollars out for every one dollar deposited. Its stock was selling at or slightly above par. The St. Louis headquarters had annual expenses of only $15,000, a sliver of its business—$1,978,000 in loans, $504,000 in exchange, $1,141,000 in deposits, and $1,450,000 in circulation.[10]

Campbell managed both markets and people with gentle but firm hands. A letter to Fayette branch president J. J. Lowry nicely captures his management style:

> Several months ago we found a great demand for our Bank Notes and a very small suppply on hand . . . and to meet the demand the Board ordered an issue of $100,000 of 50s and 100s and that so soon as that amount . . . was taken in they should be cancelled . . . This I am sorry to say will not reduce our regular Circulation which I believe to be too large both of the Bank and

9. Cable, *Bank of Missouri*, 207.
10. Ibid., 207, 213–14.

branches. We bought from the East $300,000 in American gold and from new Orleans some $150,000 in silver since April last . . . The Parent Bank will at all times be ready and pleased to redeem in Coin any balance of our notes that we may hold over what we have of your branch . . . Would it not be well for you to fortify your Branch with coin as we have done?[11]

The suggestion, of course, was a polite order.

Meanwhile, he kept a sharp eye and ear out for news of Harvey's campaign on the upper Missouri. The fruits of those efforts arrived in late spring 1847 after Harvey had the robes from his four posts sent downstream by mackinaw. Steam packets picked up the robes near St. Joseph and carried them down to St. Louis. The winter's trading was successful, with 515 packs of robes and 7 packs of furs deposited in Robert's warehouse. Yet, impressive as the opposition's take seemed, it was but a fraction brought down by the American Fur Company. The packet tributary arrived on June 21 with 750 packs of robes and 54 packs of furs from Fort Pierre alone. The *Martha* reached St. Louis on July 8 with 1,500 packs of robes, 280 of furs, 96 sacks of buffalo tongues, and a menagerie of wild animals for circuses and zoos. Hundreds of packs from American Fur Company posts reached St. Louis that summer aboard other mackinaws and packets.[12]

In 1847, two family sorrows marred any glee Campbell may have felt in eating away at the American Fur Company empire. With Virginia again pregnant, the Campbells looked forward to their fifth child. Then, on July 2, 1847, tragedy again struck when their son Robert died of unknown causes. In August, still mourning Robert's death, the family headed east to visit. The baby, Lucy Ann, who had suffered from measles and teething, died on September 1, 1847, at Germantown, Pennsyvlania. Burdened down with the deaths of two beloved children, Robert and Virginia returned to St. Louis that autumn. On November 15, 1847, Virginia gave birth to Hugh. They must have wondered how long they would hold on to him.

Before leaving for his 1847 summer trip east, Campbell had invested some of the profits from the first year's return into the steamer *Lake of the Woods* and promptly sent it up the Missouri with fifty to sixty men, a keelboat in tow, and fifty thousand dollars' worth of trade goods for the various Harvey and Primeau Company posts. The keelboat would be the company's lifesaver. On August 17, the *Lake of the Woods* struck

11. Robert Campbell to J. J. Lowry, September 23, 1847, Campbell Papers, MLA.
12. Sunder, *Fur Trade*, 97–104.

a snag near the Cheyenne River. Two steam pipes burst as the pilot fired the engine to get his boat off the snag. A fire broke out. Most passengers plunged into the Missouri to escape as the fire neared the gunpowder stores. The few who remained aboard, including Harvey, who had boarded at Fort Bouis, succeeded in dousing the blaze. The boat was too damaged to continue. Harvey ordered the goods transferred to the keelboat and accompanied it upriver. With some makeshift repairs, the *Lake of the Woods* successfully made it back to St. Louis by September 5. The keelboat reached Fort Robert Campbell in late November, just in time for the winter trade.[13]

After depositing his men and goods, Harvey struck off on foot with three other men down the Missouri. It was a hellish trip. Snow drifts slowed their trudge to a crawl. Assiniboine robbed them on the Yellowstone. They sheltered first at the Mandan and later Sioux villages. Once they stumbled on for five days without food. Mormons encamped at Council Bluffs succoured them. At Liberty, Missouri, they took a packet down to St. Louis, arriving in March 1848.

About the same time that Harvey stumbled into Campbell's store with news of their venture, word reached St. Louis that the Mexican War had ended. Under the Treaty of Guadalupe Hidalgo signed on February 2, 1848, Mexico ceded to the United States all of California, Arizona, and New Mexico above the Gila River, and Texas above the Rio Grande, in return for $15 million and Washington's assumption of all debts owed by Mexicans to Americans. Those territorial gains would eventually enrich the nation as well as Campbell.

He had little time to celebrate, let alone to ponder the business opportunities latent in the extension of America's empire to the Pacific. Throughout early 1848, he helped plan, organize, finance, and equip that year's trading campaign of Harvey, Primeau, and Company. Robert and another merchant, James Yeatman, acted as guarantors for the renewal of Harvey's trade license. On June 1, Harvey headed up the Missouri aboard the steamboat *Bertrand*. Along the way the *Bertrand* pulled ashore to drop off supplies and pick up robes. Fifty miles above the Yellowstone, it could go no farther. Harvey transferred his supplies and new recruits to a keelboat and pushed upstream to Fort Robert Campbell. Meanwhile, the heavily laden *Bertrand* turned downstream, reaching St. Louis on July 24.

Politics complicated the trading operations of both companies that summer. Indian agent Gideon Matlock ascended the Missouri aboard

13. Ibid., 100.

the American Fur Company's *Martha* to investigate charges by Yankton Sioux Chief Smutty Bear against both the American Fur Company and Harvey, Primeau, and Company that they had encouraged Indians to disrupt their respective rivals by stealing their horses and goods, and even killing their traders. Smutty Bear also complained that the American Fur Company was selling not only liquor to the Indians but also the government annuities that it had contracted to freely distribute. He asked that new, honest traders replace the corrupt ones in their midst. Finding evidence against both companies, Matlock revoked their trading licenses with the Yankton in late June. Rather than confront Matlock, both companies quickly removed the most notorious traders from their Missouri River posts. Ascending the river again in September, Matlock expressed his guarded satisfaction that the companies had cleaned up the worst abuses. Both companies brought down huge loads of robes that year. In the fall, Campbell and Primeau rejected Chouteau's offer to merge their companies.[14]

As if his diverse business, banking, civic, and family duties were not challenging enough, Campbell received a problem from a surprising quarter—William Sublette's will. Sublette had named Campbell one of his will's executors. On September 15, 1845, the will was officially recorded, and two weeks later his estate was appraised for about seventy-five hundred dollars. Campbell tried settling the estate when he returned that fall, but Sublette had left behind so many debts and disputed assets that the task would not be completed until 1857. Campbell tried to help Frances Sublette manage Sulphur Springs, but she resented his interference. For a while she lived in Independence, and there she ran into William Sublette's brother, Solomon. Solomon had courted her before his older brother had shown any interest, but retreated once his wealthy and famous brother took the field. It had been rumored that she continued to love Solomon but married William for his money. With William now three years dead, Frances and Solomon married on April 28, 1848.

Although the marriage raised eyebrows along with the old questions, that in itself was not the problem. On May 28, Solomon asked his attorney, Micah Tarver, to investigate whether Campbell had honestly executed his brother's will: "I want [you] to examine minutely into Mr. Robert Campbell's administration of the estate of William Sublette and if you should find any deficiency at all you will enforce the law to the full extent

14. Robert Campbell to William Medill, February 9, 1849, Campbell Papers, MLA.

in my name which I have informed him that you will do as my attorney."[15] Solomon especially wanted to account for Campbell's "large presents to his wife during the term of agreement previous to his wedding and no person knows where he got the money to make those presents." Solomon then asked his lawyer to inform Campbell that he would call off his investigation "If Mr. Campbell should be willing to take all of the estates and debts of the firm of Sublette and Campbell and let me and Andrew off."

Campbell rejected the blackmail offer and instead upped the ante. He told Tarver that "he will proceed to close your deed of trust immediately after the falling due of the next payment of interest in October, unless the debt is paid."[16] With this dispute burning behind him, Campbell headed east on his annual buying expedition. The attack on his good name and the shabby treatment of his old friend's estate must have deeply rankled him. The dispute would be resolved the following year just as unexpectedly as it had arisen.

Power, wielded wisely, begets yet more power. As Campbell's wealth and influence expanded, he attracted more of the same. For example, in September 1848, Captain Charles F. Ruff, the commanding officer at Fort Kearny, asked him to appoint a sutler at Fort Chiles. Campbell used the opportunity to put his old friend John Dougherty in the position. In his letter to Dougherty, he explained the advantages for them both:

> a person having the appointment of Sutler for the fort at Grand Island (Ft. Chiles) and the other posts to be established at Ft. Laramie could conduct business to great advantage and might add to the sutler business a large Indian trade, and by Indian trade I mean the keeping of a good stock of Indian goods at the forts to be sold to traders large and small in such quantities as they would be able to pay for and thus having the goods in the country . . . and after trading them for robes could . . . get for them a new supply.[17]

And Campbell, of course, would sell Dougherty the goods on credit and accept payment in hides. Dougherty accepted the offer. Within a year, he had become the sutler at Fort Laramie as well. Campbell's empire reached again across the plains.

Among the momentous decisions Campbell made in 1848 was to find someone to succeed his irreplaceable partner and friend, William Sublette. William Campbell, his nephew, eased some of the incredible

15. Solomon Sublette to Micah Tarver, May 28, 1848, Sublette Collection, MoHiS.
16. Micah Tarver to Solomon Sublette, July 7, 1848, ibid.
17. Robert Campbell to John Dougherty, September 16, 1848, 1848 Letterbook, Campbell Collection, MLA.

strain of running the burgeoning financial and mercantile empire. They made an excellent team, with William carrying out many of Campbell's plans and negotiations and helping him gather business intelligence. The firm of R. and W. Campbell would succeed beyond the dreams of Sublette and Campbell.

Campbell always carefully studied a potential investment before committing himself. He did not confine his information to those immediately involved, but also amassed as many official reports as possible. In the late 1840s, he mulled investment opportunities in the just-conquered Southwest. Among his papers were congressional testimonies on the Mexican War, along with reports on various western Indian tribes and the "Civilized tribes" of Oklahoma, and diagrams of machinery, inventions, factories, and railroads.

Railroads were his investment choice in 1848. Campbell was among hundreds who eventually invested a total of $10 million in the newly chartered Pacific Railroad Company. The directors promised to lay tracks not only from St. Louis to Jefferson City but also beyond—all the way to the Pacific Ocean! It was a grandiose plan, but one that was essential for Missouri's prosperity. With the acquisition of the Oregon Territory and the Southwest, a transcontinental railroad was inevitable. Enormous revenues would accrue to any state straddling that route. The Pacific Railroad Company promised to bring the wealth to Missouri.

Despite this vision, Campbell, like most other investors, must have been quite uneasy handing over his money to the Pacific Railroad Company. After all, Missouri had already granted charters to several dozen other railroad companies; most had quickly gone belly-up and none had laid a mile of track within the state. Campbell's investments would eventually pay off; although the Pacific Railroad never traversed the continent, it did lay several profitable tracks across Missouri.

By late 1851, the Pacific Railroad extended only from St. Louis to Cheltenham five miles to the west; by 1856, 125 miles of track linked St. Louis and Jefferson City. Campbell's long-term investment seemed sound. It was not private enterprise, however, but rather massive federal, state, county, and city aid, that made the construction possible. On February 22, 1851, Missouri's legislature approved and the governor signed into law the "Act to Expedite the Construction of the Pacific Railroad, and of the Hannibal and St. Joseph Railroad." The act pledged the state to match in bonds the respective amounts the railroad companies raised from private investors. Missouri's backing caused previously hesitant investors to pour money into the two companies. Only then was enough capital pooled to complete the railroads. The state initially loaned the Pacific Railroad $2 million and the Hannibal and St. Joseph $1.5 million in bonds. Millions of dollars more in state subsidies to those railroads would follow. Had Missouri's legislature not acted, both railroad companies would have failed like dozens of others.

Missouri was simply following the path that other states and the federal government had already taken. Railroad construction expenditures were too onerous for private investors alone to carry. Across the country, railroads succeeded only when public and private investments worked in tandem. In 1852, Congress allocated to Missouri as it did to other states alternative square miles or sections of public lands in a checkerboard pattern six miles on either side of the proposed railroads. St. Louis County and City chipped in another $1 million for the Pacific Railroad. With such massive federal, state, county, and city investments, the Pacific Railroad could not help but succeed. Even so, progress was slow. It would not be until 1865 that the Pacific Railroad's main line linked St. Louis with Kansas City, a mere 283 miles to the west. The Pacific Railroad's Southwest Branch also crept along; by 1860 it had extended only to Rolla, 113 miles from St. Louis. The cost for both branches would eventually soar past $10 million, of which taxpayers underwrote 90 percent.[18]

All that, of course, lay ahead. Campbell spent much of January 1849 politicking in Jefferson City for reappointment to the bank presidency. Politics disgusted him. In letters to his wife, he railed against "unprincipled politicians who resort to every means to accomplish their ends." Somewhat ironically, he said of a rival legislator, "I would rather have him against me than for me as he has no influence nor standing here that could do me injury."[19] He judged the reappointment a toss-up—"my friends think favorably of my prospects and no doubt my opponents feel equally sanguine of their success—I neither hope nor fear, but wish most anxiously to have it determined."

Not only did the political machinations upset him, but he was terribly homesick as well. He cared "little about what the [election] results may be compared to getting off from here as I am heartily tired of being away from home." He worried over a possible cholera epidemic and asked Virginia to get "some of the young men at the store or Jefferson's camp . . .

18. Paul W. Gates, "The Railroads of Missouri, 1850–1870."
19. Robert Campbell to Virginia Campbell, January 6, 1849, January 10, Campbell House.

to clean out the backhouse which . . . will render it less offensive." In all, "I am most anxious to get home to you and the children who occupy my thoughts much more than the election . . . I often think of little Hugh's sweet song in the morning when he wakes and I would give a great deal to have him here or to be with him and you."

Yet he managed to have some fun hobnobbing with friends. One night he dined at Judge Morrow's. He attended "a grand procession and oration" that celebrated the Battle of New Orleans anniversary. Rented rooms were scarce in Jefferson City. He crammed into a boardinghouse room with a representative, Colonel Ballow and "a very gentlemanly man—Dr. Forbes"; he had to share a bed with the latter. As always, he was gracious and appreciative of others: "I owe much to many kind friends for the interest they have taken in my behalf and whatever may be the result of the election it has afforded me the satisfaction of knowing that I have many kind friends whose high regard I do appreciate."

When the votes were tallied, Campbell had lost. A majority had voted against him because his management had been too "hard." The legislators responded to their constituents, who complained that the State Bank of Missouri was too stingy with its money, thus starving many a promising business of desperately needed finances. Those legislators who favored a "soft" credit and circulation policy voted for J. M. Hughes.

Disappointing as the loss of the bank presidency was, Campbell had all the more time now to devote to his business. New business opportunities arose unexpectedly when word arrived from California of the gold strike at Sutter's Mill. Blinded by visions of striking it rich, thousands of men were funneling through St. Louis on the way west along the California Trail. Those aspirants demanded supplies, which Campbell and other merchants sold at premium prices.

St. Louis was an increasingly dynamic place in which to make money. Three interrelated phenomena—more people, better transportation, and the strategic location—accounted for the economic expansion. The city now extended eighteen blocks west of the river before it disappeared into farmland. During the 1840s, its population had quadrupled from 16,469 to 77,860. German immigrants accounted for most of the increase. By 1850, 22,534 or slightly less than one of every three people in St. Louis had been born in Germany. Other foreign tongues could be heard as well. Survivors of failed revolutions against despots across Europe during the 1840s had come to America's shores; a portion of them found their way to St. Louis. From the perspective of Campbell and other merchants, the cacophony of languages among the city's swelling population mattered

little compared to their buying power and demand for goods and services. A parade of 2,897 steamboats in 1850 alone carried people and
products to and from St. Louis. That same year St. Louis was third in
the nation for steamboat registrations with 24,995 tons, compared with
Cincinnati's 16,906 tons and Louisville's 14,820 tons. All those people
and steamboats came to St. Louis because it was located in the nation's
heart, astride the north-south Mississippi River corridor, near the east-
west Missouri and Ohio River corridors, and near the starting point for
emigrants heading west on the Santa Fe, California, Mormon, or Oregon
Trails. The Mississippi served St. Louis in a more subtle way—the drop
in the river's depth by several feet above the city required transship-
ments between lighter upstream steamboats and heavier downstream
steamboats, which added yet more wealth and jobs.[20]

That explosive growth had a dark side. In their frenzy to make
money, the city's politicians and merchants had neglected investment in
such essential services as sewage disposal, water, garbage collection, fire
fighting, and hospitals. The arrival of immigrants into already crammed,
humid, filth-strewn streets, boardinghouses, and vacant lots ripened
St. Louis for disaster.

Not one but two tragedies ravaged St. Louis in 1849. A cholera
epidemic broke out in May and eventually killed 8,423 people that year
alone; subsequent outbreaks killed 883 in 1850 and 845 in 1851. About
one of every three victims was a child five years or older.[21]

Death again haunted the Campbell family. Among the cholera victims was their firstborn child, James Alexander, who died on June 18,
1849; he was just seven years old. His younger brother Hugh became
sick but survived. To his friend and business associate John Dougherty,
Campbell revealed that the sorrow "has caused us to be longer silent
than usual. The writer lost his oldest son in a few hours illness and
[the] remaining child is on the very verge of the grave from which we
hope . . . [he] is now recovering—everybody about the store has been
sick." Apparently, Campbell was so grief-stricken that he had to describe
himself in the third person.[22]

20. Edwin C. McReynolds, *Missouri: A History of the Crossroads State;* Wyatt Winton
Belcher, *The Economic Rivalry between St. Louis and Chicago, 1850–1880,* 47, 41–42, 1–25,
26–31.
21. John W. Reps, *Saint Louis Illustrated: Nineteenth-Century Engravings and Lithographs
of a Mississippi River Metropolis,* 64; Primm, *Lion of the Valley,* 163.
22. Robert Campbell to John Dougherty, July 21, 1849, 1849 Letterbook, MLA. For
a goulish description of what life was like during the epidemic, see Elizabeth Russell,

Amidst this calamity, a devastating fire broke out on May 17 aboard the steamboat *White Cloud*, which was tied up at the wharf. The fire spread down the row of twenty-three other steamboats and then jumped Front Street to engulf warehouses, businesses, and homes all along the river and for two blocks west. When the fire finally burned out, it had caused damage costing $6.1 million. Among those businesses burned to the ground was Campbell's store.[23]

New opportunities blossomed from the ruins. The fire wiped out the cramped, fetid old quarter and allowed architects to transform St. Louis into a modern city: "The narrow streets were widened, and the houses that have arisen on those ashes are now business palaces, built in continuous blocks of stone, brick, and iron . . . The narrow streets, the inconvenient houses, have given way to rows of four and five story stores, equal to the business purposes of those of any city in the land."[24]

More important, the City Council appropriated $50,000 for the first lines of a sewage system. By 1855, St. Louis had invested $525,000 in thirty-one sewers that drained the city's central four hundred acres. Yet, these efforts were not enough. While the rebuilding and the sewers alleviated some problems, others still festered. The first three streets running parallel to the river were surfaced with blocks of limestone, but the streets farther west were covered with soft limestone, which the traffic crumbled into either choking dust or calf-deep mud, depending on the weather. Worst of all, the problems of disease-laden drinking water and inadequate sewage remained unsolved. Epidemics would rise suddenly and persistently to kill for decades to come. The epidemics would claim more Campbell children.[25]

Although devastated by his son's death and the store's destruction, Campbell had no choice but to struggle on—he had a beloved wife and one small child to nurture. Fortunately, his business was fully insured. The settlement enabled him to pay off the last remaining debts of Sublette and Campbell. He sold off his lot and moved his operation into a larger building down the street. The same insurance award enabled Solomon Sublette to pay off his debt to Campbell. Frances Sublette admitted that the "fire was of benefit to us in the way we had not realized . . . The ground was sold at action yesterday for $440 per foot . . . and ran into

---

ed., *Persimmon Hill: A Narrative of Old St. Louis and the Far West by William Clark Kennerly*, 225–26.
  23. Primm, *Lion of the Valley*, 174.
  24. John Hogan, quoted in Reps, *Saint Louis Illustrated*, 72.
  25. Primm, *Lion of the Valley*, 163–64; Reps, *Saint Louis Illustrated*, 83.

a little more than $14000. The insurance on the house will be some 3 or 4 thousand more, which will more than pay for all the debts of Sublette & Campbell." Although hard feelings undoubtedly lingered, Campbell and the Sublettes were able to put the dispute behind them. Solomon and Frances Sublette lived out their remaining years at Sulphur Springs, selling off tracts of land when they needed money until only the main house and resort remained. Solomon died on August 31, 1857, and Frances a month later on September 28. Upon their deaths, the remnants of Sulphur Springs were sold.[26]

The May 17 fire had destroyed the American Fur Company's *Martha*, packed with forty thousand dollars' worth of trade goods to be shipped upriver. Although the *Martha* was fully insured, it would take weeks for Chouteau to lease another steamboat, the *Amelia*, fill it with goods, and send it upriver. Some of those goods would come from Campbell at premium prices. That brief advantage, however, did not enable Campbell to bridge the vast gulf in trading power between the two firms. The American Fur Company steamboats and smaller packets brought down 2,298 packs of robes that summer. Harvey, Primeau, and Company shipped down 600 packs of robes aboard the packet *Mary Blanc* in July and several hundred aboard the Campbell-owned *Tamerlane* in August. That fall, a snag split the *Tamerlane* in two on the lower Missouri. Harvey, Primeau, and Company had snagged as well. The partners quarreled; men deserted; the Indians took their robes elsewhere. Cholera swept up the Missouri, killing hundreds of buffalo hunters and robe scrapers. Indian sniping on the steamboats, trading posts, and isolated traders increased.

The epidemic, fire, and deaths delayed but did not cancel Campbell's annual buying trip east. He returned just in time for the birth of his daughter Mary on September 23. A swelling in Mary's head dampened the Campbells' joy. The child lingered until excessive water on the brain killed her on December 30, 1850. Of the Campbells' first six children, only three-and-a-half-year-old Hugh remained.

In the unbridled market economy of that era, it was impossible for even someone as prudent as Campbell to escape the speculative boom and bust cycle. He was grossly overextended on all business fronts. His June 15, 1850, accounts receivable entry revealed that he was owed $76,369.59 from various individuals and businesses he had credited. His

26. Frances Sublette to Solomon Sublette, June 30, 1849, Sublette Collection, MoHiS. Sunder, *Sublette*, 231,

warehouses bulged with the skins, robes, or furs of 12,411 buffalo, 543 water-damaged buffalo, 23 half hides, 3,250 buffalo tongues, 205 prairie wolf, 1,079 white wolf, 275 fox, 41 badger, 54 lynx, 3 grizzly, and sundry other objects. New loads sporadically arrived. Yet the national market for such products was saturated and prices were low.[27]

At times those robes were far more difficult to gather than to sell. After another perilous descent, Harvey and another trader, James Russell, arrived in St. Louis aboard a packet with four thousand robes. They had left Fort Robert Campbell on April 2 with two other men. Assiniboines fired on the boat but did not hit anyone. Two other men joined them at Fort William. They survived a three-day blizzard and later an attempt by Sioux to lure them ashore. Another man joined their packed boat. One hundred miles below Fort Bouis, heavy winds swamped the boat. Four men drowned, one froze to death, and Harvey and Russell shivered in a sandy hollow on an island. They managed to kindle a fire. Upon drying out they retrieved and bailed out the boat, then paddled it downriver with a broken paddle. At the Vermillion River, they ran into three more Harvey, Primeau, and Company mackinaws, received supplies and two more men, and then proceeded downriver. At Liberty, Missouri, Harvey transferred the robes to a packet and continued on to St. Louis. Two of the three other mackinaw loads were transferred to the packet *Saranac* at Council Bluffs and safely brought down to St. Louis. The third sank sixty miles above Council Bluffs. On June 13, after Campbell took in the robes and issued more supplies, Harvey promptly ascended the Missouri on the new company steamboat, the *Ange*, to renew the perilous cycle.

Cholera and smallpox raged across the United States and out across the plains throughout 1850 and 1851. Harvey reached St. Louis on May 21, 1851, aboard the steamboat *Sacramento* to explain that the epidemics had devastated most of the upper Missouri tribes, sharply cutting their manufacture and delivery of buffalo robes. Nonetheless, his traders had managed to collect seven thousand robes from the Sioux. Campbell and James Christy, another merchant, acted as guarantors for Harvey's trade license. On July 1, the indomitable Harvey had embarked upon the steamer *Robert Campbell* packed with two hundred tons of trade goods and bound for the high Missouri. Along the way the *Robert Campbell* deposited goods at opposition trading posts upriver. At the Yellowstone, Harvey disembarked with the remainder. The boat returned downriver with one hundred packs of robes, having lost both chimneys in a storm

27. Robert Campbell Account Book, July 1850, Campbell Papers, MLA.

near Fort Pierre. The packets *Alton* and *El Paso* also brought down loads of Harvey, Primeau, and Company robe packs that summer. One mackinaw snagged and sank with all its take. The epidemics allowed only a modest haul of robes that year.

It was not all work and no play for Campbell in 1851. The arrival of acclaimed singer Jenny Lind, the "Swedish Nightingale," for a series of five concerts briefly dispelled some of the Campbell family sorrow. P. T. Barnum himself orchestrated her national tours. The press reported virtually every detail of her visit to St. Louis. A crowd of thousands, a brass band, and a carriage pulled by six horses met Lind at the wharf when her special steamboat docked. She stayed in splendor at the Planter's House. To give Lind some peace, Barnum veiled one of her maids and led the adoring crowds through the streets. One night the Polyhymnia Society serenaded her beneath her window; at her request, they later gave a special concert in her honor. One wealthy enthusiast paid twelve hundred dollars to buy a front-row, center seat; the cheapest seats sold for the then exorbitant price of five dollars each. Robert and Virginia attended Lind's March 18, 1851, performance at Wyman Hall, and thrilled to her renditions of "Come Per Me Sereno," "Home Sweet Home," "Coming Through the Rye," "I Know that My Redeemer Liveth," "The Last Rose of Summer," "#4 Gypsy Song," and "Mountaineer Song." The Campbell family album holds Jenny Lind's picture.

That year opportunities on the plains had arisen for Campbell to widen both his business and diplomatic horizons. He would reach for both but seize only one. He accompanied Virginia and his surviving child, Hugh, to Philadelphia, where his family would stay with Hugh and Mary during the cholera months. After a quick buying trip among eastern merchants he hurried back to St. Louis to prepare for his latest public duty—he had been named a commissioner and supplier to the treaty council with the plains Indians.

Tom Fitzpatrick had more than fulfilled his duties since being named Indian Commissioner for the Upper Arkansas and Platte in 1846. From his Fort Bent headquarters, he had not only held together a fragile peace on the central plains but also deepened his already formidable reputation among the tribes for honesty, compassion, and efficiency. Despite these efforts, tensions rose as the parade of whites across the plains and decimation of the buffalo continued. Each tribe harbored resentments against not only the white intruders but also each other. As buffalo diminished, the chance grew that the plains could erupt in a war among the tribes and with the Americans. In 1847 alone, the

Comanches had killed 47 Americans, destroyed 330 wagons, and run off 6,500 livestock.[28]

By the summer of 1849, Fitzpatrick had concluded that the only way to avert war was to convene a general peace council with all the plains tribes. He sold St. Louis Indian Superintendent David Mitchell on the idea. Mitchell urged him to take his plan to Washington. The White House approved. In the Senate, Thomas Hart Benton got his chamber to approve a two-hundred-thousand-dollar appropriation for gifts on April 29, 1850, but the effort died in the House of Representatives. Then, later that year, Fitzpatrick was briefly replaced as Indian agent in an obscure political squabble.

Campbell began a lobbying campaign on Fitzpatrick's behalf, writing long letters to influential power holders in Washington extolling the virtues of his longtime friend and business associate: "I know of no person so well qualified to fill the office as Major Fitzpatrick . . . and so every man will say who is at all acquainted with the major and the duties required of that agent . . . of his thorough knowledge of Indian character and great influence with them."[29] His efforts paid off—Fitzpatrick was reinstated on February 20, 1851, just in time for him to rejoin the chorus calling for a general council.

A week later on February 27, 1851, Congress appropriated one hundred thousand dollars for gifts to the Indians and appointed Superintendent Mitchell to organize the treaty council, which was to open on September 1 at Fort Laramie. Mitchell plunged into his duties. Fitzpatrick was dispatched with presents and invitations for the tribes. By July 25, Fitzpatrick had completed his circuit of the plains and was at Fort Laramie making preparations for the general council. Meanwhile, Mitchell had to contract, collect, and convey the goods to the council. In April, he called on both R. and W. Campbell and P. Chouteau and Company to submit bids for supplying the council goods; by April 17, both companies had tendered bids. R. and W. Campbell's $60,510.84 bid just edged out P. Chouteau's $62,188.50 estimate. It was a major coup that Campbell hoped could give him the financial power to eventually underbid Chouteau on the upper Missouri.

When Mitchell submitted R. and W. Campbell's bid to the War Department, however, it was rejected. The War Department had already

28. Major Gilpin Report from Fort Mann, August 1, 1847, House Ex. Doc., DOC. 1, 30th Cong., 2d sess., 136–40.
29. Robert Campbell to R. Buchanan, December 4, 1850, 1850 Letterbook, MLA.

chosen the New York firm of Grant and Barton to supply the goods. On May 26, Mitchell received word from Commissioner Lucas Lea of what had happened, and promptly informed Campbell.

Campbell shot off a pointed letter to Lea two days later in which he explained his understanding that Mitchell was fully authorized to make the decision and that, regardless, the War Department should have informed him much sooner as he had already begun his purchases. Worst of all, it was not fair that

> . . . we should be requested to submit sealed proposals after being accepted by the Sup Ind Affs and by him sent to Washington, should then be accessible to parties not connected with the office of the Commissioner of Indian Affairs, and about a month allowed to transpire without any objections or disapproval of the actions of the Sup Ind Affs in making the contract— thus allowing parties to search the Eastern Markets and even to order from Europe if possible to underbid us without coming fairly into competition, and without once being appraised of any objection to our prices . . . All we ask is to have our contract complied with in good faith.[30]

It was a compelling argument. Lea did not reply until July 1, when he pinned the blame on Mitchell who should have known that the War Department would have the final word and thus should not have given the go-ahead to Campbell. He further argued that to "have approved the contract, when a better one could have been made, would have been a gross dereliction of official duty."[31] The army, however, would regret giving the contract to the inexperienced Grant and Barton rather than to veteran Indian traders such as Campbell or Chouteau.

A week later, on July 8, the goods Campbell had contracted reached St. Louis. With small hope of being able to sell them off, he packed them away in his warehouse. Aware of the huge costs Campbell had incurred, Lea offered him two consolation prizes. He approved a contract that Mitchell had granted to Campbell on June 25 to deliver seventy-five thousand pounds of cattle at a cost of seven dollars per hundred pounds at Fort Laramie by September 1. He also selected Campbell to be one of the commissioners to a treaty to be negotiated with the northern plains tribes at Fort Laramie that fall.

With an escort of seventy-five dragoons, Mitchell set off in mid-July. Campbell would not be able to tidy up his affairs and embark until July 29. He was now much older and wealthier than when he first headed

---

30. Robert Campbell to Lucas Lea, May 28, 1851, Campbell Papers, MLA.
31. Lucas Lea to Robert Campbell, July 1, 1851, ibid.

up the Missouri twenty-eight years before. In those days he thought nothing of spending months in the saddle. This trip west would be different. As a sign of his wealth, status, and age, he loaded his carriage and horses aboard the steamboat.

Accompanying him were fellow delegates Colonel Samuel Cooper, the army's adjutant general; Colonel A. B. Chambers, the *Missouri Republican* editor; and B. Gratz Brown, the *Missouri Republican* reporter. Their steamboat reached Kansas City on August 2. They caught up with the Mitchell party thirty-five miles above Cottonwood Springs, and together the entire group reached Fort Laramie on September 1. On his trip, Campbell mixed private business with his official business when he conferred with his agents at Fort Kearny and Fort Laramie.[32]

Mitchell and the delegation faced a difficult and dangerous situation. Bands of Sioux, Cheyenne, and Arapaho had been gathering around Fort Laramie since July to impatiently await the delegations arrival. Whatever smoldering hatreds and rivalries split those tribes, they were united in disappointment when they learned that no wagon train full of supplies and gifts accompanied Mitchell.

To worsen matters, the council almost opened with violence rather than peace. Two warriors in the Shoshone delegation had been killed en route to the council by a Cheyenne raiding party. Jim Bridger, the Shoshone's interpreter, had quieted their rage with promises of many presents and the army's protection at the council. Then, as the Shoshone approached Fort Laramie, a Sioux bent on killing the chief who had killed his father years before sprang on his horse and charged. A French interpreter pursued the Sioux, wrestled him off his horse, and subdued him. A hasty council among the Shoshone and Sioux chiefs and their white interpreters defused the crisis. For extra protection, the Shoshones camped near the dragoons.

Finally, a more immediate problem had to be resolved—fodder for the horses. The thousands of Indian ponies grazing the surrounding prairies for weeks had stripped it bare. Mitchell decided to move the council thirty-six miles back down the Platte River to Horse Creek, where the grass was rich and abundant. Mitchell, Campbell, and the others must have had mixed feelings about moving camp. The longer they put off a council, the greater the chance that some vengeful act could spark

32. Robert Campbell to John Dougherty, September 5, 1851, Campbell House. For an excellent account of the council, see John J. Killoren, *"Come Blackrobe": De Smet and the Indian Tragedy*, 131–73.

a bloodbath. Then again, would the extra time defuse the simmering passions? One thing was certain. In moving toward the wagon train, the provisions and gifts would be distributed that much sooner, thus alleviating a major portion of the tension.

They reached Horse Creek late on September 5. Mitchell prudently used the Platte River to split the most hostile Indians. The Sioux, Cheyenne, and Arapaho were assigned the north side and the Shoshone sent to the south side to camp near the dragoons and commissioners. Tensions lifted somewhat when the Sioux invited all the tribes, including the Shoshone, to a grand feast.

While the Indians, troops, and commissioners headed east down the Platte, Campbell tarried at Fort Laramie to finish his business. Father Peter John De Smet, the famous "blackrobe" who was then prosletyzing among the Blackfeet, appeared at Fort Laramie on September 6. The following day Campbell offered De Smet a ride to the council in his carriage. They arrived late on September 7.

Around ten thousand Indians continued to wait for the council's commencement and, more important, the supply train. Some of them had been camped for weeks. Mitchell delayed the council's opening in hopes that the supplies would arrive to assuage the Indians' growing irritation. He used the excuse of the Crow's failure to appear as reason to put off the proceedings. Fearing any further delay would be counterproductive, Mitchell finally convened the council on September 8.

Distrust and disappointment burned through all the Indians as they approached the council that morning of September 8. The great fear of Campbell and the other delegates that the council could explode into violence was lessened somewhat by the sheer spectacle of watching the various bands converge on them:

> the whole plains seemed to be covered with the moving masses of chiefs, warriors, men, women, and children; some on horseback, some on foot. The chiefs and braves who expected to go into the Council—for only the principal men take part in principal deliberations like this—generally came on foot; then followed the young men mounted and on foot, then the squaws and children . . . Each nation approached with its own peculiar song or demonstration . . . They came out . . . decked out in all their best regalia, pomp, paint, and display for peace.[33]

33. Letter from the Editor, September 8, 1851, "Treaty Ground, Horse Creek near Fort Laramie," *Missouri Republican,* October 24, 1851, MLA.

An arbor of lodge poles and skins had been erected. Mitchell, Fitzpatrick, Campbell, and the other commissioners and officers were seated in the center, while the tribal delegations and their interpreters from the tribes were arranged around them. Mitchell stood to deliver the opening address. After welcoming the chiefs, he reminded them that Indians and whites had different ways of swearing to tell the truth and fulfill their promises. When whites took an oath they placed their hand on the Bible; Indians smoked the pipe to the Great Spirit. A large redstone pipe was repeatedly filled, lighted, and passed among all the delegates.[34]

With the sacred pipe ceremony finished and the delegates about to make their speeches, the council was suddenly disrupted by two women, one white and one Indian. Lieutenant W. L. Elliot's wife entered after the pipe ceremony was completed. After she was seated with the commissioners, Mitchell pointed out that her presence symbolized the Americans' peaceful intentions. Not long after, a Cheyenne woman entered, leading a horse with a boy mounted upon it. She called out that one of the Shoshone chiefs present had killed her husband several years earlier, and now she was presenting the boy and horse to him as a gift. She was ushered out; the gift would await the council's conclusion.

Mitchell then began to speak, relating the Great Father's concern that the immigrants were driving off the buffalo and bringing sickness to the plains and mountain Indians. To protect his Indian children, the Great Father made four proposals. First, he requested that military posts be erected to protect the Indians. He then suggested that the land be divided so that each tribe received enough to be self-sufficient. Third, he proposed a general peace treaty among all the tribes. Finally, he called for the bands within each tribe to acknowledge one Head Chief who could negotiate with the Great Father and who would be responsible for his people's compliance with any treaties. He concluded his speech by informing them that a wagon train was approaching with presents for them all.

Fitzpatrick and each of the chiefs in turn then made short speeches of approval for the council, whereupon it broke up for the day. The following day was filled with speeches by the chiefs, many of which bitterly recounted the destruction and death the whites had brought with them to the plains. The Crow arrived on September 10 and were invited into the council the next day. That same day, on September 11, a delegation of Assiniboine, Hidatsa, and Arikara also joined the council.

34. Letter from the Editor, "Treaty Ground near Fort Laramie, September 8, 1851," *Missouri Republican*, October 26, 1851, MLA.

Over the next week, Mitchell forged a consensus behind all of his points but one—a principal chief for each tribe. In each tribe, each band desired that position for itself and gridlocked over the selection of head chief. After several days of intense debate, all of the tribes had selected a leader except for the Sioux. Mitchell broke the impasse ten days later by choosing Fighting Bear as the chief of all the Sioux. The chiefs agreed to support his choice.

Although the tribes had agreed in principal on dividing the land among them, they differed over where the boundaries should be drawn. It was this issue that Campbell and the other mountain men such as Fitzpatrick and Bridger were the most influential in resolving. They used their knowledge of the West and the tribes to demarcate boundaries grudgingly accepted by all. Mitchell alleviated some of the lingering resentment by promising the Indians that they could continue to migrate freely as they had before as long as they remained at peace. By the evening of September 16, a consensus had been hammered out on all points.

The following day, on September 17, twenty-one chiefs and fifteen white witnesses, including Campbell, marked or signed the Treaty of Fort Laramie, which included eight tenets: (1) a lasting peace among all the assembled tribes; (2) the right of the United States to build roads and forts in the territory; (3) the U.S. government's duty to protect the Indians from the whites and each other; (4) the promise of the tribes to provide restitution for any crimes against Americans; (5) the division of the territory into tribal regions; (6) the duty of each tribe to select a head chief; (7) the duty of the United States to distribute among the tribes in proportion to their respective populations fifty thousand dollars annually for fifty years; and (8) the provision that if any band or tribe violated the treaty, the United States could withhold the annuities from all the signatories.

Ideally, this would have been the time to distribute presents. The supply train, alas, was nowhere to be found. The following day, the delegations met again to discuss the possibility of creating a special land for "half-breeds" and their families, but no agreement was struck. Finally, to the relief and joy of all, the wagon train arrived on September 20, whereupon Mitchell dispensed $65,015.76 worth of goods among the ten thousand Indians who had gathered in proportion to their respective populations.

By September 24, the council's affairs were finished and the com-missioners headed east, accompanied by Fitzpatrick and eleven Sioux,

Cheyenne, and Arapaho chiefs who would journey all the way to Washington. At Fort Kearny, the commissioners met with the Pawnee and concluded a similar treaty. There the party split up, with Fitzpatrick and the chiefs heading southeast along the Blue River route while Campbell and the other officials continued down the Platte River to Bellevue.[35]

Campbell and the delegates could congratulate themselves on a brilliant diplomatic coup. They had gathered as many as twelve thousand Indians from seven tribes often hostile to both each other and Americans, and had forged among them a peace treaty. Yet, how long would the peace last? Although Campbell's thoughts have been lost, they no doubt reflected those of Fitzpatrick and the other commissioners. Fitzpatrick painted a bleak portrait of the Indians' plight: "The Cheyenees and Arrapahoes, and many of the Sioux, are actually in a starving state. They are in abject want of food half the year, and their reliance for that scanty supply, in the rapid decrease of the buffalo, is fast disappearing. The travel upon the roads drives them off, or else confines them to a narrow path during the period of emigration; and the different tribes are forced to contend with hostile nations in seeking support for their villages. Their women are pinched with want and their children constantly crying out with hunger. The arms, moreover, are unfitted to the pursuit of smaller game, and thus the lapse of only a few years presents only the prospect of famine."[36]

Like other participants, Fitzpatrick lamented the moral dilemma faced by the government:

> to leave them as they now are would be inhumanity; and . . . to isolate them in small strips of territory, where they cannot subsist under surrounding circumstances upon the large lands they now occupy, would be only to deliver them over to the ravages of disease, in addition to the miseries of famine. If penned up in small secluded colonies they become hospital wards of cholera and smallpox, and must be supported at an immense annual cost to the government. If no alteration is effected in their present state, the future has only starvation in store for them. The former would insure a gradual decline—the latter a speedy extinction.

He concluded that the only course was to open their territory to settlement and hope that the Indians would civilize themselves by

---

35. Annual Report of Thomas Fitzpatrick, Indian Agent Upper Platte and Arkansas, to Lucas Lea, Commissioner of Indian Affairs, Washington, November 24, 1851, Library of Congress, microfilm 04093.

36. Thomas Fitzpatrick, Indian Agent Upper Platte and Arkansas, to A. Cumming, Supt. Indian Affairs, St. Louis, November 19, 1852, Library of Congress, microfilm.

following the example of the surrounding whites. Yet he recognized that " 'extinguishing the Indian title' . . . is the legalized murder of a whole nation. It is expensive, vicious, inhumane." Tom Fitzpatrick's views were prescient.

Whatever sympathy Campbell may have felt for the Indians was soon swallowed by a succession of family and business crises. The Campbell family's perpetual sorrow deepened during early 1852. Virginia gave birth to Robert on October 17, 1851. The father arrived home five days later on October 22. He had little time to enjoy his new child. Scarlet fever claimed the baby on February 2, 1852. Once again, Campbell struggled to stifle his grief. He had to protect his surviving wife and child at all costs.

Business woes mounted and threatened to sink him. By 1852, Harvey, Primeau, and Company was deeply in debt to Campbell and had little chance of repaying what it owed. Harvey arrived at St. Louis in early June to once again press Campbell for credit and sponsorship. Campbell helped him streamline his company by shedding unnecessary workers and redeploying the remainder to cut costs. He again agreed to act as Harvey's guarantor. Harvey repaid Campbell's trust. That year Harvey, Primeau, and Company deposited fifty thousand dollars' worth of 16,000 robes and 450 beaver skins in Campbell's warehouses.[37]

The 1851 treaty had widened the bitter rivalry between the American Fur Company, Robert Campbell, and other entrepreneurs. They now competed not only for the robe trade but also in their bids to convey the annual annuities to the different tribes. In June 1852, Indian Super-intendent Mitchell asked both Campbell and Chouteau for bids to send annuities up the Missouri. The river was low, the season was late, and the risks were great. Campbell reluctantly declined but would bid in later years. An equally reluctant Chouteau took the job, but only after extracting a high price from the government. From then until 1864, the American Fur Company won bids eight of the twelve years; companies backed by Robert Campbell would win the other four. The competitive bids cut costs from $8.50 per one hundred pounds from St. Louis to Fort Pierre in 1853 to between $2 and $3 in the 1860s. The shipping price to Fort Union dropped even more dramatically, from $11.50 in 1853 to $2.50 in 1861. The winning bidder made a considerable profit despite the plunge in prices.[38]

37. Sunder, *Fur Trade*, 146.
38. Ibid., 144.

Politics may have been as important as low bids in determining the American Fur Company's domination of the annuities. In the 1852 election the Democratic Party candidate, Franklin Pierce, swept Whig President Millard Fillmore from office. Perhaps after receiving ample "donations," Pierce accepted Chouteau's nominees for Indian agency positions.

Campbell faced a series of business and personal disasters in 1853. As investments, steamboats were as potentially lucrative as they were risky. A 300- to 350-ton steamboat cost between twenty-five and thirty thousand dollars. Snags, boiler explosions, and fires limited the average steamboat's lifespan to 2.86 years. By 1849, 550 steamboats had been destroyed in the Mississippi River watershed.[39]

Despite the odds, Campbell had no choice but to gamble if he wanted to squeeze Chouteau from the Missouri. The first in a series of steamboat investments was his namesake, the *Robert Campbell*. Ironically, in April 1853 he leased the boat to Chouteau for thirty dollars a day. Meanwhile, Harvey returned aboard the *Highland Mary No. 1* on June 9. Campbell chartered the 254-ton steamer *St. Ange*, filled it with trade goods, and dispatched it with Harvey aboard on July 7. Business prospects seemed favorable. But later that month Campbell received the gut-wrenching word that on July 25, 1853, "three of our steamers were burned at this wharf, on one of which we had $1500 worth of goods."[40] Then, on October 13, 1853, the *Robert Campbell* itself caught fire and burned to its waterline at a St. Louis wharf.

The disastrous year culminated with the death of William Campbell in December 1853. Robert learned of his nephew and junior partner's death while he was in New York buying supplies with Tom Fitzpatrick. In January, the two aging mountain men traveled to Washington to meet with the Indian superintendent. They arrived on January 4, 1854, and checked into the Brown's Hotel. Later that month Fitzpatrick came down with a severe cold that worsened into pneumonia. Campbell was with him when he died on February 7. The following day, Campbell watched as his friend was lowered into a grave in the congressional cemetery.

Campbell hurried back to St. Louis to settle Fitzpatrick's estate. Fitzpatrick had named Campbell and Albert G. Boone executors of his June 20, 1853, will; Campbell had also witnessed the will along with B. Gratz Brown. Fitzpatrick left behind a modest estate of $10,347.86 and

39. Primm, *Lion of the Valley*, 170.
40. [?] to Campbell, July 26, 1853, Campbell Papers, MLA.

some property. After deducting various debts, on June 21, 1853, Campbell was left with $8,500 to give to Margaret Poisal, Fitzpatrick's wife of four years; his son Andrew Jackson; and his posthumous daughter Virginia Thomasine. Campbell would continue to forward to Margaret Poisal various dividends from Fitzpatrick's investments until they were completely liquidated by January 1856.[41]

As Campbell resolved Fitzpatrick's will, he was deeply involved in his perennial duel with Chouteau and Company. In 1854, he joined with Captain Joseph Throckmorton to run the 227-ton *Genoa*, a fast steamboat on the Missouri River route. He won that year's bid for the Missouri River annuities. The *Genoa* conveyed the annuities and Indian agent Alfred Vaughan to various tribes upriver. The boat proved to be a short-lived investment. Two years later, it snagged and sank near Nebraska City on September 13, 1856.

On July 20, 1854, Harvey, Primeau, and Company experienced its worst crisis yet when Harvey died at Fort William. In his will, Harvey named Campbell the executor. Harvey split his estate between his two half-Indian daughters. Not much was left after Campbell paid off Harvey's considerable debts. Campbell convinced the remaining partners, Primeau, Picotte, and Bouis, to renew their license, reorganize the firm, cut the number of traders from thirty to fourteen, and continue to battle the American Fur Company. They reluctantly agreed to do so. He then acted as guarantor for that year's license.

Three years after the 1851 Laramie Treaty, war exploded on the plains. Violence rather than peace had accompanied the annual September distribution of annuities at Fort Laramie. An 1853 dispute had resulted in six dead Miniconjou Sioux; Fitzpatrick's skillful diplomacy barely managed to prevent a war. Tensions were sky-high thereafter. On August 19, 1854, hot-headed Lieutenant John Grattan led thirty troops and two howitzers to the Brule camp to demand that Chief Conquering Bear give up for arrest a warrior who had butchered and eaten an immigrant's stray cow. When Conquering Bear refused, Grattan ordered his men to open fire. The troopers gunned down Conquering Bear but were wiped out by the Brule, who went on to destroy the nearby Chouteau and Company trading post. The Brule then packed up their camp and headed north. Although Fort Laramie received reinforcements, the troops were too few to be marched against the Sioux. Raids on individuals and stagecoaches

41. Hafen, *Broken Hand*, 317–19, 343–34; Robert Campbell to Mrs. Thomas Fitzpatrick, September 11, 1854, Letterbook, MLA.

continued that year and into the next. Campbell, Chouteau, and their respective business partners feared that the war would spread to their operations on the upper Missouri.

In late 1854, the Campbells moved into a beautiful home in an exclusive new neighborhood. The new home was one of many built in St. Louis during the 1850s to accommodate the expanding population and the overwhelming demand for lodgings. Private landowners such as Pierre Chouteau, James Lucas, John O'Fallon, and others reaped enormous riches when they sold off their large tracts west of town. In a series of auctions between 1854 and 1859, the city too sold off its land. Developers subdivided the land into residences and businesses.

The most exclusive of those developments was Lucas Place, described as

> St. Louis' first clearly defined spatial expression of class consciousness. Although several earlier neighborhoods had housed concentrations of wealthy and prominent residents, they had also been home to large numbers of people from other socioeconomic backgrounds. As the city boomed with new money and as surnames became insufficient evidence of a person's wealth or status, identification by neighborhood became increasingly important. Lucas Place, actually more of a settlement of new rich than of the city's old families, took on the aura of an elite enclave.[42]

Inspired by his study of planned, elegant, exclusive neighborhoods in eastern American cities and across Europe, James Lucas had begun work on Lucas Place in 1851. When it was finished, Lucas Place extended for four blocks west of Missouri Park between Fourteenth and Eighteenth Streets. Lucas himself moved into 1515 Lucas Place.

It was into 20 Lucas Place that the Campbell family escaped from the wharf district in November 1854. Their beautiful Greek revival–style home was at what is now 1508 Locust Street. They remained at this address for the rest of their lives. There, assisted by a half dozen or more servants, Robert and Virginia entertained other members of the city's elite circles and visiting dignitaries in a style appropriate to their wealth and social status. The Campbells were undoubtedly delighted when, in 1855, the Second Presbyterian Church was erected at Fourteenth Street and Lucas Place, facing Missouri Park and just a block from their home.

42. Richard Allen Rosen, "Rethinking the Row House: The Development of Lucas Place, 1850–1865," 20–28. See also Charles C. Savage, *Architecture of the Private Streets of St. Louis: The Architects and the Houses They Designed.*

Yet, no matter how luxurious their lifestyle, neither Robert nor Virginia could ever lift the sorrow that deepened with the death of each baby. Three new children were born in the mid-1850s—Hazlett Kyle on November 23, 1853, only to die from measles on his birthday three years later; Robert on October 8, 1855; and another baby named Hazlett Kyle on February 2, 1858. Of their previous children, only Hugh remained.

Although the Campbells had escaped the squalor and clamor of downtown, they felt compelled to journey much farther to elude the murderous diseases that stalked them and their city. Early each summer, Virginia and the children would accompany Robert east on his annual business trips to enjoy prolonged stays in Philadelphia, Cape May, New Jersey, Long Island, and New York City. With his buying complete, Campbell would leave them there until autumn, when the pestilence season in St. Louis had largely passed.

Virginia's weekly letters to Robert were filled with details of dinners with friends, the humid weather, Hugh's horseback riding progress, sea bathing, furniture purchases, and, especially, the children's health. Her June 1855 correspondences speak volumes about her concerns and delights. In her first letter she worried about the baby's "cough and hack . . . He was the cause of great anxiety to me . . . It was probably for the best [that we came east], the baby may have gotten better in St. Louis after those teeth were through and the weather turned cool but he has derived a great deal of benefit from the journey although he is very thin yet . . . he . . . has good spirits and loves everyone so much and calls them all by name . . . he's a smart little fellow." A week later she wrote that "Hugh looks so well cantering and has such a good seat in that gait and enjoys it so much, but the groom wants to teach to feel as much at home in trotting rapidly as in cantering which is much rougher . . . but Hugh tries to do just as Wm tells him." She revealed her sensitivity for her husband in her third letter that month: "I am sorry you have such hot weather. I know how you suffer when it is so oppressive—it is well we are away I should be exceedingly oppressed. The dear children are all perfectly well." In that month's final letter, she declared, "Our blessed baby is the delight of the whole house, he talks everything in his way and everybody thinks him uncommonly smart."[43]

43. Virginia Campbell to Robert Campbell, June 4, 1855, Virginia Campbell to Robert Campbell, June 11, 1855, Virginia Campbell to Robert Campbell, June 21, 1855, Virginia Campbell to Robert Campbell, June 26, 1855, Campbell House.

Those letters were wonderful diversions from Campbell's perennial business woes. In retrospect, he would have done better to bow out the previous year of 1854. The mild winter caused the buffalo to range far out on the plains. The bands skinned few robes that season. The light snowfall meant a low river that summer of 1855. Even worse, an Indian war had spread across the plains.

The American Fur Company gambled by sending the shallow-draft *St. Mary* upriver. It successfully ran the Sioux gauntlet, delivered the annuities and trade goods to the posts, and returned packed with robes. Meanwhile, Campbell's company lost its bid for the annuities. Suspecting corruption, he demanded to see all papers relating to the award. After studying them, he was unable to prove anything. With the low water, Campbell sent goods by land rather than river and managed a fair take despite the challenges. In July 1855, his warehouse held "16,866 buffalo robes, 604 Elk, 553 Antelope, 622 beaver, 5 grizzly bear, and 67 wolf," as well as a collection of lesser pelts.[44]

While Campbell's traders dodged Sioux parties, Thomas Twiss, the new Upper Platte and Arkansas agent, sent runners to the bands to bring them to Fort Laramie; those who stayed away would be considered hostile. About half the Sioux did gather at Fort Laramie for the September annuities. Chief Little Thunder had taken Conquering Bear's place as chief of the Brule and Miniconjou. When that village remained camped on the Platte River at Ash Hollow, Colonel William S. Harney led six hundred troops of the Second Dragoons, Sixth and Tenth Infantry, and Fourth Artillery out of Fort Kearny against it. On September 3, Harney's troops encircled Little Thunder's village and attacked. At a cost of four killed, seven wounded, and one missing, the troops slaughtered eighty-five Sioux and captured seventy women and children; half the band managed to escape. Harney marched on to Fort Laramie with his prisoners. Two weeks later, Harney led his force northeast across the plains and eventually reached Chouteau's old post of Fort Pierre on October 20. Chouteau was enriched by an additional forty-five thousand dollars when the army bought the dilapidated post from him. The rest of that year and into 1856, the chiefs of the hostile bands sent delegations to sign peace treaties with Harney. The first war the United States fought with the Sioux sputtered to a close.[45]

44. Robert Campbell Ledgerbook, Campbell Papers, MLA.
45. Robert Utley, *Frontiersmen in Blue: The United States Army and the Indian, 1848–1865*, 113–19.

The Sioux War's end presented new opportunities for Campbell to expand his robe trade outward from the Missouri watershed. During the 1850s, he nurtured a network of agents at trading and military posts across the plains. His key men were John Dougherty at Fort Kearny through 1855, and then Fort Laramie until 1857, and Seth Ward at Fort Laramie from 1857 to 1871. Ward was especially effective. He "compounded his own business operations through shrewd and initiatory action and in the process became a principal architect of the commercial life of his region."[46]

Diversification was essential. The robe and fur trade was changing again. During the 1840s and 1850s, by one estimate, the Indians killed at least four hundred thousand buffalo yearly across the plains. Meanwhile, the industry's value to Missouri's economy declined in both relative and absolute terms from the 1820s to the 1850s. In 1820, the fur and robe trade's $500,000 revenue accounted for one-fourth of Missouri's $2 million economy; by the mid-1850s it had fallen to around $300,000 of a $100 million economy. At that time, the upper Mississippi watershed produced more furs and robes than that of the upper Missouri.[47]

Chouteau had controlled both realms since 1843 when a near bankrupt Ramsay Crooks sold out to him. Chouteau, however, failed to keep out swarms of American and Canadian trappers and traders. Minnesota became a territory in 1840 and achieved statehood in 1853. The new government encouraged competition to erode the Northern Department's monopoly. The competitive upper Mississippi trade helped Campbell because it diverted the American Fur Company's money, time, and men from the Missouri.

Kansas City traders, however, were an increasingly sharp pain in Campbell's side. During the early 1850s, Kansas City traders took a larger cut each year of the robe and fur trade from Campbell and the American Fur Company alike. To Campbell's relief, that competition proved to be ephemeral. From the late 1850s on, Kansas City merchants shifted to easier investments like supplying emigrants to Kansas and beyond.

Yet another rival arose in the mid-1850s. In 1854, Sioux City was first surveyed. The Sioux City Company formed the next year to buy up the land and advertise for settlers. The same year that Sioux City

46. W. N. Davis, Jr., "The Sutler at Fort Bridger," *Western Historical Quarterly*, 38, 37–54; Merrill J. Mattes, "The Sutler's Store at Fort Laramie," 93–133.

47. Alfred A. Vaugn, Indian Agent, Fort Pierre, to Col. Alfred Cumming, Superintendent Indian Affairs, September 20, 1853, Library of Congress, microfilm 04093, 114. Sunder, *Fur Trade*, 18.

was incorporated in 1857, thirty steamers docked at the wharf. The largest firm in the new town was owned by David Frost and John B. S. Todd. Rather than compete head-to-head with Frost, Todd, and Company, Campbell worked closely with that firm to undercut Chouteau's monopoly.

Campbell and other St. Louis merchants would hold their own against their rivals in Kansas City or Sioux City. The greatest rival to their business proved to be Chicago. In 1848, the telegraph linked Chicago to the eastern markets, enabling its merchants to take advantage of the latest information and opportunities; it would be years before St. Louis joined the telegraph network. Also in 1848, Chicago began to divert upper Misssissippi Valley trade from St. Louis when the Illinois and Michigan Canal linked the Illinois River and Lake Michigan. Then during the 1850s, Chicago became the hub for twenty railroad lines stretching like spokes of a wheel across the Midwest, the most important of which was the Galena and Chicago Union Railroad connecting the upper Mississippi River and Chicago in 1854. Chicago took over from St. Louis in handling one product after another—St. Louis pig iron shipments, for example, dropped from 749,128 tons in 1847 to 315,677 in 1855, while Chicago's rose to 142,000. During the 1850s, Chicago invested in grain elevators; St. Louis did not. Thus, Chicago's cost of handling grain dropped to half that of St. Louis. By 1855, Chicago enjoyed twice as much grain business with one-fourth the number of men as St. Louis. Still, St. Louis prospered. The 1850s were the "golden age" of steamboating for St. Louis. In 1860, 3,454 steamboats docked at St. Louis, 557 more than a decade earlier.[48]

Washington also contributed to the business losses of St. Louis merchants in the upper Missouri region. In 1853, the Stevens-Mullan Expedition conducted a railroad survey across the West from St. Paul to Puget Sound. In 1855 at Fort Benton, the government signed a treaty with the Blackfeet in which it exchanged annuities for peace. Chouteau received the contract to supply the annual annuities to the Blackfeet at four and three-fourths cents a pound on regular goods and thirteen and three-fourths cents on future council goods. Chouteau did not even have to deliver the goods directly to the Blackfeet, but could drop them off as far upriver as it was possible for steamboats to take them. In the years ahead, Campbell would make numerous bids for the annuity contracts for the Blackfeet and other Missouri River tribes. Almost invariably,

48. Belcher, *Economic Rivalry*, 34–40, 44–45, 102–3, 48.

Chouteau won renewals by both underbidding and outlobbying Campbell in Washington and St. Louis.

Campbell's continued interests in the West embraced not only business prospects but also the people he left behind. The western plains and mountains were as much in turmoil, change, and tragedy as lands farther east. In one of his letters to Jim Bridger, he inquired after the Plume Rouge family "as they were the best Indians that I ever knew. Old Gros Pied the principal Chief who was killed by the Blackfeet in 1828 . . . was also an excellent Indian and I should like to hear about his family."[49]

The best place for Campbell to make money was Missouri itself. By the 1850s, Missouri's once largely subsistence, barter, and agrarian economy was rapidly disappearing. Better strains of seeds enabled farmers to grow more of a surplus to sell to others. Banks loaned, borrowed, and created money. A larger supply of coin and banknotes underwrote ever more trade. Transportation improved dramatically as a web of roads, steamboats, and railroads merged the state's village markets with regional and national markets. Cash crops such as hemp and tobacco were packed on trains and steamboats and transported to the country's far corners. By the same means, manufactured goods arrived from eastern factories. Entrepreneurs set up their own factories in St. Louis. Production was increasingly specialized and diversified. More products were available at cheaper prices. Rather than make their own clothes, soap, or furniture, a farm family could increasingly afford to buy them from elsewhere in the local market in exchange for their cash crop. An affluent middle class expanded within the mostly hardscrabble population. The competition for their business, however, was increasingly cutthroat. By 1855, Campbell's mercantile business was one of 444 wholesale houses in St. Louis with combined sales of $87,033,697.[50] Yet enormous wealth could still be reaped from the trade. Not only was the economic pie getting bigger, but Campbell continued to slice off larger portions.

By the mid-1850s, Robert and Virginia Campbell had managed to achieve considerable wealth, tranquility, status, security, and power despite their sorrow over their children's deaths. Campbell had diversified his economic empire to the point where it was little affected by the 1857 Panic that depressed the nation's economy. Astonishingly, his credit was

49. Robert Campbell to Jim Bridger, April 7[?], 1852, Campbell Papers, MLA.
50. Belcher, *Economic Rivalry.* See also David Thelen, *Paths of Resistance: Tradition and Dignity in Industrializing Missouri;* Steven Hahn and Jonathan Prude, eds., *The Countryside in the Age of Capitalist Transformation: Essays in the Social History of Rural America;* Miles W. Eaton, "The Development and Later Decline of the Hemp Industry in Missouri," 346–67.

even better than that of the U.S. government. In 1857, General Reynolds of the U.S. Engineer Corps was ordered to lead an expedition to explore the badlands of the middle Missouri River watershed. His expedition traveled by steamboat to Fort Pierre, from which he intended to obtain horses and supplies for the overland journey. But when he "applied to the Traders there for means . . . they refused credit to the United States, and would only accept drafts on Robert Campbell of St. Louis, whom they knew and would trust sooner than the government."[51]

Campbell's robe business up the Missouri continued to turn a considerable profit. On September 12, 1857, the *Clara* returned to St. Louis with three hundred packs of robes for his warehouse. Until 1857, Picotte had staved off all Chouteau pressure to sell out. Bouis, however, increasingly talked of dissolving their partnership. When Picotte discussed a possible sellout with Campbell, he agreed if Picotte in turn promised to serve as field commander for yet another opposition company. Picotte shook hands on the deal. Campbell joined with Frost, Todd, and Company to win that year's annuity bid. They chartered the steamboat *Twilight*, captained by John Shaw, and sent it up the Missouri on May 31 with four hundred tons of trade goods and seventy traders. The *Twilight* reached Fort William by July 5 and then churned as far as the Poplar River to unload goods and annuities for Fort Robert Campbell. On July 21, the *Twilight* was safely back in St. Louis with several thousand buffalo robes. That year, Campbell and Frost, Todd, and Company also acquired a sutlership at Fort Randall, the largest wholesale store in Sioux City, and a trading post at the James River's juncture with the Missouri.

Campbell followed up his 1857 coups by winning the 1858 annuities bid. The *Twilight*'s round trip on the Missouri in 1858 was successful. It deposited goods and men for a new trading post, Fort Atkinson, next to the American Fur Company's Fort Berthold at the Mandan-Hidatsa villages. The *Twilight* took on men and goods from Fort William, which was abandoned when the Assiniboine shifted their trade to Fort Union in fear of the Sioux. A new post, Fort Clark, was built higher up the Missouri to attract both the Assiniboine and Crow trade and deposit goods and annuities for Fort Robert Campbell and the Blackfeet. Campbell and Frost, Todd, and Company bought up land acquired from the Yankton Sioux and sold it off to settlers. The new town was called Yankton and became the territorial capital of the Dakotas.

51. Holloway, ed., *A Narrative*, 16.

Campbell had won the annuity bid for two years, and was determined to lock it up for the next several years at least. His decision to do so was prompted when, in June 1858, steamboat Captain Joseph Throckmorton tendered a four-year bid from 1859 to 1862 for the annuity business. Campbell then encouraged Edward Atkinson, representing Frost, Todd, and Company, to submit a similar bid. Indian Superintendent Alexander Robinson carefully considered both bids. Charles Chouteau, Pierre Jr.'s son, got wind of the bids and submitted a private two-year bid. Robinson finally decided to accept Chouteau's bid, and got the secretary of the interior's approval to do so. The opposition cried foul but could do nothing.

Meanwhile, gold and silver strikes in Idaho and Montana offered new ways to make money for steamboat owners on the Missouri. Hopeful miners reached those fields by traveling either up the Missouri River to Fort Benton and then overland or via the Oregon and Bozeman Trails. To the profits reaped from carrying Indian annuities and trade goods could be added earnings from passengers, soldiers, and supplies.

In 1859, Charles P. Chouteau took over operations from his father, Pierre Jr. His firm won a contract from Indian Commissioner Charles Mix that paid $2.50 per hundred pounds on goods to Fort Union and $7.50 per hundred pounds on goods to Fort Benton.[52] The American Fur Company dispatched two steamboats up the Missouri that year, the *Spread Eagle* and *Chippewa*. Neither succeeded in reaching Fort Benton, but they did return safely to St. Louis in August with forty thousand robes between them. Campbell and Frost, Todd, and Company planned a less ambitious but still lucrative journey of their own. On June 4, 1859, Captain Throckmorton steered the Frost, Todd, and Company's 399-ton *Florence* upriver to Fort Randall and returned on July 16 with twenty-five thousand robes. The robe trade would drop sharply the following year: in 1859, as the rivals were packing their huge take of robes on mackinaws and steamboats, a mysterious disease began decimating buffalo herds across parts of the plains.

Frost, Todd, and Company's last trip to the upper Missouri was made in 1859. On November 4, the partners sold off that region to junior investors Malcolm Clark and Charles Primeau and concentrated on developing their investments and political ambitions in the Yankton region. Their lobbying in Washington prompted Congress in March 1861 to create the Dakota Territory. Campbell continued to make minor,

52. Lass, *Steamboating*, 15.

mostly profitable investments in both Frost and Todd, and Clark and Primeau.

Any disappointment that Campbell may have felt in the failure of his latest attempt to topple the giant quickly dissipated. By the decade's end, the business opportunities in St. Louis were greater than ever. During the 1850s, industrialization and immigration transformed St. Louis, Missouri, and much of the nation. In 1860, 12,000 laborers worked the city's 1,126 factories, which produced $28 million worth of goods, making St. Louis the second-largest manufacturing city in the Mississippi River watershed after Cincinnati. A population explosion provided those industries with both workers and consumers. During the 1850s, Missouri's population nearly doubled, from 682,044 in 1850 to 1,182,012 in 1860. Foreign immigrants swelled the population and demanded goods and services, and they often brought with them special skills that helped develop the economy. By 1860, the city had 166,773 inhabitants, of which 60 percent were foreign—the highest proportion of foreign-born inhabitants of any American city. Included were 60,000 Germans and 39,000 Irish.[53]

Railroads linked Missouri's scattered population into one huge market. By 1860, 810 miles of railroad stretched across the state, of which four lines branched out from St. Louis. The Iron Mountain, Atlantic and Pacific, and Pacific railroads ran south of the Missouri River. The North Missouri Railroad linked with the Hannibal and St. Joseph Railroad that spanned the northern part of the state. From St. Louis and Hannibal, railroads linked Missouri with the web of lines across the northern states and into the South.

As the economy diversified, Campbell accordingly diversified his own investments. During the 1850s, he expanded his mercantile, property, steamboat, and railroad empire. And as his wealth and reputation expanded, he became an ever more influential power broker in St. Louis and Missouri politics. A letter of recommendation from Campbell could win a candidate a coveted appointment. Campaign donations or loans to allies could swing elections in their favor and lead to subsequent rewards for Campbell.

In 1859, Hugh and Mary Campbell pulled up stakes in Philadelphia, came to St. Louis, and moved into a house on Washington Avenue. Hugh became Campbell's last business partner. The Campbell house was reunited. But the nation's would soon fall apart.

---

53. U.S. Bureau of the Census, 1850, 1860; Michael Fellman, *Inside War: The Guerrilla Conflict in Missouri during the American Civil War*, 8.

Chapter 7

# Civil War (1860–1865)

**T**ensions rose steadily as the 1860 election approached. The Republican Party's nomination of Abraham Lincoln as its presidential candidate prompted southern leaders to swear that their states would secede if he became president. What happened then was anyone's guess. But few could have imagined that secession would lead to war and the horrors to come.

Until the November election, for merchants such as Campbell, perhaps the year's most important national event was the inauguration of the Pony Express between St. Joseph, Missouri, and Sacramento, California, by the freighting company Russell, Majors, and Waddell. That slender communication line threading two thousand miles of wilderness provided updated information about distant market demands that could be supplied by Campbell and other enterprising merchants. A mere year and a half after it began, however, the Pony Express died, the victim of the telegraph. Information became virtually instantaneous.

Speedy communication, of course, was not enough. It would still take nearly five months for wagon trains to plod their way from Westport or St. Joseph to Sacramento. Snows closed that route nearly half the year. Yet, only nine years later in 1869, a transportation revolution followed the communication revolution with the transcontinental railroad's completion. Meanwhile, men like Robert Campbell could dream.

Campbell had no role in organizing the Pony Express. Yet, by investing heavily in railroads and steamboats, he was on the cutting edge in advancing the transportation revolution that transformed America's eastern half into one huge market by midcentury. Although in those unregulated times virtually any investment was a roll of the dice, steamboat investments were especially risky. Campbell poured money into a succession of steamboats that operated profitably for a year or more before meeting disaster. Typical was the fate of the huge 421-ton *Robert Campbell, Jr.*, built at Jeffersonville, Indiana, in 1860. Captained by John Shaw, it ran the St. Louis–New Orleans route. In the summer of 1863, it steamed up the Missouri River for Fort Union but had to turn back because of low water. In the case of his namesake, Campbell was lucky; he sold it later that year, just before it caught fire and burned to its waterline at Milliken's Bend on September 28, 1863. Uncertain as investments in railroads and steamboats were, they made perfect business sense. Goods had to be transported somehow. Why not pay oneself for doing so?

In contrast, the Pony Express was something altogether different from the industrial-era steamboats and railroads. It was a transportation and communication method as old as the first domesticated horse. Yet, in spanning the West, the Pony Express fired the imagination of entrepreneurs for the new possibilities it promised.

Neither Campbell nor any other businessman could afford to dally long over such hopes. The hard realities of a cutthroat business world swirled all around and threatened to drown Campbell in debt. As long as the Clark and Primeau company remained a viable contender against the American Fur Company, Campbell continued to back it. But by 1860, the partners leaned toward selling out to their rival. That year, Campbell did not underwrite a steamboat for Clark and Primeau's Missouri River trade. Instead, he encouraged Clark and Primeau to contract with the American Fur Company to ship their goods up and robes down together. He then bought much of the take from both firms. Clark and Primeau finally gave in to the American Fur Company late that year, selling out their operations in return for receiving a franchise over some lucrative trading posts. With their monopoly restored, the American Fur Company promptly streamlined its operations, closing down forts Robert Campbell, Sarpy II, Clark, Stewart, and Kipp. Profits rose, along with prices charged to Indians, soldiers, and passengers alike.[1]

As luck would have it, not long after one opposition firm folded, another opened. Campbell was willing to see Clark and Primeau die because he was helping finance and organize what he hoped would be a much more viable potential contender. Charles Larpenteur had been one of his clerks way back in that frigid winter of 1833–1834 at Fort

1. *Daily Missouri Democrat*, July 27, 1860, MLA.

William. Larpenteur and one Jefferson Smith were both veterans of decades up the Missouri. They accepted as partners the former Frost, Todd, and Company clerk Henry Boller, and Robert Lemon, one of Robert Campbell's clerks.

Larpenteur explained that the partnership emerged when he and Smith lost their jobs after Clark and Primeau went under:

> On my way down the Missouri I found at Fort Berthold, Jefferson Smith, an old trader, who . . . was out of employment, and who had about $4000. There I also met a young man by the name of Boller, who said that he could raise $2000 from his father in Philadelphia. I felt sure that I could obtain my share from Mr. Robert Campbell of St. Louis. Under such an understanding we agreed to meet in St. Louis. My plan for taking up our outfit was to go around by the way of St. Paul, thence on to Pembina, and through part of the British possessions, with the view to avoid the Sioux. This was a road which no one of us had traveled. . . . it was not til the last of July [1860] that we met in St. Louis. I had arrived a few days before, and had informed Mr. Campbell of our project, of which he approved, and readily advanced me my portion of the outfit . . . one of Mr. Campbell's clerks by the name of Robert Lemon joined the company. A few days after the arrival of the other two partners we went into business.[2]

It was a bold, even risky scheme. Yet Campbell had full confidence in the principals. That confidence would prove to be misplaced. The partners took goods and eleven men by steamboat up the Mississippi to St. Paul, bought eight wagons, and then, on September 5, set off overland toward the Missouri. Troubles plagued the expedition from the start. Larpenteur and Boller squabbled incessantly over the expedition's command; they split up on the Souris River, with Smith and Boller taking four wagons to retake Fort Kipp and square off with Fort Berthold for the Mandan-Hidatsa trade, while Larpenteur and Lemon rolled the other four wagons to Fort Stewart near Fort Union and the Assiniboine trade. To their shock, they found both forts ruined. Smith and Boller erected a sod fort and opened trade. With Fort Union's hold on the Assiniboine unshakable, Larpenteur and Lemon chose to head twenty-five miles farther up the Missouri and build the Poplar River post.

Ironically, former opposition leader Malcolm Clark was now the American Fur Company bourgeois at Fort Union. He dispatched a party to the Poplar River to erect Malcolm Clark's Post. Larpenteur actually

2. Hedren, ed., *Narrative of Larpenteur*, 264–65; see also the memoir of partner Milo M. Quaife, ed., *Henry Boller among the Indians*.

welcomed the opposition fort since it diverted goods and men from Fort Union and "I knew [Clark] to be very unpopular with both whites and Indians. My equipment was not large, but well selected for the Indian trade. I made a small reduction in prices which satisfied the Indians, and I knew that if I sold out, even at this reduction, I would do well . . . Out of my four wagon loads I traded upward of 2000 robes, besides a great many other skins and hides."[3] It was a promising beginning to a venture that would end badly.

Mounting such expeditions was the highlight of Campbell's business year. Most of the time he immersed himself in the often tedious minutiae of business routine—scrutinizing accounts, bills, and shipments, firmly but politely hounding debtors, cutting big and small deals alike. Through a combination of diversified, mostly sound investments, meticulous attention to detail, and a reputation for ethical conduct he had amassed ever greater wealth, a portion of which he could afford to gamble on a succession of opposition firms up the Missouri.

As one of the city's leading citizens, he played host to any dignitaries visiting St. Louis. Typical was his experience on September 26, 1860, when he was among those who greeted the Prince of Wales and his entourage. Fellow dignitary Edward Bates wrote that

> everything . . . was conducted decently and in order—more so than was expected, considering the large and promiscuous crowd . . . The Prince and suite attended the Fair to day. I was one selected to go with them, and, with Col Rob Campbell, rode out and in the same carriage with Lord St. Germains. They seemed highly pleased with the exhibition, and especially with the order and decorum of the immense crowd (estimated by some, at 60,000) drawn by curiosity, to see the Prince and his nobles. Lord St. Germains said to me that he never saw a large, promiscuous crowd so well-dressed and well-behaved.[4]

Such events were but fleeting diversions from the worsening animosities between the free and slave states that threatened to explode into secession and perhaps even war. The ideological strains splintering America would also tear Missouri apart. Missouri politics were dominated by the so-called "Boonslick Democrats" of wealthy plantation owners and merchants along the Missouri River. Most Missourians were "Conservative Unionists," at once pro-union and pro-slavery. Three of four Missourians had emigrated from southern states and retained the

3. Hedren, ed., *Narrative of Larpenteur*, 272–73.
4. Howard K. Beale, ed., *The Diary of Edward Bates, 1859–1866*, 147–48.

belief that slavery was biblically and constitutionally justified, even if only a minority actually owned slaves. By skillfully manipulating popular sentiments and deploying their wealth and ability to grant legislative favors, the Boonslick Democrats had retained the statehouse and a majority in the legislature. Robert Campbell was a Conservative Unionist who most likely voted for Stephen Douglas to be president.[5]

When the votes for the November 1860 election were tallied, Republican Abraham Lincoln had won the presidency while Missouri had spread its votes for various Democratic Party candidates for national and state offices. Many of those Democrats, including the newly elected governor Claiborne Jackson, favored Missouri's secession if Lincoln won. Campbell pondered the election's business significance:

> It is impossible to form any conjecture of what course *political* and *financial* affairs will take as are both intimately connected with the present state of affairs. People whose opinions are of any value are so little disposed to allow themselves to believe in any dissolution of the Union that when the secession occurs we'll have to take a chance of what will be the result—in the meantime business men do not like to enter into large operations with the South and thence the monetary [system] crumbles in the South. We must hope that matters will soon assume a better phase.[6]

His reaction was understandable. Economically, Missouri was rooted firmly in the North, with a small feeder vine down the Mississippi. That southern vine would not sustain Missouri if its northern roots were ripped asunder. And if Union troops cut off Missouri from the Mississippi, the economy would die. The southern reaction to Lincoln's victory immediately shook the economy. Their impassioned calls for secession sparked a bank run. Eastern banks were the first to shut their doors. On November 28, 1860, all of Missouri's banks except for the Exchange Bank of St. Louis suspended specie payments. The country appeared to be teetering on the verge of yet another financial as well as political crisis. Despite the year's political and business calamities, its most important event for Campbell was the birth of another son, James Alexander, on March 16, 1860.

Secession swept the South as one slave state after another broke free from the United States. By March, South Carolina, Mississippi,

5. Walter H. Ryle, *Missouri: Union or Secession*, 25; William E. Parrish, *Turbulent Partnership: Missouri and the Union, 1861–1865*; Arthur R. Kirkpatrick, "Missouri on the Eve of Civil War"; Robert E. Shalhope, "Eugene Genovese, the Missouri Elite, and Civil War Historiography"; Reid Mitchell, "The Creation of Confederate Loyalties."
6. Robert Campbell to R. C. Martin, December 6, 1860, 1860 Letterbook, MLA.

Florida, Alabama, Georgia, Louisiana, and Texas had seceded to form the Confederate States of America, whose elected President Jefferson Davis called for a hundred-thousand-man volunteer army. Those troops would soon be needed.

Among the Confederate states, the United States had only two forts, Sumter in Charleston harbor and Pickens in Pensacola Bay. After South Carolina seceded, it had sent a delegation to negotiate with the White House for the takeover of Fort Sumter. Meanwhile, it blockaded the fort. Lincoln ordered a fleet readied to force through supplies to Fort Sumter. On April 9, President Davis ordered the fort captured before the fleet arrived. On April 12, rebel gunners fired the first shots at Fort Sumter. After two days of bombardment, the fort was surrendered.

The following day on April 15, Lincoln asked for seventy-five thousand volunteers for ninety days of service to quell the rebellion, with each state providing a number of troops proportionate to its population. The proclamation was the excuse secessionists had been waiting for in the upper southern states—Arkansas, North Carolina, Virginia, and Tennessee joined the Confederacy.

The election, secession of the southern states, and outbreak of fighting tore Missouri apart. On January 12, 1861, Campbell was among those prominent Missourians who tried desperately to keep the state and nation together by signing a petition, "To the People of St. Louis," calling on them to "take the management of public affairs into their own hands. The preservation of the government of the United States, is at this time, the great question, not only of this continent, but of the civilized world . . . This nation lately so happy, so powerful, and so free is now threatened with obliteration from the map of the world, and its inhabitants are filled with alarm and disarray . . . We believe the people of Missouri almost unanimously prefer being the Great Neutral State . . . And to this end, we suggest that you (the people) . . . bring out for the approaching State Convention a ticket composed of men of tried prudence and patriotism who will truly represent the union sentiment of this City and County and in whose support all those who under existing circumstances and devotedly for the union can unite."[7] Campbell also wrote to Senator Crittenden asking him to use the declaration as the basis of a compromise with the southern states.

Despite these efforts, Campbell would play a minor role in the struggle for Missouri. Throughout the crucial months of February, March, and

7. Petition Civil War Collection, MoHiS.

April, he was in the East on a business trip. Shortly after returning, he went to Jefferson City to attend his railroad business.

Throughout the war, Campbell would be in the thick of its logistics if not its fighting. Procurement orders poured into his office, and his wealth expanded with hundreds of contracts to supply the Union army. Even a small army of 10,000 men needed 250 wagons, 3,500 draft animals, and 60 tons of daily supplies.[8] He used his nationwide business network to procure such supplies for the Union forces in Missouri.

The war did not greatly change his business routine; it simply broadened it. Throughout the war, he wrote hundreds of business letters addressing a myriad of opportunities and setbacks. As usual, many of his letters concerned urging debtors to repay what they owed him. Nonetheless, in July 1861 he could confidently write that "Hugh and I are both prudent in business and will be therefore in a condition to meet the present emergencies, and I am happy to say that we are entirely out of debt, while many of our largest mercantile houses, both in St. Louis and other sections of the country, have failed."[9]

Ironically, Campbell's greatest business vulnerability was in the area where fighting was least likely, in the West. The Civil War raised risks for the robe and fur trade in several ways. Guerrillas threatened steamboats on the Missouri and Mississippi Rivers. Many, perhaps most, riverboat pilots were southern sympathizers. If the annuities were not appropriated or did not make it to the tribes, the Indians might take advantage of the Civil War to revolt against the whites. Campbell also worried that his Indian agents might be jeopardized by the new administration. In an April letter to Frank Blair, Missouri's Republican member of the House of Representatives, Campbell urged him to pressure the White House to retain his agents. Blair complied.[10]

Yet the Civil War gave Campbell and the opposition an advantage against the American Fur Company on the Missouri. The Chouteaus were Democrats and slave-owners. Fearing the loss of their empire and homes, they supported the Union. Three years after the war broke out, Charles Chouteau would even sign a loyalty oath to the United States. Nonetheless, throughout the war, Union officials suspected them of disloyalty and kept a close watch on them and their employees in St. Louis and at the trading posts.

---

8. James McPherson, *Battle Cry of Freedom: The Civil War Era*, 325.
9. Robert Campbell to Anne Campbell, July 11, 1861, Campbell Papers, MLA.
10. Robert Campbell to Frank Blair, April 16, 1861, 1861 Letterbook, ibid.

In the short run, the American Fur Company actually benefited from their Democratic Party connections. On March 3, 1861, the day before Buchanan left office, the state granted the American Fur Company a two-year contract to supply annuities to the Missouri River tribes. The award was a blow to the challenge of Campbell and the opposition. Irritated by the midnight deal and worried by reports that questioned the Chouteaus' loyalty, the Lincoln administration replaced the two-year contract with a one-year agreement.

Carelessness rather than design delivered a powerful blow to the American Fur Company that year. The *Chippewa*, loaded with sixty thousand dollars' worth of cargo, including 113,000 pounds of Blackfeet annuities, caught fire on June 23 just below Poplar River. With the fire rapidly spreading toward nearly 6,000 pounds of gunpowder, the crew and passengers jumped overboard. The *Chippewa* exploded into a million fragments.[11]

The opposition partners nearly squandered these opportunities. Unfortunately, the personality conflicts that had soured relations earlier reappeared, undercutting Larpenteur's success. Perhaps jealous of the greater number of robes Larpenteur and Lemon were gathering, Smith and Boller sent separate letters to Larpenteur and Lemon in an attempt to provoke animosities between the two. The scheme worked:

> As Mr. Lemon was a new hand in the country, he did not know how to take such stuff, which made him look and act quite cross at times. I also received letters from the same parties, in which they used up Lemon about as badly as they did me. Thus matters stood until spring [1861] when, one day, after a few sharp words, the secret cause of our ill feelings toward each other came out.

Larpenteur patched up relations with Henry Boller when he visited in March 1861. Shoving the letters in Boller's face, Larpenteur demanded to know why they had been written, especially the one "about my taking the robes and peltries to St. Paul, to cheat you two gentlemen out of them? All you see here belongs to Robert Campbell till we have a settlement with him; after which, if there is anything to divide among ourselves, each will get his share. Every hair of this goes to St. Louis, not St. Paul. All his reply was, 'Let us bury the hatchet.'"[12]

On April 5, Boller and Lemon embarked in mackinaws with the robes piled high on board. The plan was for them to descend with the robes to

11. Sunder, *Fur Trade*, 226–28.
12. Hedren, ed., *Narrative of Larpenteur*, 273.

St. Louis while Larpenteur and Smith managed their respective posts. When the mackinaws arrived at Fort Berthold, however, Smith joined them. At St. Louis, "Mr. Campbell, astonished to see him, asked what brought him down. Not liking the reception he was given by Mr. Campbell," Smith defected to the American Fur Company. A discouraged Boller dropped out and looked for another line of work. Only Lemon remained loyal; he headed upriver by steamboat to help Larpenteur bring down the remaining robes. They safely arrived in St. Louis on August 4, 1861. Unfortunately, the robe market had withered. Campbell explained, "Gentlemen, I cannot sell your robes, except at great sacrifice, which I see no necessity to make. If you wish to return I will furnish your outfit. Now make up your minds and let me know."[13] The two traders quickly agreed to form Larpenteur, Lemon, and Company, with Robert and Hugh Campbell serving as guarantors. They even talked Boller into investing a small share, although he refused to accompany them back upriver.

Campbell helped the partners buy goods and hire men, and saw them off on a steamboat bound for St. Paul. There Larpenteur and Lemon bought seven wagons and hired eight men, and, on September 14, headed back to Poplar River Post. At the last minute, however, with winter barreling down on them, they acted on a rumor that the trade would be better near Fort Union and headed there. On November 9, they reached Fort Stewart's ruins and sent out messengers to find the bands. That winter would be as harsh as the previous one had been light.

With the opposition supplied and Hugh handling business, and feeling confident that Missouri had been saved for the Union, Campbell took his family and two nurses to Newport, Rhode Island, in June. They stayed for the summer and well into the fall. Before leaving them in July to scour markets for goods up and down the eastern seaboard, Campbell wrote his sister Anne a letter full of loving pride for his family:

> Our youngest child is cutting teeth and has been quite unwell but we hope that this fine climate will restore him to health, all the other members of the family are in excellent health and little Robert who suffered so much with his leg for the past two summers here now is quite well and runs about as well as the other boys—Hazlett has always enjoyed excellent health and is very robust. Hugh is very large for his years and although only 13 and 1/2 years old is almost a man in height.[14]

13. Ibid., 281.
14. Robert Campbell to Anne Campbell, July 11, 1861, Campbell papers, MLA.

Campbell returned with his goods to St. Louis in August. On October 3 he again headed east for more purchases and a brief vacation with his family in Newport. In November the Campbells returned to St. Louis.

The year 1862 opened with an economic disaster. On December 30, 1861, most New York banks suspended their specie payments, triggering similar actions by banks across the country over the next few weeks. The treasury was forced to follow suit, cutting off its payments to soldiers and contractors alike. The Campbell home was joyful, however, on January 6, 1862, when Virginia gave birth to George Winston. Later that month, with his baby seemingly healthy, Robert journeyed to eastern markets for six weeks before returning to his family in late March.

Business on the Missouri remained as cutthroat as ever. The federal government investigated the American Fur Company operations during 1862. While the investigators could not prove disloyalty to the Union, they did find plenty of malfeasance. Upper Missouri Agent Samuel Latta described the American Fur Company as

> the most corrupt institution ever tolerated in our country. They have in-volved the government in their speculations and schemes; they have en-slaved the Indians, kept them in ignorance; taken from them year to year their pitiful earnings in robes and furs, without giving them the equivilent; discouraged them in agriculture by telling them that should the white man find that their country would produce they would come in and take their lands from them. They break up and destroy every opposition to their trade that ventures into their country, and then make up their losses by extorting from the Indians.[15]

Latta went on to accuse the American Fur Company of taking the Crow and Assiniboine annuities for itself, and then selling them to those Indians.

Despite the damning indictment, the American Fur Company was the only firm capable of handling the annuities. In 1862, Chouteau's monopoly once again won that year's annuity contract.

Meanwhile, Larpenteur and Lemon spent a long, miserable winter amidst Fort Stewart's ruins. Few Indians came to trade. Men deserted. A growing bitterness split Larpenteur and Lemon. Lemon rejected Larpen-teur's plan to take goods up to the Milk River to exploit the Blackfeet trade; he did, however, succeed in bringing in the Gros Ventres, who traded 450 robes. Larpenteur stayed at Fort Stewart to manage trade and build a mackinaw to convey their robes downstream.

15. S. N. Latta to W. P. Dole, August 27, 1862, 37th Cong., 3d sess., HED No. 1, 340–41.

Aware that Larpenteur's venture was likely to fail, Campbell helped organize yet another opposition firm, La Barge, Harkness, and Company, which included Joseph and John La Barge, James Harkness, Eugene Jaccard, and American Fur Company defector Charles Galpin, who each dropped ten thousand dollars into their pool. They invested their money in trade goods and two steamboats, the *Emily* and *Shreveport*, captained respectively by Joseph and John La Barge. As usual, Campbell would sell the opposition most of their goods and market all their robes.

John La Barge got the *Shreveport* off first, on April 30. He waited for several days at the Yellowstone for his brother to arrive on the faster *Emily*. Finally he steamed on toward Fort Benton. Delays kept Joseph from steering the *Emily* away from the St. Louis wharf until May 14. Then he was checked by a confrontation with the American Fur Company that almost ended in a sinking and bloodshed. Above Fort Berthold, Joseph La Barge caught up to and tried to pass the American Fur Company's *Spread Eagle*, which held not only Charles Chouteau but also Indian Agent Latta. The two steamboats chugged abreast for over a mile. The channel narrowed ahead. Risking an explosion, La Barge pushed the steam power to its limit. As the *Emily* edged ahead, the *Spread Eagle* rammed it. La Barge grabbed a rifle and pointed it toward the *Spread Eagle*, whose captain Robert Bailey and several passengers responded by brandishing their own weapons. Fortunately, no one fired. La Barge later pressed charges against Bailey, who briefly lost his license. When La Barge reached Fort Stewart, Larpenteur transferred to him his robes and ascended the Missouri with him to build Fort Owen McKenzie near the Assiniboine Indians, Fort Galpin on the Milk River for the Gros Ventres, and Fort La Barge just upstream from Fort Benton for the Blackfeet. The *Emily* and the *Shreveport* then descended the Missouri safely back to St. Louis with 165 packs of robes for Campbell.

Like other businessmen, Campbell spent the war keeping one eye on his investments and the other on the fighting. His beloved family, however, always came first and gave him many worries and sorrows. Any satisfaction he felt in 1862 at his own business successes and Union victories was shattered on June 9 when diphtheria killed his namesake. The following day the company clerk George Nolan wrote that his boss "is again called to mourn the death of his son, Robert, an interesting little fellow of only seven years, died yesterday of sickness of diphtheria, it is very sad, as Mr. and Mrs. C. have been so very unfortunate with their children, and it being eight they have lost." Campbell expressed a grief so deep that he could only obliquely refer to himself: "Dear little Robert died on this day a week ago. He was loved by all who knew him. We were all very sad and the writer makes an effort when he writes or speaks of him, to show his submission to the will of God."[16]

Campbell shepherded his wife, his four surviving sons—Hugh, Hazlett, James Alexander, and George—his sister-in-law Mary, and their servants east on June 26. Death continued to stalk them. On June 30, six-month-old George Winston, also stricken with diphtheria, followed his brother to the grave. While his family continued on to the resort of Bedford Springs, Pennsylvania, Campbell returned with his baby's tiny casket to St. Louis and buried George Winston. On July 8, he and his brother Hugh embarked to join their family and buy goods elsewhere on the East Coast. A month later on August 9, Campbell returned to St. Louis. In late October, he ordered a monument built in Bellefontaine Cemetery for his family: "The front of the monument will face north which will be reserved for my wife and myself—we have buried nine of our children the names of five I wish on the side to the west and four on the side south . . . I . . . wish to have the portion of scripture 'to suffer little children to come unto me, and forbid them not, for such is the kingdom of God.' "[17]

As Campbell mourned the loss of his children, hundreds of thousands of other northern and southern families struggled with the deaths of their loved ones. The war ground on as Washington systematically tried to crush the Confederacy from all sides. To mobilize, dispatch, and supply vast armies and navies, Washington had to raise vast amounts of money.[18] The Internal Revenue Act of 1862 created a Bureau of Internal Revenue that supervised tax collection on a range of products and procedures. While the measure was essential for waging war, the taxes heaped the financial burden higher on businesses and households alike. Regulations designed to curb shipments to the enemy slowed business. Treasury officials inspected every shipment that left St. Louis. To discourage unnecessary shipments on a vital waterway and to raise revenue, a 5 percent tax was imposed on merchandise sent down the Mississippi River. Corrupt officials tended to discriminate against St. Louis firms in

16. RC Company to R. C. Martin, June 10, 1861, Campbell Papers, Robert Campbell to J. and J. Stewart Company, June 16, 1861, MLA.

17. RC Company to J. and J. Stewart Company, July 1, 1862, Robert Campbell to John Beard, October 27, 1862, ibid.

18. For good overviews of these other Lincoln policies, see Leonard Curry, *Blueprint for Modern America: Non-Military Legislation of the First Civil War Congress;* Bray Hammond, *Sovereignty and an Empty Purse: Banks and Politics in the Civil War.*

favor of Chicago firms. The St. Louis Union Merchants Exchange sent a delegation to Washington in September 1862 to protest the discrimination and the tax. The White House lifted the tax and promised to clean up the corruption.

Not all of Washington's actions inhibited business. Congress enacted two other laws that summer which would help settle the West and indirectly swell Campbell's business empire. On May 20, 1862, the Homestead Act was passed granting 160 acres of public land free to anyone who farmed it for five consecutive years or paid $1.25 an acre for it. The Morrill Act of July 2, 1862, created a Department of Agriculture that would foster greater farm productivity and create land-grant colleges from public land sales.

Washington also created the nation's first paper currency, known as greenbacks. Printing the amount needed to finance the war was inflationary. Campbell discussed that problem along with several others in a letter to his agent Seth Ward at Fort Laramie:

> General Craig has ordered more of the Ohio Cavalry to winter at Laramie. Mr Bullock thinks that you did not buy nearly enough of Indian goods . . . If you can buy Mules at low prices and get them Safely to Iowa and well wintered we think you would do well . . . The price of everything must advance in the proportion that "green backs" fall below the stands of Gold. If peace were only established people would operate with Confidence and until then we are all "groping in the dark."[19]

Although Campbell unconditionally supported the Union, he did not justify all actions taken to preserve it, especially if they appeared to affect him personally. To his friend General Henry Halleck, he protested an order dated December 24, 1862, that required American flags "to be suspended over the altars of the Methodist and Presbyterian churches . . . May I beg that you will cause this crusade against the church of my fathers to be discontinued. Already two Presbyterian ministers have been banished from the city—and one congregation broken up—without a word or act of disloyalty! I beg further to suggest that it is not good *policy* to quarrel with sects—whether they be Jews, Methodists, or Presbyterians."[20] It is not clear whether the offending flags were removed.

Throughout the war none of the half dozen rebel invasions of Missouri would seriously threaten St. Louis. After the initial skirmishing in

19. Robert Campbell to S. E. Ward, November 8, 1862, Campbell Papers, MLA.
20. Robert Campbell to General Henry Halleck, January 8, 1863, Campbell Papers, MLA.

May 1861, St. Louis was spared the bloodbath soaking most of Missouri and other regions of the United States. Yet, St. Louis experienced its own horrors. Refugees flooded the city, swelling the population from 160,000 in 1860 to 204,000 two years later. Homelessness, malnutrition, robbery, prostitution, and corruption soared.

While wealthy families like the Campbells could isolate themselves from most of these problems, life during the war was austere and full of grief. Campbell family friend Jesse Benton Fremont described those times as completely "changed. There was no life on the river; the many steamboats were laid up in their wharves; their fires out; the singing, cheery crews gone—they, empty, swaying idly with the current. As we drove through the deserted streets we saw all the closed shutters to warehouses and business places; wheels and horses hooves echoed loud and harshly when one drives through the silent streets late at night." Visiting English author Anthony Trollope was also struck by the steamboats "lying idle . . . in a continuous line nearly a mile in length . . . dirty, dingy, and now, alas, mute. They have ceased to groan and puff, and if this war be continued for six months longer will become rotten and useless."[21]

Although federal troops and a majority of its people kept St. Louis firmly in the Union camp, an *Atlantic Monthly* correspondent described how the war hurt and embittered nearly everyone: "The blockade of the river reduced the whole business of the city to about one third its former amount; and yet nothing could prevent refugees from the seat of war from seeking safety and sustenance in the impoverished town. Families were terribly divided. Children witnessed daily the horrid spectacle of their parents fiercely quarreling over the news of the morning, each denouncing what the other held sacred, and vaunting what the other dispised."[22]

Did the Irish-born Campbell and North Carolina belle Virginia ever squabble over the war? All surviving letters between them are loving and supportive; none speak of politics. Like most women of that era, Virginia Campbell left politics to the menfolk and concentrated on raising children, managing the household, and entertaining. Yet she undoubtedly had cousins fighting for the Confederacy and felt an abiding sentiment for her childhood community and state. She may have been more torn

21. Jessie Benton Fremont, *Souvenir of My Time,* 166. Anthony Trollope, *North America,* 386.
22. Quoted in Reps, *Saint Louis Illustrated,* 101.

than she let on, fretted more so as news arrived of battle after battle in which North Carolina regiments were engaged, and especially worried that final year when General Sherman's army invaded and ravaged her home state. Conflicting tensions surely afflicted the Campbells as they did countless other American families during the war.

In 1863, as if Campbell did not have enough to worry about given the precarious health of his family and businesses, he was forced to spend considerable time pleading leniency or favoritism to various authorities for family or friends. In January 1863, he learned that authorities had arrested and imprisoned a friend in St. Louis's Gratiot Prison. He set aside his work to write an extraordinary letter to President Lincoln that reveals the depth of his humanitarianism:

> I respectfully ask a pardon for Wm. P. Dixon . . . now in Gratiot Prison, in this city. If you do not deem it proper to grant a pardon, then I ask a commutation of his sentence . . . so that a *fat old* man may enjoy the open air in some free state. William P. Dixon had taken the usual oath of loyalty and allegiance, and that oath has been violated. Gunpowder had been concealed on his premises, and he did not disclose the fact, as was his duty. He is therefore guilty, and I do not pretend to extenuate his guilt. I knew this man . . . in North Carolina over forty years ago. During an interval of thirty years, I knew nothing of him. Within the last four years, the slight acquaintance of youth has been renewed, and of course I feel a deep interest in him, and in the preservation of his life, which I think is now endangered. On no former occasion, have I asked you for any favor, nor do I now claim any right to trespass upon you other than what belongs to any loyal citizen. This man Wm. Dixon has erred, but I trust he has not committed an "unpardonable sin." In the event of granting either a pardon or a commutation of his Sentence, I pledge myself for his future good conduct as a citizen.[23]

A seemingly favorable response came quickly. On February 3, Campbell could convey to Mrs. Dixon his "pleasure to inform you that we have this day received a telegram from Hon. John Tucker, Asst Secre of War, dated at Washington yesterday which says your friend is pardoned . . . Accept our hearty congratulations." Campbell wrote a thank-you letter to Tucker describing what happened when "I handed your telegram to [Dixon], and I only wish that . . . you . . . had been present. The luxury of 'doing good' would have been felt." There was, however, a catch: "On applying to Gen. Curtis . . . we found that no pardon had been received by either! This was a disappointment . . . As I stand in rather a peculiar

23. Robert Campbell to Abraham Lincoln, January 12, 1863, Campbell Papers, MLA.

situation with regard to this *pardoned* and *unpardoned* man . . . I beg you will cause me to be relieved from the dilemma, by causing the pardon to be *immediately* forwarded."[24]

Dixon was released days later. His travails, however, were not yet over. Two months later, Campbell wrote Interior Secretary Usher explaining that "a little fellow named Capt. Sayles Brown, of the enrolled militia considered that the pardon only related to the *person,*—not the *property* of Mr Dixon. He therefore seized the property under forfeiture of bond! . . . I have therefore to beg, as a special favor, that you will call on your friend [Secretary of War] Stanton & request him to send the pardon forthwith."[25]

There was yet another twist to the story—Dixon was rearrested. On May 25, Campbell wrote Tucker that "after waiting since 1st Apl to hear from the War Dept, I yesterday received a letter from HeadQuarters here, stating that any 'application for pardon & release of Wm. Dixon cannot be granted.' This letter has astonished me!" In yet another letter, he argued that "if you were informed that the crime of W. Dixon was 'grave', there must have been some mistake. It was a crime of omission not commission . . . To prove how differently the crime of Dixon was regarded here . . . Gen. Curtis . . . granted a commutation of sentence before I heard from Washington!"[26]

This last letter was decisive. Campbell wrote Dixon on June 3 that he had "received a telegram from John Tucker stating that 'the Sec of War has telgraphed Gen. Scofield to release Mr. Dixon.' Thus you are again free and may defy all attempts at arrest, unless you should again become liable by subsequent acts or words."[27]

Campbell used his pull to help out three other needy people that year. Fortunately, none took the strenuous efforts demanded by the Dixon case. Seth Ward's son Dick was expelled from the Christian Brothers Academy in St. Louis after a bout of mischief. Campbell intervened with authorities and got Dick reinstated. He also helped another Ward son, James, to enter Washington University. Then Campbell experienced a far more serious problem within his own extended family. Federal troops imprisoned Andrew Campbell's son, Robert Boyle, when he was

24. Robert Campbell to Mrs. Dixon, February 3, 1863, Robert Campbell to Tucker, February 12, 1863, ibid.

25. Robert Campbell to Holt, April 6, 1863, ibid.

26. Robert Campbell to Tucker, May 25, 1863, Robert Campbell to Holt, June 2, 1863, ibid.

27. Robert Campbell to Dixon, June 3, 1863, ibid.

caught with a traveler's pass signed by Confederate General Sterling Price himself. That was evidence enough to get Boyle hanged as a spy. Campbell managed to get his nephew released.[28]

Meanwhile, of course, business went on. Despite the eruption of a Sioux war on the plains, both the American Fur Company and La Barge, Harkness, and Company had no choice but to send steamboats up the Missouri. Not only was it essential to send supplies up to their respective posts and bring down robes, but annuities also had to be distributed. This year, the opposition won that contest, along with, it turns out, another.[29]

Following the quelling of the Indian war in Minnesota of 1862, the federal government decided to remove the Santee Sioux and Winnebago to the Fort Randall reservation in the Dakota Territory. Campbell worried that the Indians would suffer terribly on the crowded steamboats that would transport them from Fort Snelling on the Mississippi River to Fort Randall on the Missouri River. He skillfully packaged his humanitarian concern with arguments that opening a military road between the two forts would save the government and promote business:

> We respectively suggest that land transportation between those forts might not only be more comfortable to the Indians, but might cost less to the Government. We have also in view the possibility of a low stage of water in the Missi. & Missouri rivers . . . and also the effect of hot weather on crowded boats. Some of the small traders, on the upper Missouri and Yellow Stone Rivers, prefer, on the score of expedition & economy, to take their outfits from here to St. Paul and from hence overland.[30]

Learning further details of the removal, he protested to Indian Affairs Secretary Clark Thompson that the contractor violated an understanding that Washington would tolerate

> no delay or difficulty in embarking the Indians . . . it appears to us that S. Boatman, would be detered from undertaking their removal, as much influence must be used (for which they are unfitted) with Traders Interpreters to induce them to leave their present homes. We deem it unfortunate that any other than Agents of the Government should be allowed to influence those Indians, in such important matters, but as you interpret your instructions & the law, the course adopted is probably unavoidable.[31]

28. Hugh Campbell to Seth Ward, October 9, 1863, 1863 Letterbook, MLA; Andrew Campbell to Robert Campbell, September 17, 1863, Campbell Collection, MoHis.

29. See Hedren, ed., *Narrative of Larpenteur,* 292–99.

30. Robert Campbell to Usher, April 3, 1863, Campbell Papers, MLA.

31. Robert Campbell to Thompson, April 15, 1863, ibid.

The solution to the problem was to retain older sutlers and agents respected by the Indians. In a letter to congressional representative Frank Blair, Campbell singled out Seth E. Ward of Fort Laramie and Joseph Turbin of O'Fallon's Bluff as especially deserving of reappointment, while condemning a

> *"new crop"* of Indian agents . . . recently sent to the plains, a majority of whom seem to think that instead of being a check on the traders, they should participate in the profits! Hence they refuse permission to the old traders, unless they become partners, or act under licenses granted to the friends of the Indian Agent! . . . The result of all this may be another sad Indian outbreak, and we therefore deem it our duty to represent . . . that unless *for cause,* no license should be refused to old traders, in whom Indians have confidence.[32]

Most notorious of all Indian agents was John Loree, a "shrewd and intelligent Man . . . We respectfully ask that you will take such steps as you may deem right to prevent Agent Loree, or any other Indian agent, from participating in trade, or giving licenses to his *schoolmates and friends.* An Agent, we believe, should be a disinterested arbitrator between the traders and Indians." Hugh Campbell joined his brother in condemning the "arbitrary and selfish action of John Loree" at Fort Laramie, who granted licenses to "his brother, brother-in-law, and a schoolmate . . . Mr. Loree proposed to give a license to one person provided he bought the goods from his (the agent's) brother!"[33]

Unheeding of such protests, the government carried through its plan to transport the Sioux and Winnebago and retain the Indian agents. Not surprisingly, on April 16, 1863, Pierre Chouteau and Company won the contract from Indian Superintendent Clark W. Thompson. That summer Chouteau's firm conveyed 3,251 Indians from St. Paul to the Missouri River reservation for twenty-five dollars a head.[34]

The opposition did score a victory in 1863 when La Barge, Harkness, and Company won that year's annuity contract from William Dole, Commissioner of Indian Affairs. The fees included eight different rates, ranging from seventy-five cents for every hundred pounds of goods sent to Omaha to five dollars for every hundred pounds sent to Fort Sarpy or the Milk River mouth. In addition, La Barge won a contract to deliver

32. Robert Campbell to Frank Blair, September 21, 1863, ibid.
33. Robert Campbell to W. P. Dole, Indian Affairs Commissioner, October 23, 1863, Hugh Campbell to W. P. Dole, December 23, 1863, ibid.
34. Lass, *Steamboating,* 25.

supplies to the American Exploring and Mining Company that exploited Montana's gold fields. With these two contracts in hand, the opposition could make an enormous profit if they delivered the goods.[35]

On April 20, John La Barge's *Shreveport* set off packed with one hundred tons of goods and eighty passengers. Meanwhile, Joseph La Barge waited impatiently with the *Robert Campbell* at St. Louis for the annuities shipment. The Sioux war diminished that year's robes. McKenzie's Post had suffered the most. Sioux had killed two of its men and run off its livestock. John La Barge ordered it evacuated and pushed on upriver. Low water prevented the *Shreveport* from getting much beyond the Milk River. There, on June 20, La Barge unloaded supplies for Fort La Barge and headed back downriver. Meanwhile, the *Robert Campbell* had departed on May 13 with 650 tons of goods to be distributed at reservations up the Missouri. At the Heart River, the two steamboats met, then continued upstream together for protection. Above Fort Berthold, Sioux fired on them when they stopped to take on wood. Cannon aboard the *Robert Campbell* were fired and the Sioux were dispersed.

Disaster struck at a place called Tobacco Garden, halfway between Fort Berthold and Fort Union. There the steamboats stopped when a Sioux war party demanded a council and annuities. Seven men rowed a boat to shore to pick up the chiefs. The Sioux walked up to the boat and, after shaking hands with the boatmen, opened fire. Three men were killed, and the others plunged into the river and swam for the steamboats. The men on the steamboats opened fire, killing and wounding eighteen to thirty warriors.

Undaunted, the La Barge brothers pushed upstream. At the Yellowstone, the Assiniboine and Crow annuities were unloaded and stored in Fort Union. The river was too shallow for them to proceed farther, so they headed back downriver. Eighty miles below Fort Pierre II, a military detachment impressed the *Shreveport* into supply service back upstream. The boat's robes were transferred to the *Robert Campbell*. The brothers switched boats. The *Robert Campbell* continued downstream and arrived at St. Louis on August 6 with 889 packs of robes. The *Shreveport* was sent downstream to haul military supplies between Fort Leavenworth and Sioux City. These fortunes of war caused the opposition to fail to deliver the goods for the American Exploring and Mining Company, which promptly sued La Barge, Harkness, and Company for violating their contract.

35. Ibid., 43.

Although it would ultimately win that legal battle, like the succession of opposition firms before it, La Barge, Harkness, and Company folded. In November 1863, it disbanded after lasting only one round with the American Fur Company. More lawsuits followed as plaintiffs tried to recover money lost from broken contracts. The largest suit came from the freighters John Roe and Nicholas Wall, who claimed twenty-four thousand dollars for losses suffered when La Barge, Harkness, and Company failed to supply their wagon train at Bird's Rapids near Fort Benton. In 1865, the Montana Territorial Supreme Court ruled in favor of Roe and Wall. To raise money for these and other lost lawsuits, the former partners sold off their trading posts up the Missouri to the American Fur Company. La Barge estimated that his company lost more than one hundred thousand dollars from 1862 to 1865.[36]

The American Fur Company had its own difficulties that year. Its two steamers, the *Nellie Rogers* and *Alone,* survived the round trip. Sioux war parties sporadically fired on the boats. As the *Alone* was tied up at Roulette's Post, Assiniboine attacked the fort, killed all seven traders, and looted the goods. Those aboard the *Alone* cut its cable and escaped downriver. The *Nellie Rogers* meanwhile brought twenty thousand robes to St. Louis.

The military had successfully crushed the Santee Sioux rebellion in Minnesota in 1862. In 1863, a new Indian war burst out, this time with the Lakota Sioux straddling the Missouri River.[37] The army campaign against the Sioux did not begin until late summer. Two armies were sent against the Lakota, one led by General Henry Sibley from St. Paul and the other by General Alfred Sully from Sioux City. Private enterprise would supply and convey Sully's force upriver to Fort Pierre. Pierre Chouteau and Company won that contract. Low water impeded the expedition; Sully's troops did not reach Fort Pierre until mid-August. Sully defeated the Sioux at White Stone Hill on September 2, 1863. The war, however, would drag on for another year.

Amidst this Indian war, Campbell's son Hugh ventured out onto the plains. He was fifteen years old in 1863 and determined to follow in his father's footsteps. That year when the Campbells planned to summer in Milwaukee, Hugh begged permission to travel up the Platte River valley and visit family friend Seth Ward. How much Hugh had to cajole each parent to gain permission will remain unknown. After losing one child

36. Sunder, *Fur Trade,* 252.
37. Utley, *Frontiersmen in Blue,* 261–80.

after another, Virginia Campbell certainly must have protested the lad's plans. In the end, his father let him go.

Hugh had a glorious time. From Fort Laramie, he wrote his parents a letter filled with boyish excitement over his adventures: "Maj. Lowie said that he thought if the Indians knew who I was they would give me a dog-feast . . . I have just returned from shooting . . . All of them said that I could have killed an antelope. The distance was about 75 feet."[38] Hugh also met Friday, the Arapaho Indian boy that Campbell had escorted back to the mountains in 1833 after two years of schooling and life in St. Louis. Hugh recalled that upon "offering my hand to him [and saying] 'Come Friday let us shake hands for old acquaintance sake,' his eyes filled up instantly, and I was very much afraid that he would cry."

By late summer Hugh was safely back at the Campbell home in St. Louis. Despite his young age, Robert and Virginia must have feared that if the war dragged on much longer, they would have had to watch stoically as their son volunteered or was pressed into service.

Throughout the military, political, economic, and social battles engulfing the nation, Campbell systematically amassed more wealth. Despite the death of yet another opposition firm, the year had been profitable for him. His war contracting business flourished. With land prices low and a future boom anticipated, he invested much of the profits in real estate. As always, he spread his business chips as widely as possible to exploit possibilities and limit losses. Among those far-flung ventures were supply contracts with old mountain compañeros such as Jim Bridger in Wyoming Territory and Ceran St. Vrain and William Bent in New Mexico Territory. Even California was within Campbell's grasp.

Collecting debts owed him, however, remained as tedious and uncertain as ever. He opened one letter to a friend supervising investments in California by noting he had just returned "from a fishing excursion to Rock Island," perhaps intending to set a relaxed mood before launching into a request that debts be repaid: "You are aware that neither my broker nor myself derive any profit or advantage from those investments—except the pleasure which it affords us to serve our friends. Hereafter we will try to avoid action in those matters—for the 'times are out of joint' and I am getting old."[39]

38. Hugh Campbell, Jr., to Robert Campbell, August 15, 1863, Campbell House. Robert Campbell to Seth Ward, July 6, 1863, 1863 Letterbook, MLA.
39. Robert Campbell to Thompson Campbell, May 20, 1863, Campbell Papers, MLA.

Once again, the new year opened with joy, only to be followed by crushing sorrow for Campbell and his family. Virginia Campbell gave birth to John on January 30, 1864; spina bifida killed the baby on February 13. As if God had cursed their family, Robert and Virginia conceived one child after another only to watch helplessly as diseases killed ten out of thirteen of them. The childhood mortality rate for the Campbell family was appalling even for that time. Most of the children died in infancy; none enjoyed more than seven years of life. From then on Robert and Virginia could only cling to and pamper their three surviving children—Hugh, Hazlett, and James Alexander. Those boys enjoyed not just loving parents but also seven servants, luxury, wealth, and the best schooling available. Virginia tutored them when they were young. As teenagers they attended Smith Academy, Washington University's preparatory school. Although they all would live into adulthood, none would ever follow in their father's successes of character or business.

As 1864 unfolded, Campbell's business prospered everywhere but the perennial exception of the upper Missouri. The collapse of La Barge, Harkness, and Company the previous year assured that the American Fur Company would win the 1864 annuities contract for the Missouri. While the collapse of yet another opposition firm undoubtedly disappointed Campbell, he still raked in money from the Missouri. He bought up many of the robes brought down by independent traders and helped outfit many of those venturing to Idaho's gold fields. He did wrangle an important contract in September when the federal government authorized him to deliver $120,000 in payroll to troops in New Mexico. After an anxious month, the payment reached New Mexico in late October.

The business difficulties Campbell and other merchants and investors suffered during the war seemed to improve as 1864 opened. To William Bullock at Fort Laramie, he wrote that "Business is reviving. The military (or Treasury) restrictions on trade have been removed, and we begin to 'breathe more freely.' "[40] A deeply sincere humanitarianism continued to underwrite Campbell's business philosophy. In the same letter, he warned Bullock that "the Idaho gold mine fever seems to increase. You will have a large immigration passing through your region. We fear that many of them will suffer . . . without experience of the plains & mountains."

40. Robert Campbell to Bullock, March 8, 1864, ibid.

But what seemed like a ripe business year soured. The Campbell brothers had overextended their investments and loans, thus stifling their cash flow. Rather than threaten debtors with lawsuits, Campbell preferred to appeal to their sense of ethics and compassion. To one long-standing debtor, he wrote a psychologically astute letter that gently squeezed the other's emotions and pocketbook: "If you can spare a part of the principal of the loan made to you some years ago it would be received with pleasure. Both of us have been making investments and our cash balances are not so large as usual. We need some money. You will understand this is a *suggestion* merely—as we do not wish you to make any sacrifices whatever in order to pay us."[41] Most debtors responded in kind. Campbell, of course, still wielded a lawsuit when all else had failed and the stakes were high enough. But, in all, kindness and understanding probably made him more money over both the short and long term than did lawsuits.

No matter how close he skated to the edge of financial disaster, Campbell remained aloof from the unsavory business practices swirling beneath him. When pressed to buy up banknotes after the price dropped he disdainfully rejected the idea: "Gentlemen. In reply . . . we have merely to . . . not purchase the notes of our neighbors however good they may be."[42] Not taking advantage of the weak was only one of many ways that Campbell practiced the biblical injunction "to do unto others . . ." Throughout his life, he tried not only to remit money to his family in Ireland but also to contribute to worthy causes in St. Louis.

The Civil War even split churches. Reverend Henry A. Nelson of the First Presbyterian Church was a fervent abolitionist. He caused a stir when he entered a restaurant with several black ministers and tried to get service. Nelson remained defiant until they were finally served. In July 1864, three-fourths of the congregation abandoned Nelson's church to found the more conservative Walnut Street Presbyterian Church. The Campbells were among those who moved to the new church. That move symbolized Robert Campbell's position as pro-Union but tolerant of slavery and discrimination against free blacks.

By the end of 1864 the war was beginning to wind down. Union armies had conquered or blockaded much of the Confederacy. Abraham Lincoln was overwhelmingly reelected to the White House. The

41. Robert Campbell to R. Buchanan and Sons, May 15, 1864, ibid.
42. Robert Campbell and Co. to Odells and Barnes, New York, September 19, 1864, ibid.

Campbells could pass the holidays "joyously and pleasantly in this city. You would scarcely suppose that civil war existed, if you were now in Fourth Street. All of us are well."[43]

The year 1865 would bring peace to the reunited states. But before that occurred, Campbell would clash with the Radical Republicans, who had captured Missouri's state house. Dominated by Radical leader Charles Drake, a constitutional convention opened at St. Louis's Mercantile Library Hall on January 7, 1865; it would continue for three months. Drake and the Radicals pushed through three measures that racially, electorally, and judicially transformed Missouri. The first was to write slavery's abolition into the constitution. The next step was to push through a measure designed to disenfranchise Missouri's "rebels." Those who wanted to vote or hold public office, along with lawyers, jurors, teachers, and corporate executives and trustees had to take an "iron-clad oath" that they were innocent of all of eighty-six separate acts of disloyalty. The iron-clad oath law applied to all who had committed rebellious acts from the beginning of hostilities, effectively canceling amnesties for those who had taken them. The Radicals ignored arguments that the law was ex post facto.

By mid-March, Drake had lined up the votes to follow up his electoral revolution with a judicial revolution. By a 43 to 5 vote, the convention declared all state court judicial positions vacant as of May 1, 1864, thus allowing the governor to put Radicals in more than eight hundred positions through Missouri's supreme court, circuit courts, county courts, and special courts, including not only judges and clerks at each level but also all county recorders, attorneys, and sheriffs.

By April 8, a constitution had been hammered out and was submitted to the convention's vote. The delegates approved it 38 to 13. To become law, the constitution had to pass a referendum. Just after the convention ended and the campaign opened to push the constitution through in the referendum, word arrived of Abraham Lincoln's assassination. The tragedy fueled the Radical flames. Nonetheless, when the votes were all counted by July 1, the proposed constitution had passed by a very thin margin—1,862 of 85,478 ballots cast. On July 4, Governor Fletcher officially declared it Missouri's new constitution.

Campbell vainly protested this legal revolution. He wrote Representative Holt that, regarding "the new Constitution, it may be proper to say that as an organic law, it is generally looked upon as very objectionable.

43. Robert Campbell to Seth Ward, December 27, 1864, ibid.

A majority of the members of the Convention were unfitted for the discharge of the important duties assumed. They have produced a spiteful, vindictive . . . document and have shown the least possible respect for vested rights, while they repudiate every thing like conciliation."[44] Campbell would be among a minority who voted against the proposed constitution when it was presented to a referendum that summer.

Another "revolution" startled Campbell early in 1865. His nemesis of more than three decades, Pierre Chouteau and Company, the American Fur Company's last incarnation, abandoned the Missouri River trade. There were good reasons to sell out. Lincoln's election in 1860 had not only curbed the American Fur Company's patronage power but also opened it to investigations that crimped its operations and profits. With Lincoln's reelection, the company faced at least another four years of lean times. The Sioux war and diminishing buffalo herds had reduced the robe take. The price for robes had dropped with the demand for them while the heavy overhead of supplying trading posts remained as burdensome as ever. In all, the robe trade had been a losing enterprise for years. The only good money to be made on the Missouri these days came from carrying freight, annuities, and passengers. But a succession of opposition firms, most of which were partly underwritten by Campbell, had sapped profits from that trade. Although Chouteau and Company had always managed to crush the opposition, the victories were costly and ultimately Pyrrhic. The struggles had exhausted Pierre Chouteau, who would die in September 1865.

Nonetheless, the American Fur Company's demise came unexpectedly. For months, Charles Chouteau had debated with himself and other executives as to whether or not to fold. In March 1865, he was in Washington lobbying for that year's annuity contract and an extension of his trading license when he ran into James Boyd Hubbell, a rich Minnesota entrepreneur who had been trading on the Missouri River. Chouteau asked Hubbell to buy the Upper Missouri Outfit, lock, stock, and barrel. Hubbell agreed. Although the price was never revealed, Hubbell and his partners were rich enough to pay half the price immediately in cold cash. On March 23, 1865, Hubbell, Alpheus Hawley, James Smith, and Francis Bates signed a contract creating the Northwestern Fur Company for an initial four-year run. Hubbell and Hawley contributed ten thousand dollars each and their trading posts to the new company, while Smith and Bates chipped in fifty thousand dollars in goods and cash. Profits

44. Robert Campbell to Holt, June 27, 1865, ibid.

would be split equally among the investors. Campbell would sell that new firm much of its supplies.

Although Campbell's greatest opponent had toppled, yet another foe remained—corrupt, inefficient, arrogant Indian agents. Campbell continued to crusade against them as fiercely as ever. Although the army had defeated the Sioux, problems with all the plains tribes still festered

> owing to the remarkable selection of Indian agents. We became acquainted with several of those agents, & (with one exception) we have not known a set of men less fitted to represent the U. States amongst Indians . . . most of them represented themselves as *traders*, driving out all competition . . . We entertain the highest respect for the Sec. and the Commissioner, but we firmly believe that the outside political pressure has caused them to sanction appointments of selfish and incompetent agents;—who are the chief causes of existing troubles. Add to those evils, the imprudence (we will use no more severe language) of some *improvised* military commanders; and the Indian War is explained.[45]

Although over the decades Campbell had scored some victories by getting trusted friends such as Fitzpatrick, Ward, or Dougherty named as agents or sutlers, it was a war that he would and could never win. Indian agencies were prized political plums. It was understood that the appointee would use the position to skim a fortune into his own pockets from government appropriations that legally were to go to the Indians.

The year's greatest news, of course, was the Union's war victory and America's reunification. Characteristically, Campbell saw the war's end in largely business terms. He wrote: "The surrender of Lee's army, and the other remarkable events of the last few days, have disturbed the market, and upset all the calculations of speculators. Many failures are expected amongst those who have little, and risk much."[46] Campbell would watch those speculators bankrupt themselves as he continued to enrich himself.

45. Robert Campbell and Robert Twist, Washington, D.C., January 19, 1865, ibid.
46. Robert Campbell to Major W. Moore, April 11, 1865, ibid.

# New Directions (1865–1879)

**C**ampbell was sixty years old when the war ended. He was about to enter the last stage of his life, one that coincided with the nation's reconstruction. In that tumultuous era of dislocation, corruption, crime, reform, and unbridled industrial and population expansion, Robert Campbell achieved ever greater heights of wealth and prominence. While Reconstruction offered possibilities for great profits, the potential risks and costs were just as formidable. As always, Campbell's business acumen and forthright character, along with ample doses of luck, carried him successfully through the economic and political maelstrom in which many of his fellow capitalists were led astray by bad investments or outright corruption.

The war had profited a few and devastated millions. Reconstruction would cost the nation hundreds of millions of dollars, a necessity that would enrich the contractors.[1] The war devastated much of Missouri. Four years of guerrilla fighting had gutted the populations and economic vitality of entire regions across the state. Many fled to the safe haven of St. Louis, which swelled by 43,000 inhabitants during the war, bringing its population to 204,327 by 1866. Few of those refugees found better lives in St. Louis than they had enjoyed before the war. Most were on various forms of relief or barely eked out an existence. Thus all those extra mouths to feed were a net liability for St. Louis and a skimpy market for businessmen. It would take years before most of

1. McPherson, *Battle Cry*, 818–19. For overviews of reconstruction, see Eric L. Mc-Kitrick, *Andrew Johnson and Reconstruction*; Kenneth Stampp, *The Era of Reconstruction, 1865–1877*; David Gilcrest and W. David Lewis, eds., *Economic Change in the Civil War Era*; Ralph Andreano, ed., *The Economic Impact of the American Civil War*; Patrick O'Brien, *The Economic Effects of the Civil War*.

the refugees were resettled into comfortable, productive lives. A year after the war ended, Campbell complained of "the enormous quantity of unemployed persons here; seeking situations and starving from want of employment."[2]

Though exhausted from the strain of four years of war, Campbell was too swamped managing old and acquiring new businesses to take a much needed vacation. On July 6, he saw off his family and their servants on what was supposed to be an extended vacation through Minnesota and Canada to the East Coast. They got no farther than Minneapolis. Hazlett fell ill with scarlet fever in August. Upon getting a telegram of the news on August 12, Robert hastened to his son's side. This time death kept its distance. By the time he reached Hazlett, his son had recovered. The enthusiasm for a family vacation, however, had ended. Campbell returned with his family to St. Louis. By mid-October Hugh could confidently relate that "Little Hazlett has entirely recovered, and is bright and hearty. Jemmie [James Alexander] is well and both of them are affording great pleasure to the writer."[3]

Campbell returned again to the daily grind of managing a financial and mercantile empire. The speed and safety of the mails was of enormous importance to Robert Campbell with his far-flung business interests. In October, he felt compelled to scold Major William Moore at Fort Union for failing his "duty to devote some attention to the transmission of the mail through your place . . . This has caused great delay and a long detour. The mail for this or eastern places should be sent to Kansas City. From there they come in 19 hours to St. Louis, thus saving four or five days in time."[4]

Andrew Johnson, like his political predecessors, used the spoils system to fire federal officials and replace them with party loyalists. With the Johnson administration in power, Campbell and his associates lost much of their lobbying influence in Washington: "It is a matter of regret to us that we cannot intervene in some way in Washington . . . At this moment we did not know a single person connected with either of the executive or legislative departments of government on whom we have any claims. So much for keeping aloof from politics."[5]

2. Robert Campbell to P. Kyle, April 6, 1866, 1866 Letterbook, MLA; Primm, *Lion of the Valley*, 280.

3. Thomas Ranken to [?], August 15, 1865, Hugh Campbell to Mrs. John A. Clark, October 18, 1865, Campbell Papers, MLA.

4. Robert Campbell to W. H. Moore, October 17, 1865, ibid.

5. Hugh Campbell to John A. Clarke, October 30, 1866, ibid.

Those lines sum up Campbell's view of politics. He was not a crusader nor interested in political power for its own sake. Indeed he preferred to distance himself from the whole distasteful practice. Politics was important to him only as far as it affected his life; his involvement was limited to lobbying those in power who could enhance his ability to make money or help others.

As usual, he did all he could to help relatives and friends. In May 1865, he and Hugh wrote a letter to Lieutenant General Ulysses S. Grant recommending their nephew, artillery captain John Hamilton, for promotion, notwithstanding the "intended reduction and reorganization of the army." Despite his lack of political pull, Campbell was able to convince Grant to delay firing W. H. Moore, Fort Union's sutler, until a successor bought him out. Campbell also helped Seth Ward hang on as Fort Laramie's sutler. Less satisfying must have been the many times when friends asked him to use his pull to extract those rightly or wrongly thrown into jail. In January 1866, he talked General John Pope into releasing Joseph Turgeon, who was jailed on charges of illegally trading with the Indians. Two months later, he did the same for Michael Williams, this time asking Missouri Governor Thomas C. Fletcher for his release. Williams was pardoned the following month.[6]

In the postwar era, Campbell's business empire was concentrated in the interrelated fields of finance, railroads, and real estate, while he turned over his merchandise business to his brother Hugh and David Ranken. He would finally close his merchandise business in 1871 in order to pursue the other more lucrative businesses.

Playing the financial markets was his greatest source of wealth. Campbell was a magnet for those with money who wanted it invested by someone honest, capable, and connected. In 1865, for example, old mountain comrade Jim Bridger sent him $5,000 to invest, adding to the $3,000 he had earlier sent. The year's biggest deal landed in his lap from Hugh Ranken of Ireland, who wished to sell off his St. Louis property and reinvest the profits. Campbell sold the property for $410,000 and put most of it into treasury bills yielding 6 percent, along with $25,000 into St. Louis County bonds. The commission he took from that deal alone would have made him a wealthy man. While Campbell made

6. Hugh and Robert Campbell to U. S. Grant, May 13, 1865, Robert Campbell to W. H. Moore, May 27, 1866, Hugh Campbell to Joseph Turgeon, January 5, 1866, Robert Campbell to Thomas Fletcher, March 1, 1866, Hugh Campbell to Michael Williams, March 23, 1866, ibid.

money for others, he, in turn, depended on eastern financiers to make money for him. In July 1866, for example, he sent $32,411.76 to the eastern financiers Stewart and Company, followed by an additional $14,938.99 on July 16. And he continued to lend people money. By February 28, 1867, he had $11,106.37 in outstanding loans to people in Missouri, $3,140.54 in Illinois, $13,940.17 in Arkansas, $27,989.42 in Montana and Idaho, $9,074.15 in Iowa and Texas, $3,782.76 in Kansas, $1,474.22 in Nebraska and Utah, $13,839.47 in the Creek Nation, $50,564.46 in New Mexico and Colorado. Few of the entries had the word "paid" penciled in beside them.[7]

During the war, Campbell had expanded his investments in the Pacific Railroad to the point where he became one of three directors, along with Hudson Bridge and David Ranken. In 1865, the directors pooled enough of their own money to not only complete the Pacific Railroad's track to Kansas City but also buy up land and construct a terminal, train yard, and machine shop. The investments in Kansas City would pay off enormously for Campbell and the other directors in the coming years. Yet Campbell resigned as director that same year. It is likely he did so to avoid being involved in a bribery scandal that included George R. Taylor, the Pacific Railroad's president since 1860, and other executives. The scandal became public in 1867. Campbell's probable awareness of the corruption would have put him in a tough ethical and legal quandary. Should he inform on his friends and business partners, or turn a blind eye to the whole sordid mess? Whatever Campbell knew, he kept to himself. At best, he avoided the investors' lawsuits against those accused of corruption.[8]

Despite the scandal, it was essential for Missouri's economic development to expand the railroad. On the war's eve, Missouri had 810 miles of track. Construction of new track had ground to a halt during the war; it was difficult enough to keep repairing the tracks destroyed by guerrillas. Starting in late 1865, public policy and private interests meshed in developing the railroads in Missouri and across the nation. The federal government gave away public lands to the railroads. The Missouri legislature and St. Louis City Council passed various bond issues, tax reductions, grants, low-interest loans, and other subsidies for the railroads at the taxpayers' expense. The railroads again expanded,

7. Jim Bridger entry, 1865, Robert Campbell to Hugh Rankin, August 5, 1865, Campbell Ledgerbook, February 28, 1867, Robert Campbell to Stewart and Co., 1866, Ledger, MLA.
8. Primm, *Lion of the Valley*, 221–29.

but at an enormous cost. By January 1, 1868, the state's total railroad debt was $31,735,840 in bonds and interest due. Of this huge debt, the railroads would only pay back $6,131,496, while $25,604,344 was extracted from the taxpayers. That money had bought a mere 1,540 miles of new railroad track—a cost of $16,626 per mile.[9]

Notwithstanding the scandal and debts, St. Louis too had to invest in the railroads to maintain its economic dynamism. In 1868, St. Louis raised a $5 million bond to bridge the Mississippi. Engineer James B. Eads would complete the two-level rail and vehicular bridge, the world's first large-scale bridge built of steel rather than wrought iron, in 1874. Campbell was undoubtedly among the dignitaries in the fourteen-mile-long parade held to celebrate its opening. Although the final price tag was $9 million, the bridge linked St. Louis directly with eastern markets, and would soon pump millions of dollars into the local economy.

As a prominent stockholder in the Pacific Railroad and, more recently, the Illinois and St. Louis Railroad and Coal Company, Campbell played an important role in lobbying for these public policies. Not all of his efforts were successful. The Pacific Railroad received an unexpected setback in 1866 when Missouri farmers blocked Texas cattlemen from reaching the railhead at Sedalia, claiming that the longhorns carried Spanish fever that would devastate local cattle. The cattlemen turned their herd west toward Kansas railheads that fed into the Hannibal and St. Joseph Railroad. The Pacific Railroad lost fees on twenty-five thousand head of cattle that year alone. Campbell also failed to prevent the loss to St. Louis of an important industry, livestock yards, to rivals Kansas City and East St. Louis. The railroads converging on St. Louis hurt themselves when they refused to help local businessmen invest in a stockyard there. Kansas City opened its Union Stockyard in 1870 and East St. Louis its own stockyard in 1871.

These setbacks merely reduced potential profits. More troubling was the unsavory side to being a railroad tycoon. Campbell's railroad investments definitely brought into collision his capitalist and humanitarian values. Railroad monopolies unblinkingly gouged both passengers and shippers alike with exorbitant prices, and paid off politicians to kill bills that would regulate prices or improve river navigation for rival steamboats. Whether Campbell approved of the "monopoly rents" his railroads charged is unknown. He certainly did not hesitate to lobby hard for as big a share as possible from the public pork barrel.

9. William E. Parrish, *A History of Missouri: Volume III, 1860–1875*, 216.

He did understand well the impact the westward-creeping railroads would have on relations with the Indians:

The building of Rail Roads creates a necessity for the settlement of White people along the line of the Road and we know from sad experiences that where the White Men settle along side the Indians the latter must have less. The Rail Road interest has unfortunately too great influence . . . to be easily frustrated in obtaining any legislation that may be regarded to accomplish these objects, in running a road any where that is desired, and I have great fears of our being able to Keep the indian country clear of them. I will do all in my power to aid the Indian friends in advancing their interest.[10]

And then there was Campbell's real estate empire. Eventually, he succeeded in making the Southern Hotel his flagship investment. The idea for building what became the Southern Hotel dated back to the mid-1850s, when civic leaders recognized the need for a luxury hotel in St. Louis. On December 8, 1855, the Missouri legislature approved the incorporation of the Southern Hotel Company, in which Campbell would be a prominent investor. A subscription was issued and the entire block bordered by Sixth, Walnut, Seventh, and Elm Streets was purchased. Lack of funds, however, delayed construction. In 1860, the Missouri legislature exempted the Southern Hotel Company from taxes for a decade to spur development. The outbreak of the Civil War, however, prevented the Southern Hotel's completion and opening until December 6, 1865.

In August 1866, seeking to buy a controlling interest in the newly built "Southern Hotel," Campbell requested from Stewart and Company "$100,000 tomorrow provided I get the deed all right." Within days he got his deed in return for $500,000, half of which was borrowed from Boatman's Savings Institution. Triumphantly, he immediately embarked east to join his family in "Rye Beach [Connecticut] and after spending a few days then will visit New York."[11]

Over the years, through continual investments Campbell would convert the Southern Hotel into a luxurious palace and social magnet for St. Louis elites, of whom Robert and Virginia were among the leading royalty. In 1871, the *St. Louis Republican* reported the changes he had brought to the Southern Hotel, whose

10. Robert Campbell to Enoch May, esq., August 16, 1870, Campbell Papers, MLA.
11. Robert Campbell to Stewart and Co., August 14, 1866, ibid.

magnificent structure has for years been regarded as one of the finest hotels in the west. Perhaps in the United States . . . no hotel presented so many attractions to the traveler intent upon . . . enjoyment . . . but the Southern as it was known will be known no more. The hand of change is upon it. Improvement is the order of the day and the old house so magnificent . . . will become still more . . . grand . . . The changes effected—the grand billiard hall on Elm Street is gone, and replaced by a wide corridor extending back from the . . . rotunda . . . On either side of this marble paved passageway there are room fitted up for guests . . . Where the old bar was, are large rooms . . . for committees, clubs etc. Adjoining these are small rooms opening up to them for the use of subcommittees . . . Walls of these rooms are set back from the lines of columns so that one looking south from the grand entrance would have an unobstructed view of the line of columns through the street to street. The old staircase is to be replaced with a new and more elegant structure. A new and elegantly fitted washroom has been installed [behind] the grand stairway . . . There will be a new bar. The dining room has been redecorated. The ceiling has been newly canopied and the place fresh and cheery. The grand hall leading from the rotunda to the dining hall has been paved with marble tiles . . . All through the hotel it has been cleaned, redecorated, the great pier mirrors regilded, new curtains, . . . covered with elegant Royal Wilton carpets . . . Renovation has cost $60,000.[12]

Campbell's social responsibilities for his church may have taken as much time as that for his hotel. He was one of five trustees for the Walnut Street Presbyterian Church, having left the Second Presbyterian Church in 1864 during the schism over its liberal minister. His new church was a beehive of activity. Its "Manual" details such duties for members as the Sabbath services, expository lectures every Wednesday, prayer meetings every Friday, communion on the first Sabbaths in February, April, June, August, October, and December, Baptism rites preceding communion, meetings for "all who are concerned and anxious about their souls" every alternate Monday evening, meetings of the deacons every other Monday evening, the Sabbath school, business meetings for the school the evening of the second Tuesday in January, April, July, and October, neighborhood prayer meetings "among females living in destitute parts of the city, by the ladies of the church, and in the evening by young men," the "Ladies Society, organized to work in connection with the Synod's Committee of Missions [which] meets every Thursday from November to May; and the Ladies Prayer Meeting is held every Saturday," and the collection

12. *Missouri Republican,* September 1, 1874. Franciscus Catherine Lenzie, "St. Louis Social Customs"; St. Louis Hotel, Vertical File, MoHiS.

"taken up in the morning of each Lord's day in order to defray all the necessary expenses."[13]

In addition to attending the appropriate meetings, members were required to ask themselves a range of spiritual questions "frequently and solemnly." Those questions involved examining the nature of one's sins, one's trust in Jesus as the Savior, the depth of one's faith, the degree to which one tries to emulate the love of Jesus, the amount of time committed to doing good works through the church or on one's own, the ability of one to forgive the sins and trespasses of others, and the earnestness with which one tries to convert the impenitent. How often Robert Campbell asked himself these questions is impossible to say, but his letters reveal that those values guided his daily life to a degree few achieve.

While the Southern Hotel and Walnut Street Presbyterian Church were the pillars of the Campbells' social world, other cultural institutions were also important. Campbell served his ethnic roots by financial and social contributions to the fraternal Ancient Order of Hibernians. The Philharmonic Society, Haydn Orchestra, and St. Louis Oratorio Society, along with five theaters, offered regular performances. By one count, 233 theater troupes and individual artists performed across Missouri during the Reconstruction era; virtually all of them passed through St. Louis. The Public School Library Society of St. Louis sponsored lectures. Agricultural and mechanical fairs were annually held. Circuses were popular. While the Campbells undoubtedly attended many of the performances, they would have been less likely to be seen at more common entertainments that took place at cycling, baseball, ice skating, and horse racing arenas, and they most certainly shunned the less reputable ones such as cock fighting and boxing. At times, the Campbells certainly strolled or took a carriage ride in the new city parks. Until developer and Campbell friend Henry Shaw created Tower Grove Park in 1867, Lafayette Park was the city's only large public green space. In 1874, St. Louis bought 1,309 acres of farmland west of the expanding city and named it Forest Park.

Affluence, high culture, and education are clearly linked. Missouri's private and public schools blossomed after the Civil War. In 1867, Washington University in St. Louis opened Missouri's first law school. The

13. Church Manual for the Communicants of the Walnut Street Presbyterian Church of Saint Louis (Saint Louis: A. P. Cox, Printer, Office of the Missouri Presbytery, 1869), Campbell Papers, MLA.

1870 Census revealed that in higher education, Missouri held six private medical schools, three theology schools, three art and music academies, and eight commercial schools, and on the lower school level, thirty-seven private colleges, forty-five academies, and 586 private and boarding schools. An ever more literate public demanded more newspapers, journals, and books. By 1870, Missouri had 279 newspapers with a combined circulation of 522,866, of which there were 21 dailies with a circulation of 86,555.[14]

In 1867, Campbell felt his investments were secure enough that he could fulfill his wife's long-standing wish to undertake a grand tour of Europe. On June 26, Robert, Virginia, Hazlett, James Alexander, Hugh, and a servant embarked on the Cunard steamer, the *Persia*. After visiting his family in Ireland, they traveled through parts of Germany, Austria, Switzerland, Italy, and France, along the way visiting Paris, Geneva, Berlin, Lausanne, Baden, Prague, Vienna, Leipzig, Munich, Strasbourg, and Rome; marveled at glaciers, aristocrats, Sunday gambling at Baden, Garibaldi's speech before the Geneva peace congress, and magnificent palaces and mountains; bought up home furnishings; and dodged cholera epidemics. After all this, Campbell was eager to get back to business: "I would return at any moment, but Virginia and Hugh are desirous of seeing Italy before our return. I feel it right that they should be gratified as our family are all together."[15] They finally returned to St. Louis in May 1868.

Campbell had chosen a secure time for an extended vacation. The nation had suffered a sharp recession immediately after the war that required all of his efforts to keep his business empire intact. The demobilization of millions of troops, factory workers, teamsters, and contractors caused massive unemployment. Yet, after a harsh recession for a year, the economy expanded powerfully until the Panic of 1873. Massive investments in railroads both directly and indirectly spurred the expansion. The railroads demanded massive amounts of raw materials, steel, iron, and machinery to build and run, and they also, along with steamboats, linked communities across Missouri and between states to create one national market. In Missouri, the miles of railroad track nearly doubled, from 810 to 1,540 from 1865 to 1870 alone. The demand for goods to replace those lost during the war or fulfill new needs stimulated a

14. Parrish, *History of Missouri*, 186–97.
15. RC and Company to Stewart and Co., April 23, 1867, Campbell Papers, MLA; Robert Campbell to Andrew Campbell, November 3, 1867, Virginia Hamilton Collection, Estate Papers, MoHiS, p. 418.

manufacturing boom. By 1870, Missouri had 11,871 factories capitalized with $80,257,244 and employing 65,354 workers who turned out $206,213,429 worth of production. About 75 percent of that production was in St. Louis, which had 4,579 factories capitalized at $60,357,001 and employing 40,856 workers who produced $158,761,013 of goods. That output made St. Louis the nation's third-largest industrial city, after New York and Philadelphia. By 1871, St. Louis had spread over "an area twenty square miles with a hundred and seventy-five miles of improved streets; extending fourteen miles along the river with an average width of two miles, and terminating everywhere in the most beautiful of suburbs."[16]

A population explosion and the release of pent-up demands for goods and services fueled much of the economic expansion. The war had thinned the population across much of Missouri. Perhaps as many as 300,000 of 1,182,012 Missourians counted in 1860 fled the state. Many of the refugees returned after the war. The birth rate jumped. The government created the Missouri State Board of Immigration in February 1865 to encourage new settlers. Nearly two hundred thousand immigrants surged throughout the state to reclaim their own homes or buy property abandoned and seized by courts for back taxes. About 184,000 of the 193,728 immigrants came from northern states, solidifying Radical rule. In all, between 1865 and 1870, the state's population had doubled, to 1,721,295, while the population of St. Louis jumped from 204,000 to 310,864 and Kansas City's rose from 4,418 to 32,260.[17]

Unregulated population and industrial growth had made St. Louis an ever fouler cesspool of polluted streets, alleys, air, and water, and, at times, a charnel house of cholera victims, as the Campbells could mournfully attest. Households and businesses simply dumped their garbage into drainage ditches alongside the streets. Most of the city's sewage drained into Mill Creek, a fetid breeding stream for diseases and noxious odors. The city drew most of its water from polluted wells and pumped it into people's homes. As the visitor Edward Dicey noted, "the smokeless anthracite coal is not to be had, and therefore the great factories by the riverside cover the lower part of St. Louis with an English-looking haze of smoke."[18] That "haze" would aggravate Campbell's lung problems and eventually kill him.

16. U.S. Bureau of the Census, 1870; Parrish, *Missouri History*, 3:200–201, 223. Quote from Rep, *Saint Louis Illustrated*, 114.

17. U.S. Bureau of the Census, 1860, 1870; Fellman, *Inside War*, 242.

18. Quoted in Reps, *Saint Louis Illustrated*, 102.

Though Campbell remained a moderate Democrat, one Radical Republican he did back was St. Louis Mayor James Thomas, first elected in 1864 and then reelected in 1865 and 1867. Thomas was one of the city's most progressive mayors, fighting hard for and achieving programs and bond measures that dramatically changed St. Louis. He succeeded in pushing through city ordinances that required competitive bidding for private garbage collection, a new sewage and water system, and ward committees charged with solving local sanitation problems. He also received funding to expand and develop the wharfs along nineteen blocks of waterfront. St. Louis got its first grain elevator in autumn 1865, and investors erected others as the city's transportation links improved. The wharf and grain elevator development boosted St. Louis's ability to compete with Chicago's railroads and the steamboat lines of other midwestern cities. St. Louis had a long way to go to catch up to Chicago: in 1869, the city's total wholesale business was $195,970,000, less than half of Chicago's $400 million volume the following year. Although St. Louis's population of 310,864 was higher than Chicago's 298,977 in 1870, its per capita income was much lower.[19]

The reforms were expensive—the city's debt soared from $4.8 million in 1864 to $13.4 million in 1868. To manage that debt, Thomas pushed through city property tax increases to 1.3 percent. The combined county and state taxes were 1.5 percent. While minuscule by today's standards, the combined tax load was considered little short of confiscatory then.[20] As today, property owners hypocritically applauded the improvements in infrastructure that helped expand their incomes and improve their quality of life, but deplored the taxes vital for paying for them.

While the Radicals tried to reform Missouri, Ulysses S. Grant, upon assuming the presidency in 1869, acted upon the advice of Campbell and others to target Indian policy for a drastic overhaul. In his inaugural address, Grant declared his dedication to ensuring "the proper treatment of the original occupants of this land—the Indians."[21] For years, not just Indians but also knowledgeable Americans such as Campbell had blasted the Interior Department's Indian Bureau for outrageous and pervasive corruption, mismanagement, arrogance, and ignorance in the

19. Belcher, *Economic Rivalry*, 175, 177.

20. Primm, *Lion of the Valley*, 282.

21. Quoted in Francis Paul Prucha, *The Great Father: The United States Government and the American Indian;* see also Robert Utley, *Frontier Regulars: The United States Army and the Indians, 1866–1891,* 134–39, 188–92, 236–42; Mark Wahlgren Summers, *The Era of Good Stealings,* 192, 197–98, 201.

discharge of its duties. Tensions burned among all the tribes against the Indian Bureau. A crisis had erupted in the spring of 1869 when Red Cloud brought his Oglala band to Fort Laramie for annuities, only to be ordered to receive them at Fort Randall on the Missouri River three hundred miles away. War seemed imminent just a half year after the 1869 Fort Laramie Treaty ended the war Red Cloud successfully fought against the U.S. Army from 1866 through 1867 on the Bozeman Trail. The Fort Laramie Treaty assigned each Sioux band to a reservation and promised annual annuities that would provide adequate food, clothing, and shelter. The 1867 Medicine Lodge Treaty had provided similar promises for tribes on the southern plains. It was bad enough that Congress had delayed ratifying those treaties and appropriating the money. Much worse was that the legislature was required to allow the Indian Bureau to dispense the allocations.

To eliminate corruption, President Grant proposed a "peace policy" that entailed giving church groups the power to nominate agents and superintendents, and a Board of Indian Commissioners whose members served without pay to oversee those officials and the distribution of annuities. Each of the commission's ten members was to be a Christian philanthropist so wealthy that he would not be tempted by any conflict of interest. Grant had asked Ely Parker, his longtime aide and a Seneca chief, to head the commission and choose its members. Robert Campbell led the list of those Parker tapped to join.

Campbell was not only the commissioner most experienced in Indian affairs but also the only one living west of Pittsburgh. The commission's fieldwork fell to Campbell and Felix R. Brunot, the board's president. Accompanied by William Fayel, the commission's secretary, Campbell and Brunot journeyed to Fort Laramie in August 1870 to negotiate with Red Cloud. When Red Cloud and his band did not arrive, the commissioners headed farther west to talk the Utes into moving onto a reservation. Upon returning to Fort Laramie, they had to wait for weeks until Red Cloud appeared in early October. The commissioners failed to convince him to use Fort Randall for their annuities. After the negotiations broke up, the commissioners traveled across the plains to Tahlequah, Oklahoma, to meet with the Cherokees, who were attempting to form a territorial government. Finally, they went east to Washington to share their findings with the other commissioners and write up a report. The Board of Indian Commissioners boldly concluded that the only path for the Indians to take was eventual assimilation into white society. To that end, they called for the abolition of the treaty system and tribal sovereignty. Upon asserting, paradoxically, that "the white man has been the chief obstacle in the way of Indian civilization," they condemned the federal government's policies as "almost uniformly thwarted by the agencies employed to carry them out."[22]

The commission formed a Purchasing Committee to supply provisions for the Indians, and delegated to Campbell the duty of gathering those supplies. Campbell was determined to avoid any appearance of profiteering at the expense of the Indians and government alike. In the spring of 1872, he described such efforts:

> I have just completed another purchase of groceries and provisions for the Cheyenne, Arapahos, [and] Kiowas at the request of the commission and will have the last of these shipped today and I got them at very satisfactory prices. In order to get the flour I bought it on change with the assistance of an expert so as to be certain of no complaints which was made last year by some Indians. In order to purchase the best terms it was necessary to pay *Cash* on delivery.[23]

To Indian Affairs Commissioner F. A. Walker he wrote,

> I have purchased and shipped the provisions named in your letter and upon quite satisfactory terms . . . There have been so many complaints about the quality of flour *delivered* when bought by samples that I felt that the safest course to pursue would be to select a reliable merchant who would purchase the flour and have each barrel inspected and then have it packed in *double sacks* and thus be certain . . . This required that each purchase be paid for in cash on delivery and I determined to advance the money for this purpose and have paid the flour and all the expenses attending the sacking . . . I send herewith each bill and each item of expense.[24]

Despite his efforts, corruption continued to permeate relations with the Indians. The commission could not supervise each of the more than eight hundred officials in the Indian Bureau. By 1872, thirteen different Christian denominations were given quotas to nominate agents and supervisors, a portion of whom were anything but saintly in the discharge of their duties. Then there was the "Indian Ring" that included Interior Department Secretary Jacob Cox, his underlings, and other senior officials throughout the Grant administration who reaped fortunes from the treaty appropriations.

22. U.S. Congress, House Report of Commissioner of Indian Affairs, Ex. Doc. 1, 41st Cong., 2d sess., 1870.

23. Robert Campbell to George Stuart, April 12, 1872, Campbell Papers, MLA.

24. Robert Campbell to F. A. Walker, April 13, 1872, ibid.

In May 1874, the commission resigned in protest. Campbell explained that having

made up our minds that our commission could do no good any longer or serve as any check on the officers of the Interior Department, and at the same time we are subject to annoyance, and will be in some degree identified with wrong that we cannot prevent . . . Our board of commissioners . . . originally . . . was composed of gentlemen that it was pleasant to be associated with and I enjoyed our intercourse very much, but lately we have met with so much annoyance in the conduct of affairs, that . . . I cannot consent to continue. I may say that personally I have no reason to complain of anything by any officer . . . but the frequency of differences between the Indian bureau and Interior Department and our board that I do not want to subject myself to such annoyance any longer.[25]

Campbell visited President Grant to explain the corruption and the perverse policies. Grant was sympathetic but unable to curb the corruption rotting his administration. As Hugh shrewdly noted to Robert, "the prompt appointment of your successors . . . being all the secretary's selection will only serve to enlarge the 'Indian ring.'"[26]

Although Campbell had contributed to the commission little more than his reputation among the Indians for fair dealing, he did leave an enduring gift to historians. En route to the Fort Laramie negotiations in 1870, he dictated a "narrative" of his decade in the mountains to William Fayel, the commission's secretary. Fayel recalled that the "notes were taken by installments after various intervals on our trip, while the narrator was in the reminiscent mood, and each recital was suspended as soon as he found it tiresome." The narrative was important, Fayel rightly maintained, because "no connected account of that portion of Col. Campbell's life, had ever been given to the public. In fact, this is the only record ever authorized or made of Col. Campbell's experiences. With a modesty characteristic of him, he avoided notoriety."[27]

Several factors prompted Campbell to relate his narrative. Fayel's admiring and inquisitive presence, of course, was essential. But Campbell was also motivated to set the record straight. The mythic version of him contrived by Washington Irving in his historic novel, "The Adventures of Capt. Bonneville," had rankled Campbell since its publication a quarter century earlier. Fayel maintained that Campbell, "instead of

25. Robert Campbell to John V. Farwell, May 15, 1874, ibid.
26. Hugh Campbell to Robert Campbell, August 4, 1874, ibid.
27. Holloway, ed., *A Narrative*, 14.

feeling flattered and indisposed to criticism, told me that the account there given on the Blackfeet fight at Pierre's Hole, in which he participated was erroneous, and mixed up with incidents that transpired in other encounters. He . . . designed to have that account corrected." Yet in Campbell's own account, the nearly four decades that split the experiences from his memory blurred, highlighted, or obscured many incidents. The narrative was further muddied when Fayel neglected to write up his notes until 1881, and only then after being pressured by Campbell's son Hugh. Nonetheless, it remains the most comprehensive contemporary account of his life.[28]

The bittersweet flood of memories unleashed by Fayel's gentle but persistent prodding of Campbell's memory were revisited the following year. In late 1871, Campbell received a letter and manuscript from William Marshall Anderson, who had accompanied Bill Sublette on his 1834 expedition to establish Fort William on the Platte River and supply that year's rendezvous. The manuscript was a narrative of Anderson's trip. Anderson wrote that he hoped his manuscript,

> though covered with the dust of nearly forty years, may, through the magic power of memory, bring before you, with all the vividness of yesterday, places and persons, almost forgotten. You and I have looked upon the same bold and beautiful scenery, the same noble and manly faces, with expressions too dear to die. I am aware, in desiring you perusal of these, my old campfire records, that I am subjecting you to both pleasant and painful reminiscences. Such are the unaccountable, perhaps unavoidable, caprices of the mind. Of all that brave and hardy band of pioneers, companions of Ashley, successors of Sublette and Jackson, I know not how few are left . . . Who are left? Who are gone? I know not, but it is certain that the survivors must follow their file-leaders. "Time is passing and we are passing with it." The question is, not when, but where we shall go. Let us be armed and prepared to march when the trumpet sounds.[29]

Those questions must have ever more persistently echoed through Campbell's mind for the last half dozen years of his life. His old lung problems arose more frequently and severely, aggravated by the thick, sulfurous fog unleashed by the soft coal burned in thousands of factory, business, and household furnaces that smothered St. Louis. Summer sojourns at Saratoga Springs, New York, or Cape May, New Jersey, could lighten his suffering, but they could not cure his ailments.

28. Ibid., 14. See Holloway's introduction and notes for *A Narrative*.
29. William Marshall Anderson to Robert Campbell, September 15, 1871, in Morgan and Harris, eds., *Rocky Mountain Journals of William Marshall Anderson*, 3.

Starting with the Panic of 1873, the economic health of the nation and St. Louis seemed similarly entrapped in a depression that lingered across the nation throughout the mid-1870s, throwing thousands from their jobs and slashing the paychecks of those who remained.

During this time, welcome political news for Campbell and most other Missourians dispelled some of the economic gloom. In 1873, the Democratic Party recaptured Missouri's statehouse and assembly. The victorious party quickly set to work revising the constitution. A new state constitution was approved in November 1875 by an overwhelming 91,205 to 14,517 margin. The 1875 constitution included thirty-two tenets protecting civil rights, compared to the 1865 constitution's thirteen. However, the "protection" that some of these tenets promoted was dubious. Whites and blacks were protected from one another through legal apartheid in both marriages and schools. Many clauses limited the state's ability to favor business through land, bond, tax, and other subsidy giveaways. County and local governments were expressly prohibited from giving credit to corporations. The state was empowered to regulate and tax railroads. To pay off the state debt, the property tax was set at 20 cents on every hundred dollars, to be reduced to 15 cents once revenues reached $900 million. Eliminating corporate welfare allowed both taxes and the debt to fall. The St. Louis tax rate dropped from $3.49 on each $100 of property in 1875 to $1.90 in 1901. By 1903, the state had eliminated the $21.8 million debt of 1875.

These reforms were not strong enough to arrest, let alone reverse, the stranglehold of huge industrial monopolies on the state's economy. The economy was locked into a vicious cycle spun as monopolies pushed up prices and forced down wages, which caused consumer spending to plummet. As it did, corporate profits fell, which provoked another round of price hikes and wage cuts. Rage among most citizens and workers rose steadily, making some explosion ever more likely.

The explosion came in July 1877 when railroads across the country laid off workers and cut paychecks 10 percent for those who remained. Inspired by railroad strikes in West Virginia earlier in the month, St. Louis railroad workers shut down the system on July 22 and demanded a "living wage," an eight-hour day, the abolition of child labor, and other benefits; within three days railroad workers across Missouri had joined the demonstrations. As railroad workers marched through the St. Louis streets on July 25, they convinced thousands of workers from other industries to join a "general strike" that paralyzed the entire city.

Once again Campbell's humanitarian and business interests ground against each other. Although his reaction has been lost, the general strike must have frightened a conservative, wealthy businessman like Campbell. The city's business elite fought back, raising twenty thousand dollars to equip a militia to squash the strike. By July 27, the troops had broken the strike and restored order. Thankfully, despite all the rage, the city had escaped with only a few broken windows and a soldier who fell and stabbed himself with his own bayonet.

Crime too worsened as ever more people squeezed into a city with a stagnant economy. The city's population grew from 310,864 in 1870 to 350,518 in 1880, of which 54,901 were German, 28,566 Irish, and 22,356 black. Although they made up only 43 percent of the population, blacks and immigrants accounted for 74 percent of the city's crime.[30]

As a millionaire, Campbell could easily shield himself and his family from such ugly problems. During the 1870s, the Campbells spent considerable time and money entertaining a parade of distinguished guests, including Washington Irving, Father De Smet, Kit Carson, and William Tecumseh Sherman. The most luminous of their guests was President Grant. The *St. Louis Times* reported that on April 21, 1873, the president enjoyed

> a brilliant reception . . . at the residence of Colonel Robert Campbell, Indian Commissioner . . . An Elegant dinner was served up in the early part of the evening, at which General Grant and his family, General Babcock, General and Mrs. Harney and a few others, personal friends of the President and of Mrs. Campbell, were present, after which the reception took place. Although intended to be strictly of a private character, in consequence of the absence from home of Colonel Campbell, yet by 11 o'clock, the elegant parlors were literally thronged by the youth, beauty, and fashion of the city . . . dancing proved to be not the least interesting feature of the evening . . . At 12 o'clock precisely, the President was serenaded by the Arsenal band, whose charming music caused a large gathering of people in the neighborhood notwithstanding the lateness of the hour. The President retired at a reasonable hour, but the festivities were kept up for some time afterwards.

The *St. Louis Daily Globe* offered juicier details:

> The President expressed his regrets at the unavoidable absence of Hon. Robert Campbell, at New York. About half-past nine o'clock the party retired to other apartments, and prepared for a . . . young folks reception, given by Mr. Hugh Campbell for Miss Nellie Grant, at which most of the elite of the

30. Thelen, *Paths of Resistance,* 107.

city were present, and the ladies were very richly attired . . . Fifty-five ladies and sixty gentlemen participated in the festivities . . . Mr. Campbell was the escort to Miss Grant, and introduced her to the visitors in a very graceful and dignified manner. About midnight the full Arsenal Band . . . arrived . . . and serenaded the [notoriously tone-deaf] President for nearly an hour . . . The President . . . remarked to the lady with him, "This is very tiresome to me—having to go through this so often." The lady replied, "Yes General, it must be; but it is to please the people, who honor you."[31]

Whether at home or elsewhere, Virginia Campbell was often at the center of the whirl of upper-crust social events and arrangements. The eminent citizen Edward Bates recorded in his diary one of countless such social encounters. Virginia brought by carriage to Bates's door the "learned and dignified" Reverend Boardman and introduced the two men, who then enjoyed "an hour or two of very pleasant conversation."[32]

Campbell's health was in a slow, steady decline during the late 1870s. The old lung problems that had periodically visited him over the decades assailed him during a dinner party for General Sherman. The attack was so severe that Campbell remained confined to bed for a month. To recover, he and his family traveled to Saratoga Springs for the waters and social life.

Saratoga Springs was America's premier resort. Although the Indians had used its soothing mineral waters for centuries, the resort dated from 1815 when Gideon Putnam acquired the land, laid out a village, and built a spa. Saratoga's popularity increased steadily over the following decades as transportation to it improved, America's wealthy and middle classes expanded, and the plethora of seemingly endless activities to be enjoyed there expanded throughout the summer season. By midcentury, Saratoga Springs was renowned as America's playground.

31. *St. Louis Times,* April 22, 1873; *St. Louis Daily Globe,* April 22, 1873.
According to one story, probably apocryphal, not all guests at the Campbell House were "so distinquished. The very proper butler was horrified to find on the door-step a group of Indians in full regalia, feathered head-dress and painted faces. They had come to pay their respects to their friend and benefactor, Robert, whom they had made an honored member of their tribes, the Blackfeet. Mrs. Campbell was equal to the occasion. The story goes that the Indians squatted in a circle on the floor and were served fire-water from a large silver punch bowl. They had brought gifts too, beaded vests and moccasins, a long peace pipe, and befeathered war bonnets. When they took their departure, Mrs. Campbell who apparently had no liking for red savages ordered the downstairs thoroughly aired and rose-water sprinkled." (Mary Scott Crabbes, a relative of Virginia Campbell, "Campbell House," 3.) The story was family lore that went unrecorded until the 1940s.
32. Beale, ed., *Diary of Edward Bates,* 560.

The Congress, Union, and United States Hotels were the most prominent among the half dozen large hotels lining Broadway Avenue. By 1875,
the U-shaped, five-story Grand Union Hotel was the largest and Campbell's favorite; it fronted Broadway Avenue, held 840 guest rooms, sat
1,400 at meals served by 240 Negro waiters, and included a mile of mar-
bled piazzas lined with a thousand wicker chairs. Campbell undoubtedly
incorporated many ideas of service, design, cuisine, and events for his
own Southern Hotel from his many visits to Saratoga Springs.

Soaks in the mineral springs remained popular but were overshadowed by more pressing events. One could join the fashion show of those
strolling the piazzas, streets, or Congress Park, or embark in one of the
carriages clattering through town and the surrounding countryside. The
nation's most eligible young men and women promenaded, preened,
and intrigued for rich spouses; the wealthiest young ladies wore a different dress each day. None of Campbell's sons would court a young
lady there or anywhere else; they remained bachelors all their lives. But
the Campbells enjoyed themselves at fancy balls at one of the hotels
or private mansions in town, or attended concerts, plays, lectures, and
performances by comedians, magicians, and ventriloquists. Meals at the
elite hotels or at Lake House on Lake Saratoga a couple miles from town
were gargantuan affairs of eight courses and with arrays of delicacies
spread over two hours of dining. By the mid-1860s, thoroughbred horse
and intercollegiate boat races had become popular; an elegant casino
opened in 1869. Billiards, gambling, and bowling were popular among
the middle classes; some men of all stations slipped away to boxing
matches, cock fights, or brothels. The Campbells were present in August
1879 when the Grand Union was illuminated by the first electric lights.
Perhaps most important of all, the spa was a great place to cut deals;
Campbell could smoke cigars and bargain with such leading American
robber barons as Cornelius Vanderbilt and his sons, or Jay Gould, James
Fisk, J. Pierpont Morgan, John D. Rockefeller, and an array of lesser
millionaires like himself.[33]

Saratoga Springs could offer but fleeting relief from Campbell's ailments. His handwriting deteriorated throughout his last years to the
point where it was largely illegible. On February 14, 1877, he signed
his will, which was witnessed by Virginia, his sons Hugh, Hazlett, and
James, and business associates Thomas T. Gantt and David Ranken.
He left their Lucas Place home to Virginia for "her natural life, free

33. George Waller, *Saratoga: Saga of an Impious Era*.

of rent, taxes, and insurance," along with "all household and kitchen furniture, carriages and harness, together with the carriage horses" and "all pictures and jewelry." Virginia and Hugh would jointly manage the estate for the benefit of all surviving members of the immediate family. Before March 16, 1885, Hazlett and James were each entitled to twenty-five thousand dollars if they married and if Virginia and Hugh agreed to the match. This was an ironic provision considering Campbell's long wait to wed Virginia. After that date, the two youngest boys would also receive twenty-five thousand dollars each for any business they chose to pursue, again only if Virginia and Hugh approved. Upon March 16, 1885, the estate would be "divided into four parts, as nearly equal as may be," to "be awarded by lot." Any indivisible parts of Campbell's empire would be held in common. And any division to Hazlett or James depended on whether they remained free of "misconduct or irregularity of life." Virginia and Hugh were free to dispose of their inheritance as they wished; Hazlett and James had to hold on to theirs.[34]

Unfortunately, Campbell lived to see the destruction of his treasured Southern Hotel. On April 11, 1877, a fire broke out in the basement and rapidly spread throughout the building, totally destroying it and twenty-one people. Joseph Pulitzer was among those who escaped. The Southern Hotel was valued at $374,420, $92,000 more than the amount covered by insurance. Campbell appealed to the Tax Board to write off his loss.[35]

The disaster aggravated his lung problem. He returned to Saratoga Springs in the autumn of 1878 before returning for one last winter in his home. In June 1879, he and his family again summered at Saratoga Springs. Apparently the spa had done Campbell some good. With the family back in St. Louis, his son Hugh could write that "I am happy to say that my father is now convalescing—having had the strength to sit up two hours yesterday."[36]

The upturn was fleeting—Campbell's health steadily weakened. A crisis erupted on October 16 when he had trouble breathing and suffered terrible pains. At 10:50 that night Robert Campbell died. The following day he was interred in Bellefontaine Cemetery beside the ten tiny children with whom he enjoyed so much love and so little time.[37]

---

34. R. Campbell et al., H. Campbell, Jr., et al., Trustees, Book 622, Office of Recorder of Deeds, Campbell Papers, MLA.

35. Southern Hotel, Vertical File, MoHiS; Robert Campbell to Board of Appeals, April 10, 1878, Campbell Papers, MLA.

36. Hugh Campbell, Jr., to Bernard Donnelly, September 26, 1879, Campbell Papers, MLA.

37. "Robert Campbell," *Missouri Republican*, October 17, 1879.

Just what did Robert Campbell leave behind? If asked about his most important legacy, Campbell would most likely have named his wife Virginia and three surviving children. He deeply loved both his immediate family and his mother and siblings. It would not be long before his loved ones began joining him. Within months Hugh, Robert's brother, confidant, and last business partner, followed him to the grave.

Three years later, on January 30, 1882, Virginia Campbell joined Robert in death; she was sixty years old when she died. She and Robert had enjoyed an affectionate, mutually supportive marriage. Virginia had happily fulfilled all her wifely duties of supporting her husband, raising and tutoring her children, and managing the household. With a husband of Robert's wealth and status, she had been the perfect hostess, entertaining with equal graciousness and aplomb everyone from presidents to Indian chiefs.

None of Campbell's sons ever matched their father's strengths of character or business. They did not marry or have any known children. The oldest surviving son, Hugh, came closest to matching his father's sense of duty and ability to manage the $2 million estate Campbell left behind. Hugh had gone to Smith Preparatory School from 1859 to 1863, and then matriculated to Washington University, where he studied law from 1864 to 1867. That legal training undoubtedly helped Campbell in his last decade, and Hugh himself as he managed the estate and cared for his mother and brothers after his father passed away. With thirteen and fifteen years separating him from his younger brothers Hazlett and James Alexander, Hugh became a surrogate father to them. With only two years separating them, James and Hazlett became very close friends. Hazlett also attended Smith Academy, but preferred horses and baseball to study. From an early age, Hazlett displayed wide swings in mood and may have suffered from manic depression. Those problems worsened after his mother died. After attending Smith Academy, James Alexander went on to study law at Yale University from 1879 to 1882. His mother's death brought him home to stay. In 1885, he returned to law school, this time at Harvard, and graduated with honors in 1888. Like Hugh, he never practiced law. In 1888, the three brothers journeyed to Europe for a tour that lasted nearly two years. It came to a tragic and abrupt end when James died in Paris of lung congestion and pneumonia on July 13, 1890. His brothers brought him home to be buried in the Campbell plot at Bellefontaine Cemetery.

James's death devastated Hazlett and worsened his emotional problems. Hugh spent the rest of his life managing the estate and his brother.

He took Hazlett to specialists in America and Europe, but none were of any help. Through prudent investments, Hugh kept his father's estate intact. But Hugh too seemingly suffered from some psychological twist that made him increasingly reclusive in his later years. The social life of both Hugh and Hazlett seemed to center on the neighborhood children they befriended. Then, in 1924, Hazlett suffered a stroke that left him speechless. The following year, Hugh badly injured his hip in a fall.

The brothers spent the last years of their lives barricaded as recluses in their home and attended by servants. It is said that Hazlett even had a special lattice grill built over a balcony so that he could see without being seen.[38] He spent hours there watching the world go by. The estate survived the 1929 stock market collapse and subsequent Great Depression. When Hugh died on August 9, 1931, at age eighty-three, he left behind an estate of $1.8 million. As doctors had declared Hazlett of "unsound mind," trusted lawyers managed the estate for him. When pneumonia claimed Hazlett on March 27, 1938, Robert Campbell's line died with him.

With Hugh's probable prior agreement, Hazlett had willed one-third of his estate to Yale University to build a memorial to his deeply beloved brother, James Alexander. The memorial was never built. Eventually twelve hundred people used Hazlett's "unsound mind" and their own respective claims to be heirs to file suits for a cut of the Campbell fortune. The suits dragged on for three years. Among the claimants, 161 were eventually found to be legitimate. The estate was sold off and its assets distributed among the descendants. As Hazlett stipulated, the home went to Yale University.

Just when it seemed that the furnishings and keepsakes of Robert Campbell and his family were to be scattered forever, a local preservation group, the William Clark Society, mobilized a fund-raising drive. Enough money was raised to purchase from Yale not only the home but also most of its furnishings. In 1943, the Campbell House Museum opened. In the half century since then, many of those who have toured the beautifully restored Campbell home would probably have maintained that it was Campbell's greatest legacy.

To those who knew him, Campbell's enduring legacy would have been memories of his virtuous character. As one eulogist put it, Robert Campbell was universally known as

38. A theory believed by some at the Campbell House Museum.

a man of great generosity and warm, benevolent impulses, but always shunned publicity in his benefactions. Privately he gave much and gave continuously, but always with thoughtful discrimination and to good purpose, and accomplished an amount of good that will never be known . . . Mr. Campbell's honest and earnest qualities brought him many friends, yet he was not lavish of his friendship. Where he could not feel respect he never professed to be a friend. But if slow to admit strangers to his intimacy, he never forgot the claims of those whose worth he had proved. To use Shakespeare's striking figure, he grappled such to his soul with hooks of steel, and his friends were the friends of a lifetime. Their attachment to him rested on the solid basis of respect for all that is valuable in human nature . . . And for over fifty years he lived, a most conspicuous citizen of St. Louis, and yet during that long period, detraction never once ventured to bring a colorful charge against him.[39]

And yet, Robert Campbell's legacy goes far beyond the well-being and fond memories of those he touched throughout his life. The "bold and dashing life" that Campbell sometimes enjoyed and often stoically endured helped transform the West from wilderness to civilization, and America from an agrarian into an industrial nation. The greater those revolutions and the greater a role Campbell played in leading them, the more wealth and power he amassed.

But a Faustian dilemma clouded Campbell's rise from rags to riches. Those revolutions of civilization and industry enriched a few, improved the lives of most, and destroyed the lives and cultures of many. Campbell himself, as a man rooted in his time, place, and ever rising station, believed that those metamorphoses were largely progressive. Still, he was not blind to the devastation that "progress" wrought on the native peoples, wildlife, and landscapes of the West. Indeed, he deplored all that while accepting its inevitability. He understood that his own ruthless efforts to enrich himself through the fur and robe trade had left behind human and natural ruins. From his middle years, as business and pleasure took him east rather than west, that carnage became increasingly abstract. He could not escape, however, the effects of living in an increasingly crowded, polluted, and unsanitary St. Louis. Here again in pursuing wealth he helped lead a revolution, in this case urban and industrial, the transformation of a town into a metropolis. But unlike in the West, this revolution affected him personally. Disease killed ten of his thirteen children while pollution shortened and fouled his own life.

39. John Thomas Scharf, *History of St. Louis City and County,* 2 vols. (Philadelphia: Louis H. Everts and Company, 1883), 1:371–72.

Such were the dilemmas of Robert Campbell's life. But he differed from most other industrialists in two key ways. He recognized the dilemmas. More important, he acted on his awareness. He tried to compensate for whatever ills he helped create through countless acts of charity for the poor, hearty support for his friends, virtue in business, and love for his family. What more could he or anyone else have done?

# Robert Campbell Family Lifespans

Robert Campbell: February 12, 1804, to October 16, 1879

Virginia Campbell: January 1, 1822, to January 30, 1882

James Alexander Campbell: May 14, 1842, to June 10, 1849

Hugh Campbell: October 9, 1843, to February 15, 1844

Robert Campbell: November 27, 1844, to July 2, 1847

Lucy Ann Campbell: July 4, 1846, to September 1, 1847

Hugh Campbell: November 15, 1847, to August 9, 1931

Mary Campbell: September 23, 1849, to December 29, 1850

Robert Campbell: October 17, 1851, to February 12, 1852

Hazlett Kyle Campbell: November 23, 1853, to November 23, 1856

Robert Campbell: October 8, 1855, to June 9, 1862

Hazlett Kyle Campbell: February 2, 1858, to March 27, 1938

James Alexander Campbell: March 16, 1860, to July 13, 1890

George Winston Campbell: January 6, 1862, to June 30, 1862

John Campbell: January 30, 1864, to February 13, 1864

# Bibliography

## Collections

American Fur Company Account Books, 1822–1860. Missouri Historical Society (MoSHi).

American Fur Company Letterbooks. New York Historical Society, New York City.

Annual Reports of Thomas Fitzpatrick, Indian Agent, Upper Platte and Arkansas (1842–1857). Library of Congress, microfilm file 04093.

Annual Reports of D. D. Mitchell, Supt. of Indian Affairs (1849–1857). Library of Congress, microfilm file 04093.

Ashley, William Henry. Miscellaneous Papers. New York Public Library, New York City.

Ashley, William Henry. Papers, 1811–1840. MoSHi, St. Louis.

Bancroft, Hubert Howe. *California Pioneer Register and Index, 1842–1848.* Baltimore: 1964.

Bellefontaine Cemetery Records, 1868. Bellefontaine Cemetery, St. Louis.

Benton, Thomas Hart. "Proceedings of the Senate of the United States on the Bill for the Protection of the Fur Trade." St. Louis, 1824.

Billon, Frederic. "A Few Brief Notes of My Personal Knowledge of Gen. Wm. H. Ashley." Billon Collection, MoSHi.

Carrington, Henry B. *History of Indian Operations on the Plains: Hearings before Special Commission.* Fort McPherson, Nebr., 1867.

Chouteau, Pierre, Collection. MoSHi.

Chouteau Family Papers. MoSHi.

Chouteau-Mafflit Collection, 1828–1854. MoSHi.

Chouteau-Papin Collection, 1794–1872. MoSHi.

Chouteau-Walsh Collection, 1794–1869. MoSHi.

Clark, William. Papers, 1766–1899. MoSHi.

Clark, William. Papers, 1825–1832. Kansas State Historical Society.

Crooks, Ramsay. Manuscripts. MoSHi.

Documents on Microfilm from the Records of the Department of the Interior now in the National Archives Relating to the Fur Trade of the Missouri River Area, 1823–1840. MoSHi.

Dougherty, John. Papers. MoSHi.

Drips, Andrew. Papers. MoSHi.

Fur Trade Envelope. MoSHi.

Indian Trade Papers. MoSHi.

La Barge Collection. St. Charles County Historical Museum, St. Charles, Mo.

Lucas, J. B. C. Letters of Hon. J. B. C. Lucas from 1815 to 1836, ed. B. C. Lucas. St. Louis, 1905.

O'Fallon, John, Collection. MoSHi.

Selected Items Relating to the Fur Trade. Bancroft Library, University of California, Berkeley.

Sibley Family Papers, 1803–1865. Lindenwood College, St. Charles, Mo.

Smith, Jedediah S. Letters, 1827–1831. Kansas State Historical Society.

Smith, Jedediah S. Papers. MoSHi, Kansas State Historical Society.

Sublette, William L. Papers. MoSHi.

Sublette Family Papers, 1819–1860. MoSHi.

Superintendent of Indian Affairs, 1823–1832. Kansas Historical Society.

U. M. O., Letter Book B (P. Chouteau Collection), 1823–1835. MoSHi.

### Newspapers

*Daily Missouri Democrat* (St. Louis), 1853–1862, 1865.

*Daily Missouri Republican* (St. Louis), 1837–1865, October 17, 1879.

*Independent Patriot* or *Southern Patriot* (Jackson), 1821–1824.

*Missouri Advocate* and *St. Louis Enquirer*, 1825–1826.

*Missouri Gazette* (St. Louis), 1816–1855.

*Missouri Intelligencer* and *Boon's Lick Advertiser* (Franklin, Fayette, and Columbia), 1819–1835.

### Official Reports

Annual Statement of the Trade and Commerce of St. Louis.

"Report of the Secretary of War for 1823." 18th Cong., 1st sess., Sen. Doc. no. 1, pp. 55–108.

19th Cong., 1st sess., H. Doc. 117 (Atkinson-O'Fallon Expedition of 1825).

20th Cong., 2d sess., Sen. Doc. 67 (Ashley to Benton, November 12, 1927).

21st Cong., 2d sess., Sen. Ex. Doc. 39 (Ashley Trapper Travel Routines; Pilcher's Expedition 1827–1830; and Smith, Jackson and Sublette, by Smith).

### Primary Published Sources

*Annual Review, History of St. Louis, Commercial Statistics, Improvements of the Year, and Account of Leading Manufactures, etc., from the Missouri Republican, January 10, 1854.* St. Louis: Chambers and Knapp, 1854.

Ashley, William H. "Diary and Accounts, 1925." Edited by Dale L. Morgan. *Bulletin of the Missouri Historical Society.* St. Louis: October 1954, and January and April 1955.

Atkins, C. J., ed. "Log of the Steamer Robert Campbell, Jr. from St. Louis to Fort Benton, Montana Territory." *Collections of the State Historical Society of North Dakota,* vol. 2 (1908), 267–84.

Beale, Howard K., ed. *The Diary of Edward Bates, 1859–1866.* Washington, D.C.: Government Printing Office, 1933.

Bonner, T. D. *The Life and Adventures of James P. Beckwourth.* Edited by Delmont Oswald. Lincoln: University of Nebraska Press, 1972.

Brooks, George R. "The Journal of Hugh Campbell." *Bulletin of the Missouri Historical Society* 23, no. 3 (April 1967): 241–68.

Brooks, George R., ed. "The Private Journal of Robert Campbell." *Bulletin of the Missouri Historical Society* 20 (1963–1964): 3–24, 51–80.

———. *The Southwest Expedition of Jedediah Smith: His Personal Account of the Journey to California, 1826–1827.* Lincoln: University of Nebraska Press, 1977.

Brown, David L. *Three Years in the Rocky Mountains.* New York: 1950.

Campbell, Robert. Papers, 1825–1879. MoSHi. Papers, 1832–1842. William H. Semsrott, "Correspondance of Robert Campbell, 1834–1845" (edited by Stella M. Drumm and Isaac H. Lionberger). *Glimpses of the Past.* January–June 1941, pp. 3–65.

Dale, Harrison Clifford, ed. *The Explorations of William H. Ashley and Jedediah Smith, 1822–1829.* Lincoln: University of Nebraska Press, 1941.

Davis, Thomas, and Karin Ronnefeldt, eds. *People of the First Man: Life among the Plains Indians in their Final Days of Glory—the Firsthand Account of Prince Maximilien's Expedition up the Missouri River, 1833–34.* New York: E. P. Dutton, 1976.

"Diary of James Harkness, of the Firm of La Barge, Harkness, and Company." *Contributors to the Historical Society of Montana,* vol. 2 (1896), 343–61.

Dickens, Charles. *American Notes for General Circulation.* Clinton, Mass.: The Colonial Press, n.d.

Eberstadt, Charles, ed. *The Rocky Mountain Letters of Robert Campbell.* Printed for Frederick W. Beinecke. 1955.

Elliot, T. C., ed. "Peter Skene Ogden—Journal of Snake Expedition, 1827–1828, 1828–29." *Oregon Historical Society Quarterly* 11 (December 1910): 355–79.

Ellison, William, ed. *The Life and Adventures of George Nidever.* Berkeley: University of California Press, 1937.

Ewers, John C., ed. *Zenas Leonard, Fur Trapper.* Norman: University of Oklahoma Press, 1959.

Fremont, Jessie Benton. *Souvenir of My Time.* New York: 1887.

Fremont, John Charles. *Memoir of My Life.* Chicago and New York: 1887.

"Glimpses of the Past: Correspondence of Robert Campbell, 1834–1845." *Missouri Historical Society* 8, nos. 1–6 (January–June 1941): 1–65.

Haines, Aubrey L., ed. *Journal of a Trapper: Osborne Russell.* Lincoln: University of Nebraska Press, 1985.

Hall, James. *The West: Its Commerce and Navigation.* Cincinnati: H. W. Derby, 1848.

Hasselstrom, Linda, ed. *James Clyman: Journal of a Mountain Man.* Missoula, Mont.: Mountain Press Publishing, 1984.

Hedren, Paul, ed. *Forty Years a Fur Trader on the Upper Missouri: The Personal Narrative of Charles Larpenteur.* Lincoln: University of Nebraska Press, 1989.

Herr, Pamela, and Mary Lee Spence, eds. *The Letters of Jessie Benton Fremont.* Urbana: University of Illinois Press, 1993.

Holloway, Drew Alan, ed. *A Narrative of Colonel Robert Campbell's Experiences in the Rocky Mountain Fur Trade from 1825 to 1835 (as dictated to William Fayel).* Fairfield, Wash.: Ye Galleon Press, 1991.

Jones, John Beauchamp. *Life and Adventures of a Country Merchant*. Philadelphia: J. B. Lippincott and Company, 1882.

Keelme, Charles, ed. *St. Louis Directory for 1836–37*. St. Louis: Charles Keelme, 1836.

Kennerly, James. "Diary of James Kennerly, 1823–1826." Edited by Edgar B. Wesley. *Missouri Historical Society Collections*, vol. 6, October 1928, pp. 41–97.

McDermott, John Francis, ed. *The Early Histories of St. Louis*. St. Louis: St. Louis Historical Documents Foundation, 1952.

Maximilian, Prince of Wied. Neuwied, *Travels in the Interior of North America, 1832–34*. Vols. 22–24 of Thwaites, R. G., ed., *Early Western Travels*. Cleveland: Arthur H. Clark, 1904–1907.

Mooney, Michael MacDonald, ed. *George Catlin Letters and Notes on the North American Indians*. New York: Gramercy Books, 1975.

Morgan, Dale L., ed. *The West of William H. Ashley*. Denver: Old West Printing Company, 1964.

Morgan, Dale, and Eleanor Towles Harris, eds. *The Rocky Mountain Journals of William Marshall Anderson*. Lincoln: University of Nebraska Press, 1987.

Ogden, Peter Skene. "Snake Country Journals, 1824–29." Edited by T. C. Elliott. *Oregon Historical Society Quarterly* 10 (December 1909), 11 (April 1910); also published by the Hudson's Bay Record Society, London, 1950.

Paxton, John A. *The St. Louis Directory and Register Containing the Names, Professions, and Residence Heads of Families and Persons in Business . . .* St. Louis, 1821.

Powers, Kate N. B., ed. "John Ball: Across the Continent Seventy Years Ago." *Oregon Historical Quarterly* 3 (March 1902): 82–106.

Quaife, Milo M., ed. *Henry Boller among the Indians*. Chicago: 1959.

*Reports of Explorations and Surveys from the Mississippi River to the Pacific Ocean*. Washington, D.C.: Government Printing Office, 1861.

*A Review of the Trade and Commerce of St. Louis, for the Year 1849, as Compiled for and Published in the* Missouri Republican. St. Louis: Chambers and Knapp, 1850.

Russell, Elizabeth, ed. *Persimmon Hill: A Narrative of Old St. Louis and the Far West by William Clark Kennerly*. Norman: University of Oklahoma Press, 1948.

Scharf, John Thomas. *History of St. Louis City and County.* 2 vols. Philadelphia: Louis H. Everts and Company, 1883.

Stewart, William Drummond. *Edward Warren.* 1854. Missoula, Mont.:
Mountain Press, 1986.

Taylor, J. N., and M. O. Crooks. *Sketch Book of St. Louis.* St. Louis: George
Knapp and Company, 1858.

Trollope, Anthony. *North America.* Edited by Donald Smalley and Brad-
ford Allen Booth. New York: Alfred A. Knopf, 1951.

Thwaites, Reuben Gold, ed. *Early Western Travels.* 32 vols. Cleveland:
Arthur H. Clark, 1904–1907.

Victor, Frances Fuller. *The River of the West.* Hartford, Conn.: Columbian
Book Company, 1870.

Waldo, William. "Recollections of a Septuagenarian." *Glimpses of the Past.
Missouri Historical Society* 5 (April–June 1928): 59–94.

Wesley, Edgar B., ed. "Diary of James Kennerly, 1823–1826." *Missouri
Historical Society Collections* 6 (October 1928): 41–97.

Wetmore, Alphonso. *Gazeteer of the State of Missouri* . . . St. Louis: Charles
Keemle, 1837.

Young, F. J., ed. "The Correspondance and Journals of Captain Nathaniel J. Wyeth, 1831–36." *Sources of the History of Oregon,* vol. 1,
pts. 3–6. Eugene, Ore.: University Press, 1899.

## Secondary Published and Unpublished Sources

Adams, William Forbes. *Ireland and Irish Emigration to the New World from
1815 to the Famine.* New York: Russell and Russell, 1967.

Alcott, William Andrus. *Physiology of Marriage.* Boston: J. P. Jewett, 1855.

———. *The Young Husband.* Boston: C. C. Strong, 1951.

Alter, J. Cecil. *Jim Bridger.* Norman: University of Oklahoma, 1962.

Anderson, Harry. "The Controversial Sioux Amendment to the Fort
Laramie Treaty of 1851." *Nebraska History,* 201–20.

Anderson, Hattie M. "Frontier Economic Problems in Missouri, 1815–
1828." *Missouri Historical Review* 34 (1939–1940): 43–52, 56–68, 182–
203.

———. *The Social and Economic Bases of the Rise of the Jackson Group in
Missouri, 1815–1828.* Columbia: State Historical Society of Missouri,
1940.

Andreano, Ralph, ed. *The Economic Impact of the American Civil War.* New
York: Harper and Row, 1971.

Arthur, Timothy Shay. *The Mother*. Philadelphia: 1845.

Ashworth, John. *"Agrarians and Aristocrats": Party Ideology in the United States, 1837–1846*. London: 1983.

Athearn, Robert G. *Forts of the Upper Missouri*. Englewood Cliffs, N.J.: Prentice Hall, 1967.

Atherton, Lewis E. *The Frontier Merchant in Mid-America*. Columbia: University of Missouri Press, 1971.

———. *The Pioneer Merchant in Mid-America*. New York: Da Capo Press, 1969.

———. *"Western Mercantile Participation in the Indian Trades." Pacific Historical Review* 9 (September 1940): 281–85.

Baldwin, Leland D. *The Keelboat Age on Western Waters*. Pittsburgh: University of Pittsburgh Press, 1941.

Baym, Nina. *Women's Fiction: A Guide to Novels by and about Women in America, 1820–1870*. Ithaca, N.Y.: Cornell University Press, 1978.

Beecher, Catharine Esther. *The Duty of American Women to their Country*. New York: 1845.

Belcher, Wyatt Winton. *The Economic Rivalry between St. Louis and Chicago, 1850–1880*. New York: AMS Press, 1968.

Bemis, Samuel Flagg. *John Quincy Adams and the Foundations of American Foreign Policy*. New York: 1956.

Boyce, D. George. *Nineteenth-Century Ireland: The Search for Stability*. Dublin: Gill and Macmillan, 1990.

Brown, Jennifer S. H. *Strangers in Blood: Fur Trade Company Families in Indian Country*. Vancouver: University of British Columbia Press, 1980.

Cable, John Ray. *The Bank of the State of Missouri*. New York: AMS Press, 1969.

Carter, Harvey L. "Robert Campbell." In Leroy R. Hafen, ed., *Trappers of the Far West: Sixteen Biographical Sketches*. Lincoln: University of Nebraska Press, 1983. Pp. 297–308.

Child, Lydia Maria. *The Frugal Housewife*. New York: 1830.

———. *Good Wives*. New York: 1849.

———. *The Mother's Book*. New York: 1849.

Chittenden, Hiram Martin. *The American Fur Trade of the Far West*. 2 vols. New York: F. P. Harper, 1902; New York: Press of the Pioneers, 1935; Lincoln: University of Nebraska Press, 1986.

———. *History of Early Steamboat Navigation on the Missouri River: Life and Adventures of Joseph La Barge.* 2 vols. New York: F. P. Harper, 1903.

Chittenden, Hiram Martin, and A. T. Richardson, eds. *Life, Letters, and Travels of Father Pierre-Jean De Smet.* 4 vols. New York: 1905.

Christman, G. M. "The Mountain Bison." *American West* 8 (1971): 44–47.

Clokey, Richard. *William H. Ashley: Enterprise and Politics in the Trans-Mississippi West.* Norman: University of Oklahoma Press, 1980.

Cott, Nancy. *Bonds of Womanhood: "Women's Sphere" in New England, 1780–1835.* New Haven, Conn.: Yale University Press, 1977.

Cowan, J. M. "The Fur Trade and the Fur Cycle, 1825–1857." *British Columbia Historical Quarterly* 2 (1938): 19–30.

Crampton, C. Gregory, and Gloria G. Griffen. "The San Buenaventura, Mythical River of the West." *Pacific Historical Review* 25, no. 2 (May 1956): 163–71.

Cullen, L. M. *Life in Ireland.* New York: G. P. Putnam's Sons, 1968.

Curry, Leonard. *Blueprint for Modern America: Non-Military Legislation of the First Civil War Congress.* Nashville: Vanderbilt University Press, 1968.

Dale, Harrison C. *The Ashley-Smith Explorations and the Discovery of a Central Route to the Pacific, 1822–1829.* Glendale, Calif.: Arthur H. Clark Co., 1941; Lincoln: University of Nebraska Press, 1991.

———. *The Explorations of William H. Ashley and Jedediah Smith, 1822–1829.* Lincoln: University of Nebraska Press, 1991.

Dary, David. *Entrepreneurs of the Old West.* Lincoln: University of Nebraska Press, 1986.

Davis, W. N. "Post Trading in the West." *Exploration in Entrepreneurial History* 6 (October 1953): 30–37.

———. "The Sutler at Fort Bridger." *Western Historical Quarterly* (January 1971): 38–51.

Degler, Carl N. *At Odds: Women and the Family in America from the Revolution to the Present.* New York: Oxford University Press, 1980.

———. *Out of Our Past: The Forces That Shaped Modern America.* New York: Harper and Row, 1959.

Denig, Edwin Thompson. *Five Indian Tribes of the Upper Missouri: Sioux, Arickaras, Assiniboines, Crees, Crows.* Norman: University of Oklahoma Press, 1961.

Devoto, Bernard. *The Year of Decision: 1846.* Boston: Houghton Mifflin, 1946.

Dollar, C. D. "The High Plains Smallpox Epidemic of 1837–38." *Western Historical Quarterly* 8 (1977): 15–38.

Dorsey, Dorothy B. "The Panic and Depression of 1837–1843 in Missouri." *Missouri Historical Review* 30 (October 1935).

Douglas, Deane C. *The Ulster County.* Belfast, Northern Ireland: The Universities, 1985.

Eaton, Miles W. "The Development and Later Decline of the Hemp Industry in Missouri." *Missouri Historical Review* 43 (July 1949): 345–67.

Evans, E. Estyn. *Irish Folkways.* London: Routledge Press, 1988.

Ewers, John C. *The Blackfeet: Raiders on the Northwest Plains.* Norman: University of Oklahoma, 1958.

———. "Influence of the Fur Trade on Indians of the Northern Plains." In M. Bolus, ed., *People and Pelts.* Winnipeg: Peguis Publishers, 1972. Pp. 1–26.

Ewers, John C., ed. *Five Indian Tribes of the Upper Missouri.* Norman: University of Oklahoma Press, 1961.

Fellman, Michael. *Inside War: The Guerrilla Conflict in Missouri during the American Civil War.* New York: Oxford University Press, 1989.

Flores, Dan. "Bison Ecology and Bison Diplomacy: The Southern Plains from 1800–1850." *Journal of American History* 78, no. 2 (1991): 465–85.

Foley, William E. *The Genesis of Missouri: From Wilderness Outpost to Statehood.* Columbia: University of Missouri Press, 1989.

Freeman, Thomas W. *Ireland: Its Physical, Historical, Social, and Economic Geography.* London: Methuen and Co., 1950.

Frost, Donald Mackay, ed. "Notes of General Ashley, the Overland Trail, and South Pass." Worcester, Mass.: American Antiquarian Society, 1945.

Gates, Paul W. "The Railroads of Missouri, 1850–1870." *Missouri Historical Review* 26 (January 1932).

Gaul, R. W. "Death of the Thunderbolt: Some Notes on the Final Illness of Milton Sublette." *Bulletin of the Missouri Historical Society* 18, no. 1 (October 1961): 33–36.

Gilcrest, David, and W. David Lewis, eds. *Economic Change in the Civil War Era.* Greenville, Del.: Elutherian Mills-Hagley Foundation, 1965.

Gill, Conrad. *The Rise of the Irish Linen Industry.* London: Methuen and Co., 1925.

Goetzman, William H. "The Mountain Man as Jacksonian Man." *American Quarterly* 15 (1963): 402–15.

Goodrich, Carter. *Government Promotion of American Canals and Railroads, 1800–1890.* New York: Columbia University Press, 1960.

Gowans, Fred R. *Rocky Mountain Rendezvous: A History of the Fur Trade Rendezvous, 1825–1840.* Layton, Utah: Peregrine Smith, 1985.

Graebner, Norman A. *Empire on the Pacific: A Study in Continental Expansion.* New York: 1955.

Guthrie, Chester L., and Leo L. Gerald. "Upper Missouri Agency: An Account of the Indian Administration on the Frontier." *Pacific Historical Review* 10 (March 1941): 47–56.

Hadfield, Andrew, and John McVeagh, eds. *Strangers to that Land: British Perceptions of Ireland from the Reformation to the Famine.* Gerrards Cross, Buckinghamshire: Colin Smythe Limited, 1994.

Hafen, Leroy R. *Broken Hand: The Life of Thomas Fitzpatrick, Mountain Man, Guide, and Indian Agent.* 1931. Lincoln: University of Nebraska Press, 1973.

Hafen, Leroy R., ed. *Fur Traders and Mountain Men of the Upper Missouri.* Lincoln: University of Nebraska Press, 1995.

———. *Mountain Men and Fur Trappers of the Far West: Eighteen Biographical Sketches.* Glendale, Calif.: Arthur H. Clark, 1965; Lincoln: University of Nebraska Press, 1982.

———. *Trappers of the Far West: Sixteen Biographical Sketches.* Lincoln: University of Nebraska Press, 1983.

Hafen, Leroy R., and Frances M. Young. *Fort Laramie and the Pageant of the West, 1834–1890.* Glendale, Calif.: Arthur H. Clark, 1938.

Hahn, Steven, and Jonathan Prude, eds. *The Countryside in the Age of Capitalist Transformation: Essays in the Social History of Rural America.* Chapel Hill: University of North Carolina Press, 1985.

Hammond, Bray. *Banks and Politics in America from the Revolution to the Civil War.* Princeton, N.J.: Princeton University Press, 1957.

———. *Sovereignty and an Empty Purse: Banks and Politics in the Civil War.* Princeton, N.J.: Princeton University Press, 1970.

Hanson, C. E., Jr. "Castoreum." *Museum of the American Fur Trade Quarterly* 1 (1965): 3–7.

Hassrick, Royal B. *The Sioux: Life and Customs of a Warrior Society.* Norman: University of Oklahoma Press, 1964.

Hawver, Marlene. "Robert Campbell: Expectant Capitalist." Master's thesis, University of Nebraska–Omaha, 1980.

Hayden, Willard C. "The Battle of Pierre's Hole." *Idaho Yesterday* 16 (summer 1972): 2–11.

Helderman, Leonard C. *National and State Banks: A Study of their Origins.* Boston: Houghton Mifflin, 1931.

Hesseltine, William B. "Military Prisons of St. Louis." *Missouri Historical Review* 23 (April 1929): 380–99.

Hill, Burton S. "The Great Indian Treaty Council of 1851." *Nebraska History* 47 (March 1966): 85–110.

Holder, P. "The Fur Trade as Seen from the Indian Point of View." In J. F. McDermott, ed., *The Frontier Reexamined.* Urbana: University of Illinois Press, 1967. Pp. 129–39.

Holt, Charles F. *The Role of State Government in the Nineteenth Century American Economy, 1820–1902: A Quantitative Study.* New York: Arno Press, 1977.

Hunter, L. C. *Steamboats on the Western Rivers: An Economic and Technological History.* Cambridge, Mass.: Harvard University Press, 1949.

Huss, Stephen. "Take No Advantage: The Biography of Robert Campbell." Ph.D. diss., St. Louis University, 1989.

Irving, Washington. *The Adventures of Captain Bonneville.* Edited by Robert A. Rees and Alan Sandy. Boston: Twayne Publishers, 1977.

Jackson, Donald. "The Indian and the Frontier in American History—A Need for Revision." *Western Historical Quarterly* 4 (1979): 43–56.

———. *Voyages of the Steamboat* Yellow Stone. New York: Ticknor and Fields, 1985.

Jackson, John C. *Children of the Fur Trade: Forgotten Metis of the Pacific Northwest.* Missoula, Mont.: Mountain Press, 1995.

Jacobs, W. R. "Frontiersmen, Fur Traders, and Other Varmints, An Ecological Appraisal of the Frontier in American History." *American Historical Association Newsletter* 8 (November 1970): 5–11.

Johannsen, Robert W. *To the Halls of Montezuma: The War with Mexico in the American Imagination.* New York: 1985.

Jones, Hoyle. "Seth C. Ward." *Annals of Wyoming* 5 (July 1927): 5–18.

Jones, John Beauchamp (alias Luke Shortfield). *The West: Its Commerce and Navigation*. Philadelphia: Gregg, Eliot and Company, 1849.

Kardulias, Nick P. "Fur Production as a Specialized Activity in a World System: Indians in the North American Fur Trade." *American Indian Culture and Research Journal* 14, no. 1 (1990): 25–60.

Kay, Jeanne. "The Fur Trade and Native American Population Growth." *Ethnohistory* 31, no. 1 (1990): 25–60.

Kennedy, Liam, and Philip Ollerenshaw. *An Economic History of Ulster*. Manchester, England: Manchester University Press, 1985.

Kennedy, Michael Stephen. *The Assiniboines*. Norman: University of Oklahoma Press, 1961.

Killoren, John J. *"Come Blackrobe": De Smet and the Indian Tragedy*. Norman: University of Oklahoma Press, 1994.

Kirk, Sylvia Van. *"Many Tender Ties": Women in Fur Trade Society in Western Canada, 1670–1870*. Winnipeg: Watson and Dwyer Publishing Ltd., 1980.

Kirkpatrick, Arthur R. "Missouri on the Eve of Civil War." *Missouri Historical Review* 55 (January 1961): 99–108.

Larkin, Jack. *The Reshaping of Everyday Life, 1790–1840*. New York: Harper-Perennial, 1988.

Lass, W. E. *A History of Steamboating on the Upper Missouri River*. Lincoln: University of Nebraska Press, 1962.

Lavender, David. *Fist in the Wilderness*. New York: Doubleday, 1964.

Lenzie, Franciscus Catherine. "St. Louis Customs." *Missouri Historical Society Bulletin* 19, no. 2 (1954).

Lowie, Robert H. *The Crow Indians*. Lincoln: University of Nebraska, 1983.

McAleer, P. *Townland Names of County Tyrone*. Draperstown, Northern Ireland: Moyola Books, 1983.

McClelland, David C. *The Achieving Society*. Princeton, N.J.: Van Nostrand, 1961.

McClelland, David C., et al. *The Achievement Motive*. New York: Appleton-Century-Croft, 1953.

McCormick, Richard P. *The Second American Party System: Party Formation in the Jacksonian Era*. Chapel Hill: University of North Carolina Press, 1966.

McKitrick, Eric L. *Andrew Johnson and Reconstruction*. Chicago: University of Chicago Press, 1960.

McPherson, James. *Battle Cry of Freedom: The Civil War Era.* New York: Oxford University Press, 1988.

McReynolds, Edwin C. *Missouri: A History of the Crossroads State.* Norman: University of Oklahoma Press, 1962.

Mann, Horace. *Lectures on Education.* Boston: 1850.

Martin, C. "Wildlife Diseases as a Factor in the Depopulation of the North American Indian." *Western Historical Quarterly* 7 (1976): 47–62.

Mattes, Merrill J. "The Sutler's Store at Fort Laramie." *Annals of Wyoming* 18, no. 2 (July 1946): 93–133.

Mattison, Ray H. "The Upper Missouri Fur Trade: Its Methods and Operations." *Nebraska History* 42 (1961): 1–28.

Mering, John V. *The Whig Party of Missouri.* Columbia: University of Missouri Press, 1967.

Merk, Frederick. *Albert Gallatin and the Oregon Problem.* Cambridge, Mass.: Harvard University Press, 1950.

———. *The Oregon Question: Essays in Anglo-American Diplomacy and Politics.* Cambridge, Mass.: Harvard University Press, 1967.

Miller, Kirby. *Emigrants and Exiles.* New York: Oxford University Press, 1985.

Mitchell, Reid. "The Creation of Confederate Loyalties." In Robert Abzug and Stephen Maizlish, eds., *Race and Slavery in America.* Lexington: University of Kentucky Press, 1986.

Moodie, D. W., and A. J. Ray. "Buffalo Migrations in the Canadian Plains." *Plains Anthropologist* 21 (1976): 45–54.

Morgan, Dale L. *Jedediah Smith and the Opening of the West.* Lincoln: University of Nebraska Press, 1953.

———. "New Light on Ashley and Jedediah Smith." *Pacific Historian* 12 (May 1968): 14–23.

Morrell, Alfred. *Beaver Behavior.* Happy Camp, Calif.: Naturegraph Publications, 1986.

Moss, James Earl. "William Henry Ashley: A Jackson Man with Feet of Clay, Missouri's Special Election of 1831." *Missouri Historical Review* 61 (October 1966): 1–20.

Nute, Grace Lee. "The Papers of the American Fur Company: A Brief Estimate of Their Significance." *American Historical Review* 32 (April 1927): 519–38.

O'Brien, Patrick. *The Economic Effects of the Civil War.* Atlantic Highlands, N.J.: Humanities Press International, 1988.

Parrish, William E. *A History of Missouri: Volume III, 1860–1875.* Columbia: University of Missouri Press, 1973.

———. *Missouri under Radical Rule, 1865–1870.* Columbia: University of Missouri Press, 1965.

———. *Turbulent Partnership: Missouri and the Union, 1861–1865.* Columbia: University of Missouri Press, 1963.

Phillips, Charles. *Missouri: Mother of the American West.* Northridge, Calif.: Windsor Publications, 1988.

Phillips, Paul Crisler. *The Fur Trade.* 2 vols. Norman: University of Oklahoma Press, 1961.

Pletcher, David. *The Diplomacy of Annexation: Texas, Mexico, and the Mexican War.* Columbia: University of Missouri Press, 1973.

Porter, Kenneth Wiggins. *John Jacob Astor: Business Man.* 2 vols. Cambridge: Harvard University Press, 1931.

Porter, Mae Reed, and Odessa Davenport. *Scotsman in Buckskin: Sir William Drummond Stewart and the Rocky Mountain Fur Trade.* New York: Hastings House Publishers, 1963.

Primm, James Neal. *Economic Policy in the Development of a Western State, 1820–1860.* Cambridge: Harvard University Press, 1954.

———. *Lion of the Valley: Saint Louis, Missouri.* Boulder, Colo.: Pruett Publishing Co., 1990.

Prucha, Francis Paul. "Army Sutlers and the American Fur Company." *Minnesota History* 40 (spring 1966): 22–31.

———. *The Great Father: The United States Government and the American Indian.* Lincoln: University of Nebraska Press, 1986.

Ray, Arthur J. "Some Conservation Schemes of the Hudson's Bay Company, 1821–50: An Examination of Resource Management in the Fur Trade." *Journal of Historical Geography* 1 (1975): 49–65.

Reps, John W. *Saint Louis Illustrated: Nineteenth-Century Engravings and Lithographs of a Mississippi Metropolis.* Columbia: University of Missouri Press, 1989.

Roe, F. G. *The North American Buffalo: A Critical Study of the Species in Its Wild State.* Toronto: University of Toronto Press, 1951.

Rosen, Richard Allen. "Rethinking the Row House: The Development of Lucas Place, 1850–1865." *Gateway Heritage* (summer 1992): 20–28.

Rowe, David G. "Government Relations with the Fur Trappers of the Upper Missouri, 1820–1840." *North Dakota History* 35 (spring 1968): 480–505.

Ryan, Mary P. *The Empire of the Mother: American Writing about Domesticity, 1830–1860*. New York: Haworth Press, 1982.

Ryle, Walter H. *Missouri: Union or Secession*. Nashville: George Peabody College for Teachers, 1931.

Saum, Lewis. *The Fur Trader and the Indian*. Seattle: University of Washington Press, 1987.

Savage, Charles C. *Architecture of the Private Streets of St. Louis: The Architects and the Houses They Designed*. Columbia: University of Missouri Press, 1987.

Schlesinger, Arthur M. *The Age of Jackson*. Boston: Little, Brown and Co., 1945.

Sedgwick, Catherine Maria. *Home*. Boston: 1837.

Seton, E. T. *Life Histories of Northern Animals: An Account of the Mammals of Manitoba*. Vol. 1. New York: Constable and Co., 1910.

Shade, William G. *Banks or No Banks: The Money Issues in Western Politics, 1832–1865*. Detroit: Wayne State University Press, 1972.

Shalhope, Robert. "Eugene Genovese, the Missouri Elite, and Civil War Historiography." *Bulletin of the Missouri Historical Society* 26 (July 1970): 271–82.

———. "Thomas Hart Benton and Missouri State Politics: A Reexamination." *Bulletin of the Missouri Historical Society* 25 (1969): 171–91.

Sharp, James Roger. *The Jacksonians versus the Banks: Politics in the States after the Panic of 1837*. New York: Columbia University Press, 1970.

Shuskey, Ernest L. "The Upper Missouri Indian Agency, 1819–1868." *Missouri Historical Review* 65 (April 1971): 249–69.

Smith, Page. *The Shaping of America: A People's History of the Young Republic*. Vol. 4. New York: Penguin Books, 1989.

Stampp, Kenneth. *The Era of Reconstruction, 1865–1877*. New York: Alfred A. Knopf, 1960.

Summers, Mark Wahlgren. *The Era of Good Stealings*. New York: Columbia University Press, 1993.

Sunder, John E. *Bill Sublette: Mountain Man*. Norman: University of Oklahoma Press, 1959, 1987.

———. *The Fur Trade on the Upper Missouri, 1840–1865*. Norman: University of Oklahoma Press, 1965.

———. *Joshua Pilcher, Fur Trader and Indian Agent*. Norman: University of Oklahoma Press, 1968.

Swagerty, William R. "Marriage and Settlement Patterns of Rocky Mountain Trappers and Traders." *Western Historical Quarterly* 11, no. 2 (April 1980): 159–80.

Thelen, David P. *Paths of Resistance: Tradition and Dignity in Industrializing Missouri*. New York: Oxford University Press, 1986.

Trollope, Francis, ed. *Domestic Manners of Americans*. New York: Vintage Books, 1949.

Utley, Robert M. *Frontier Regulars: The United States Army and the Indians, 1866–1891*. Lincoln: University of Nebraska Press, 1973.

———. *Frontiersmen in Blue: The United States Army and the Indian, 1848–1865*. Lincoln: University of Nebraska Press, 1981.

Verdon, Paul E. "David Dawson Mitchell: Virginian on the Wild Missouri." *Montana the Magazine of Western History* 27 (April 1977): 2–15.

Walker, Henry Pickering. *The Wagonmasters: High Plains Freighting from the Earliest Days of the Santa Fe Trail to 1880*. Norman: University of Oklahoma Press, 1966.

Waller, George. *Saratoga: Saga of an Impious Era*. United States: George Waller, 1966.

Ward, John William. *Andrew Jackson: Symbol for an Age*. New York: Oxford University Press, 1955.

Wilson, Elinor. *Jim Beckwourth: Black Mountain Man, War Chief of the Crows, Trader, Trapper, Explorer, Frontiersman, Guide, Scout, Interpreter, Adventurer, and Gaudy Liar*. Norman: University of Oklahoma Press, 1972.

Wishart, David J. "Agriculture at the Trading Posts on the Upper Missouri prior to 1843." *Agricultural History* 47 (1973): 57–62.

———. "Cultures in Cooperation and Conflict: Indians in the Fur Trade on the Northern Great Plains, 1807–1840." *Journal of Historical Geography* 2 (1976): 311–28.

———. *The Fur Trade of the American West, 1807–1840: A Geographical Synthesis*. Lincoln: University of Nebraska Press, 1979, 1992.

Wyllie, Irwin G. *The Self-Made Man in America: The Myth of Rags to Riches*. New Brunswick, N.J.: Rutgers University Press, 1954.

# Index

American Fur Company, 2, 3, 15, 17, 18, 27, 28, 53, 54, 61, 68, 68, 70, 75, 78, 82, 83, 97, 98–99, 100, 104, 105, 111, 129, 168, 169, 178–79, 185, 191, 196, 199, 205, 207, 208, 217
Anderson, William Marshall, 101–2, 238
Arapaho, 24, 59, 63, 80, 185, 218
Arikara, 106, 185
Ashley, William, 1, 11, 13–15, 16, 17, 20, 23, 26, 27, 28, 29, 31, 33, 38, 40, 41, 52, 53, 58, 59, 60, 71, 130
Assiniboine, 88, 90, 91, 183, 195, 200, 216
Astor, John Jacob, 27, 69, 84, 97–98, 99
Astor, William, 97–98
Audubon, John James, 86

Bannock, 18, 104
Bates, Edward, 201, 241
Battle of Pierre's Hole, 1, 65–67
Becknell, William, 56
Beckwourth, Jim, 1, 15, 16, 18, 20, 38, 39, 40, 41, 45
Bent, Charles, 41
Bent, St. Vrain, and Company, 130
Benton, Thomas Hart, 28, 149
Blackfoot, 1, 24–25, 26, 32, 33, 35, 36, 37–40, 41, 45, 59, 63, 76, 80, 85, 194, 238
Blair, Frank, 204
Bodmer, Karl, 86, 96, 101
Boggs, Lilburn, 125
Boller, Henry, 200, 205
Bonneville, Benjamin, 61, 76, 237
Bradbury, John, 86

Bridger, Jim, 20, 21, 42, 53, 60, 118

Calhoun, John, 52
Campbell, Andrew (brother), 5, 6, 51, 214
Campbell, Ann (sister), 5, 6, 47, 48, 50, 51
Campbell, Elizabeth (sister), 5, 6, 12, 51
Campbell, George (son), 207, 209
Campbell, Hazlett (son), 190, 225, 219, 225, 232, 242, 243–45
Campbell, Hugh (brother), 5, 6, 7–8, 10, 11, 12, 46–47, 48, 50, 56, 72, 80–81, 99–100, 105, 106, 108, 109, 110, 119–23, 127, 130, 197, 244
Campbell, Hugh (father), 5
Campbell, Hugh (son), 145, 167, 174, 176, 178, 190, 206, 217, 219, 225, 232, 238, 240–41
Campbell, James Alexander (brother), 5, 6
Campbell, James Alexander (son [1842–1849]), 138, 174
Campbell, James Alexander (son [1860–1890]), 202, 207, 209, 225, 232, 242, 243–45
Campbell, John (son), 219
Campbell, Lucy (daughter), 163, 167
Campbell, Mary (sister-in-law), 50–51, 56, 58, 105, 109, 110, 176, 197, 209
Campbell, Robert: Boyhood, 4–8; Campbell-Sublette, 59–80, 82–109, 110–11; Character, 2, 3, 12, 38–41, 51–52, 73–74, 76–77, 78, 82–83, 93, 94–97, 118–22, 126, 132–33, 143–44, 145, 161, 214, 246–47; Immigration,

267

8–9; Importance to Irish family, 5, 7, 11–12, 46–48, 50–52, 53, 58–59, 72, 106; Indian commissioner, 179–86, 234–39; Missouri Bank Board, 133–34, 142, 145, 172–73; Politics, 52–53, 201–2; Railroads, 171–72, 197, 227–29; Relations with other women, 19, 58, 59, 77, 118–22, 127, 143–44; Religion, 3, 82, 91, 126, 189, 210, 220, 230–31; Robert and William Campbell Company, 170–71, 179–80; Southern Hotel, 229–30, 231; Steamboats, 174, 177–78, 197, 199, 216

Campbell, Robert (son [1844–1847]), 149, 167

Campbell, Robert (son [1851–1852]), 186

Campbell, Robert (son [1855–1862]), 206, 208

Campbell, Sarah Elizabeth (mother), 5

Campbell, Virginia (wife), 118–23, 126–28, 132, 134, 139–40, 145, 167, 186, 190, 194–95, 206, 211–12, 217–18, 219, 229, 241, 243, 244

Campbell, William (nephew), 170–71

Carson, Kit, 240

Catlin, George, 43, 86

Charbonneau, Jean Baptiste, 83

Chardon, Abel, 93

Cheyenne, 19, 24, 59, 80, 106, 181–85

Chouteau, Auguste, 10

Chouteau, Charles, 196, 204, 208, 222

Chouteau, Pierre, Jr., 28, 29, 70, 97–98, 111, 112, 180, 186, 189, 192, 196, 222

Chouteau and Company, 129–30, 179, 215

Christy, Edmund T., 75

Civil War, 2, 198–223

Clark, George Rogers, 10

Clark, Malcolm, 196, 200, 201

Clark, William, 10, 31, 59, 60, 62, 74, 83, 89, 100

Clay, Henry, 52, 59, 123

Columbia Fur Company, 11, 28, 85

Comanche, 56, 59

Conquering Bear, Chief, 188, 191

Cree, 24, 88

Crooks, Ramsey, 28, 98, 192

Crow, 24, 34, 41, 43–44, 79, 80, 183–85, 195, 216

Democratic Party, 52, 58, 123, 146–47, 239

Deschamp family, 93–95

Dixon, William P., 212–13

Dole, William, 215

Dougherty, John, 83, 136, 170, 192, 223

Drake, Charles, 221

Drips, Andrew, 2, 41, 42, 53, 104

Edwards, John C., 148

Fighting Bear, Chief, 184

Fillmore, Millard, 187

Fitzpatrick, Thomas, 1, 20, 45, 53, 55, 60, 63, 76, 77, 79, 101, 104, 112–13, 118, 163, 165, 166, 181, 184, 186–87, 187–88, 223

Flathead, 18, 24, 34, 36, 59, 64, 65, 104

Flathead Post, 26

Fontenelle, Fitzpatrick, and Company, 104

Fontenelle, Lucien, 41, 53, 104

Fort Atkinson, 195

Fort Benton, 193, 208, 217

Fort Berthold, 195, 206, 208, 216

Fort Cass, 79

Fort Clark, 195

Fort Colville, 42

Fort Floyd, 69

Fort Kearny, 170, 185, 191, 192

Fort Kiowa, 27

Fort Kipp, 199, 200

Fort Laramie, 84, 98, 170, 181, 188, 192, 210, 219, 235 237

Fort Laramie Treaty, 179–87, 188

Fort Leavenworth, 162

Fort Lookout, 27

Fort Nonsense, 61, 76

Fort Pierre, 163, 167, 195, 217

Fort Randall, 195, 214, 235

Fort Robert Campbell, 168, 195, 199

Fort Stewart, 207

Fort Tilton, 27

Fort Union, 2, 69, 70, 71, 82, 84, 88, 89, 98, 165, 199, 200, 206–7, 216, 225

Fort Vancouver, 48

Fort William (Missouri River), 82–107

Fort William (Platte River), 102–3, 105, 106, 130

Fraeb, Henry, 53, 60, 64, 104

Fremont, Jessie, 145, 211

Fremont, John C., 145
French Fur Company, 11, 27
Frost, Todd, and Company, 193, 195, 196, 200

Gantt and Blackwell Company, 63
Gervais, Jean Baptiste, 53
Grant, Ulysses S., 226, 235, 237, 240–41
Greenwood, Caleb, 45
Gros Ventres (Atsina), 24, 58, 63, 64, 65–67, 72, 88

Hamilton, Alexander, 52, 123
Harney, William S., 191
Harris, Moses, 15, 16, 20, 29, 30
Harvey, Alexander, 163–65, 167, 177, 188
Harvey, Primeau, and Company, 163, 167–68, 176–77, 186
Hidatsa, 183, 195
Hudson's Bay Company, 1, 23, 25, 26, 27, 35, 42, 53, 54, 55, 85, 98

Immell, Michael, 27
Iron Wristband, Chief, 80
Iroquois, 25, 33–34
Irving, Washington, 237

Jackson, Andrew, 52, 123
Jackson, David, 20, 24, 27, 42, 48, 53, 54, 55, 56, 57
Jefferson, Thomas, 52, 123
Jones, Robert, 27

Kansa, 30
Kearny, Stephen Watts, 162–63, 165
Kiowa, 59
Kutanai, 24
Kyle, Eleanor (Lucy), 126–27, 132–34, 138

La Barge, Harkness, and Company, 208, 214, 217
La Barge, John, 208, 215–16
La Barge, Joseph, 208
Laclède, Pierre, 10
Larpenteur, Charles, 73, 88, 199–201, 205–6
Larpenteur, Lemon, and Company, 206, 207
Lea, Lucas, 180
Lemon, Robert, 200, 205–6

Lewis, Meriwether, 62, 83
Lincoln, Abraham, 198, 203, 212, 220–21, 222
Lind, Jenny, 178–79
Little Thunder, Chief, 191
Long Hair, 44–45
Loree, John, 215

McKenzie, Kenneth, 2, 70, 83, 84, 85, 86, 88, 93, 94, 95, 98–99
Mandan, 83, 195
Maximilian, Prince of Wied, 86, 96
Meek, Joe, 3, 45, 60, 63, 69
Mexican War, 161–63, 168
Miller, Alfred Jacob, 86, 108
Missouri Fur Company, 11, 27, 28
Missouri State Bank, 123–26, 133–34, 142
Mitchell, David, 136, 179–85
Mohave, 48

Navaho, 80
Nez Perce, 18, 67
Nez Perce Post, 26, 64, 104
Northwest Company, 85
Nuttall, Thomas, 86, 101

O'Fallon, Benjamin, 73
O'Fallon, John, 10, 11
Ogden, Peter Skene, 1, 27, 35
Ojibwa, 24

Pacific Fur Company, 27
Parker, Ely, 235
Pawnee, 15–16, 30, 55, 107
Pierce, Franklin, 187
Pilcher, Joshua, 41, 42, 54, 135
Pilcher and Company, 41, 43, 54
Polk, James K., 148, 149
Pope, John, 226
Poplar River Post, 200, 205, 206
Potts, Daniel, 21, 25, 38
Pratte, Bernard, 27, 28, 29, 70, 97, 111
Pratte, Chouteau, and Company, 30, 31, 129–30

Red Cloud, Chief, 235
Republican Party, 198, 221
Rocky Mountain Fur Company, 53–54, 60, 67, 68, 75, 77, 78, 100, 104, 105

Sacajawea, 83

St. Vrain and Company, 105
Sherman, William, 212, 240
Shoshone (Snake), 18, 24, 32, 34, 35, 36,
    41, 59, 77, 80, 104, 146, 181–85
Sibley, Henry, 217
Simpson, George, 23, 26, 42, 48
Sioux, 83, 106, 181–85, 188–89, 191, 214,
    217, 222, 223
Smith, Jedediah, 1, 15, 16, 17, 20, 21, 27,
    32, 33, 41, 46, 48, 53, 54, 55, 56–57
Smith-Sublette-Jackson, 20, 53, 54, 55,
    59, 60
Sonnant, Chief, 91–92
Stewart, William Drummond, 3, 75, 77,
    108, 113, 143, 146
Stone, Boswick, and Company, 28
Sublette, Andrew, 106, 118
Sublette, Frances, 143–44, 146, 147, 150,
    175–76
Sublette, Milton, 48, 53, 60, 65–67, 78,
    100, 104
Sublette, Solomon, 147, 176
Sublette, William, 1, 19–20, 21, 24, 27,
    30, 31, 32, 42, 45, 46, 52–53, 54, 55, 56,
    57, 58, 59, 60, 64, 65–67, 73–75, 84, 95,

97, 99, 100, 104, 105, 107–8, 110, 111,
    116, 119–23, 125, 126–27, 130, 145,
    146, 149–50

Thompson, James, 234
Thoreau, Henry David, 59
Throckmorton, Joseph, 188
Tracy, Frederick, 58
Tullock, Sam, 35, 36, 46

Umpqua, 48
United States Bank, 52, 123–24
Ute, 32, 59, 80

Van Buren, Martin, 52, 148
Vanderburgh, Henry, 2, 41, 69, 76
Vasquez, Louis, 75, 79, 118, 135

Ward, Seth, 192, 210, 213, 215, 217, 223,
    226
Whig Party, 52, 58, 123, 130, 131
Williams, Bill, 3
Winnebago, 214
Wyeth, Nathaniel, 2, 61, 78, 84, 99,
    100–102, 103